E DUE

THE DOW JONES-IRWIN GUIDE TO INTERNATIONAL SECURITIES, FUTURES, AND OPTIONS MARKETS

The Dow Jones–Irwin Guide to International Securities, Futures, and Options Markets

William E. Nix
Susan Wilkinson Nix

DOW JONES–IRWIN
Homewood, Illinois 60430

This book was set in Times Roman by Better Graphics, Inc.
The editors were Richard A. Luecke, Ethel Shiell, and Merrily D. Mazza.
The production manager was Irene H. Sotiroff.
The designer was Bob Mummert.
The drawings were done by Ron LaRue.
The Maple-Vail Book Manufacturing Group was the printer and binder.

ISBN 0-87094-771-0
Library of Congress Catalog Card No. 87–71358
Printed in the United States of America
1 2 3 4 5 6 7 8 9 0 MP 5 4 3 2 1 0 9 8

DEDICATIONS

*The authors dedicate this book to our parents
and other persons who are special to us.
Pauline Nix Cress
Donald Nix, In Memoriam
Ruth L. Wilkinson
John Wilkinson, In Memoriam
Ross Cress, In Memoriam*

*Our brothers and sister, family, and friends who gave us moral support
during the difficult times in researching and writing the book.*

ACKNOWLEDGMENTS

We want to thank the following persons who assisted us by granting interviews, providing information, and reviewing and editing the chapters in preparation of the book; we give special thanks to Joseph D. Astalos, who spent several months helping us review and edit material for the final manuscript:

Sir Nicholas Goodison, Chairman of the Stock Exchange of London, President of Fédération Internationale Des Bourses de Valeurs.

Paul J. Greenslade, Institutional Sales/Research, Paribas-Quilter Capital Markets, London.

Jean-Pierre Monmart, Director, and Henri Carpentier, Public Relations, of Brussels Stock Exchange, Brussels, Belgium.

Philippe A. Humbert, Roland Hoffman, and Rainer Maas, Vice-Presidents, CEDEL, S.A., Luxembourg.

Gary C. Link and John A. Nordstrom, Jr., Vice Presidents, Euro-clear Operations Centre, Brussels, Belgium.

Warren Shore and Stephen W. Schoess, officials of the Chicago Board Options Exchange, Chicago.

Marc Douezy, Documentation and Information Official, Chambre Syndicale de la Campagnie des Agents de Change, Paris Bourse, Paris, France.

Phillippe Moser, Vice President, Bourse de Geneva, Geneva, Switzerland.

Michel Maquil, Sous Director, Bourse de Luxembourg, Grand Duchy of Luxembourg.

G.G.A. Jeuken, Hoofd Public Relations, Amsterdamse Effectenbeurs, Amsterdam, Netherlands.

Jos J. Dreesens, Managing Director, and Jaap Hoff, Amsterdam Options Traders N.V., Amsterdam, Netherlands.

R. F. Sandelowsky, Director, Goudtermijnmarkt, Amsterdam B. V., Amsterdam, Netherlands.

J. Th. Vermeulen, Managing Director, Effectenbank VanMeer & Co. NV, Amsterdam, Netherlands.

Dr. Michael Hamke, Informationdienst der Frankfurter Wertpapierborse, Frankfurt am Main, FRG.

Heiko Thieme, Vice President, Deutsche Bank Capital Markets, New York.

Peter Kytzia, First Vice President, Deutsche Bank AG, Frankfurt am Main, FRG.

Malcomb G. Duncan, Director of International Relations, and Dr. Giovanni Bottazzi, officials of the Milan Stock Exchange, Milano, Italy.

G. M. Tobias Faccanoni, Direzione Commerciale, DATABANK-SASIP Spa, Milano, Italy.

Debra L. Lopez Redmond, Public Relations Manager, The London International Financial Futures Exchange, London, UK.

Donald R. Enruh, Vice President International Relations, Toronto Stock Exchange, Toronto, Canada.

Andrew G. Clademenos, Public Relations, Toronto Futures Exchange, Toronto, Canada.

Kevin M. Heerdt, Vice President, Union Bank, Los Angeles.

Hugh Sigmon, Marketing Manager, Commodity Exchange of New York.

Robert Probert, Director, Jesup & Lamont International, New York.

Officials of the Los Angeles Consulate Generals of Japan, the Federal Republic of Germany, France, the United Kingdom, Australia, Sweden, Switzerland, Canada, Italy, and the Netherlands.

Special thanks to my associates at Bear Stearns & Co.: Dan Greene, Michael Snowden, Philip Waters, Nicholas Benachi, Sue Patton, Carli Hagen, and Jackie.

William E. Nix
Susan Wilkinson Nix

CONTENTS

Investment Strategies, Portfolio, and Risk Management of International Equities and Debt Securities

CHAPTER ONE

Introduction

Why should investors consider the international markets? Historical research has shown that, from 1970 to 1985, portfolios selected on the basis of international diversification outperformed U.S. stock market indexes by a factor of two to three. The world index outperformed the U.S. markets during the same 15-year period. As an example, a dollar invested during this period in the U.S. market

TABLE 1.1 Growth Rates of World Markets 1970–1985 Compared to United States

Country	Primary Exchange	Growth Rate, 1970–1985	Percent Difference Compared to U.S.
United States	New York	7.8%	0
Japan	Tokyo	18.0	10.2
United Kingdom	London	9.8	2.0
West Germany	Frankfurt	11.3	3.5
Canada	Toronto	9.1	1.3
France	Paris	8.2	0.4
Italy	Milan	3.7	-4.1
Switzerland	Zurich	11.1	3.3
Australia	Sydney	3.9	-3.9
Sweden	Stockholm	12.0	4.2
Hong Kong	Hong Kong	18.2	10.4
Belgium	Brussels	11.2	3.4
Singapore	Singapore	13.1	5.3

Note: Growth rates 1970 to 1985 were compounded annually with dividends reinvested.
SOURCE: Morgan Stanley Capital International Perspective.

deficits caused by import/export trade imbalances. The U.S. economy is importing more than it is exporting and thereby losing foreign exchange earnings. The large governmental debt burden and noncompetitive foreign trading practices could produce economic stagnation.

THE EFFECTS OF DEREGULATION AND PRIVATIZATION

Many conservative governments in Asia and Western Europe have initiated programs to deregulate their capital markets, financial institutions, and stock exchanges. Great Britain instituted the most recent deregulation when the London Stock Exchange underwent the "Big Bang." The ramifications of the Big Bang are discussed in Chapter 9.

Many foreign governments have adopted policies to privatize state-owned enterprises in their countries. England, France, Italy, West Germany, and Japan have started active denationalization programs that will transfer the ownership of hundreds of state-owned companies to the private sector—making them more efficient and less of a financial drain on state treasuries.

The study of international investing is exciting because of the rapid changes and developments in communication technologies. Government and business leaders in noncommunist countries are recognizing the interrelationships in an evolving global economy. Events that occur in one country can have an immediate effect on production and distribution decisions made in other countries. Investors gain greater appreciation for and greater understanding of domestic markets when they study the historical and contemporary developments of non-U.S. equity and debt markets.

WHAT ARE THE OBJECTIVES OF THIS BOOK?

The formula for earning superior rates of return is to **buy undervalued securities in countries that have undervalued currencies with comparable credit risks.** These securities can be common shares, convertibles, corporate, or government bonds denominated in their respective currencies.

The material covered in this book will help readers determine the quality and timeliness of an investment. They will gain understanding of the process of selecting investment criteria, methods for determining actual value of a security, credit worthiness of a security, and evaluation of foreign currency risks. This is achieved by providing primary and secondary references, structural guidelines, and factual material about:

1. How to formulate investment policies and strategies.
2. How to use risk management techniques to manage portfolios.
3. How to obtain up-to-date information regarding the primary international financial markets.
4. How to evaluate macroeconomic data, country, industry, company, and foreign exchange risks.

But more importantly, we want to stimulate the readers' creative processes by having them ask questions. Often it is better to know which questions to ask than to be an encyclopedia of knowledge. The arena of international investing is changing rapidly and requires constant reading to keep abreast of the changes. We have the following objectives in writing this book:

1. To describe the main benefits of trading foreign listed securities, futures, and options markets.
2. To present the primary risks and opportunities of foreign investments.
3. To show how to obtain price quotations for stocks, options, and futures contracts.
4. To show how to obtain and analyze research on foreign economies, industries, companies, and financial markets.
5. To develop basic and advanced strategies for trading and investment in foreign markets.
6. To develop hedging strategies for protection against risks associated with foreign exchange rates, interest rates, and market valuations.
7. To present a selection process for determining which investments are appropriate, such as matching the criteria set by an investor.
8. To develop a multifactor assessment model for quantifying risks and profit potential of selected securities.
9. To present information on the history, demographics, and relevant information that might affect decisions to invest in a particular country.

AUTOMATED TRADING, ORDER EXECUTION, CLEARANCE, AND SETTLEMENT

Many foreign stock exchanges are automating their trading, order execution, clearing, and settlement procedures to implement 24-hour trading between electronically linked exchanges. The Toronto Stock Exchange has installed the Computer Assisted Trading System (CATS). It allows trading on less active securities. The Paris Bourse is implementing the CORES system, which was purchased from Toronto. The Stock Exchange of London has installed the SEAQ system to link up with other markets.

The creation of new investment products and services will revolutionize capital investment in world markets. For example, European currency unit (ECU) denominated securities, dual-currency bonds, zero-coupon bonds, options on stock indexes, futures contracts on government securities, and interest rate and foreign currency swaps were introduced as innovative products to fit the specific needs of a borrower or lender of capital. Another example is *savings shares* listed on the Milan Exchange. Savings shares are similar to preferred shares except that Italian companies receive special tax incentives to issue these shares.

We expect to see many additional innovative financial products and services introduced globally in the next decade. During the past 10 years, tremendous advances have occurred in investment methodology and technology. The introduction and application of Modern Portfolio Theory (MPT) techniques have allowed investment managers to define investment risks and returns in statistical terms. MPT has provided the framework for developing quantitative models to simulate real-life data and measure investment performance.

INVESTMENT TECHNOLOGIES

Personal computers, computer programs to enhance fundamental and technical analyses, computer-readable databases, and accessible telecommunications have added powerful new tools to investment technology. Further advances on the way include the applications of artificial intelligence and advanced decision-theory models for making investment decisions.

This sophistication is necessary because of the destabilization of national economies due to wars and political and economic uncertainties. Widely fluctuating oil prices, basic commodity prices, and foreign exchange rates have created opportunities for international investors who know how to analyze and profit from these changes. Economic and political realities can change suddenly and unpredictably—leading to unexpected opportunities for profit or loss. Borrowers and lenders of capital want new ways to protect themselves from the vagaries of the world marketplace.

This book presents various scenarios where opportunities exist and discusses the instruments that can be used to profit from them. The investment climate changes in response to changes in political and economic environments. Investment philosophies and instruments appropriate for one set of conditions may be inappropriate for a different set of conditions. We will elaborate on this subject throughout the book.

TYPES OF SECURITIES AND FINANCIAL INSTRUMENTS AVAILABLE FOR TRADING

Until 10 years ago, investors were limited in the types of investment alternatives available. Capital stock, corporate bonds, and government securities constituted the major instruments. We have recently seen innovative instruments created in response to changing investor needs and sophistication. The following list briefly describes the types of securities and financial instruments available in both U.S. and foreign markets. The securities can be denominated in a specified currency or in a supranational currency such as the European currency unit (ECU).

Common Shares. Voting shares issued by a corporation representing ownership.
Preferred Shares. Shares (usually nonvoting) issued by a corporation representing a security senior to common stock. Convertible preferred stock can be converted to common stock at a specified conversion price.
Savings Shares. A new type of nonvoting share with a cumulative fixed dividend issued by an Italian corporation. The Italian government allows a corporation to deduct the distributed dividends from its taxes.
Bonds, Debentures. Debt instruments issued by a corporation represent-

ing a liability to the bond owners. Bonds are secured by specific assets of an issuing corporation. Debentures are secured by the general assets of the issuing corporation. These securities are senior to common and preferred stock.

Convertible Bonds, Debentures. Bonds or debentures issued by a corporation that may be converted to common stock at a specified conversion price.

Listed Options. Securities created by an exchange that permit a holder to offset or exercise for the delivery of a specified common stock's underlying shares.

Index Options on the Market. Listed options created by an exchange that permit a holder to offset or exercise for a cash settlement on an underlying market index such as the Standard & Poor's 100, the Financial Times Index, or the Toronto Stock Exchange Index.

Financial Futures Contracts. Highly leveraged contracts created by a futures exchange that allow speculation or hedging on underlying interest rate instruments, government debt securities, stock market indexes, and foreign currencies.

Options on Financial Futures. Put and calls created by a futures exchange that can be offset or exercised for an underlying futures contract.

Zero-Coupon Bonds. Debt securities issued at a discount and maturing at par. Unlike regular bonds, these securities pay no interest during the holding period.

European Currency Denominated (ECU) Issues. Debt instruments issued by foreign government or corporate entities denominated in a basket of non-U.S. currencies.

Warrants, Rights. Securities issued by a corporation attached or separable from the common stock that can be converted into common stock at a specified parity price.

Foreign Currency Denominated Issues. Debt or equity securities issued and traded on the basis of a foreign currency. For example, Bankers Trust 12.45 percent fixed rate three-year notes issued in Australian dollars.

ADRs. American Depository Receipts substitute certificates for stock in a foreign company. These certificates are held in trust by a U.S. bank. The bank then issues depository receipts that are traded on U.S. securities exchanges.

Each of these securities and financial instruments serves a purpose in the marketplace, even though many financial experts question the wisdom of having so many types of products available. Through examples and case studies we will show how these instruments can be used for investing in foreign markets.

APPROACHES TO INVESTING
IN FOREIGN SECURITIES

There are four approaches to investing in foreign securities: mutual funds, closed-end investment companies, foreign securities listed on U.S. exchanges, and direct investment.

1. Some mutual funds specialize in foreign securities. Mutual funds are open-ended funds managed by professionals who select and manage shareholders' moneys. Their shares are issued and redeemed by a management company, and they are not traded on listed exchanges. Investors may buy shares in these funds for as little as $500. Mutual funds compute their net asset value (NAV) once daily. The NAV reflects the actual value of the securities in the underlying portfolio.

Mutual fund shares can be sold only after a customer has received a prospectus. A prospectus is a legal document written to disclose potential investment risks and opportunities in a specific fund. A prospectus also describes the objectives, restrictions, and limitations placed on the portfolio's managers. The Securities and Exchange Commission (SEC) can neither determine an investment's merits nor approve a specific fund. The SEC can only qualify a prospectus for distribution to broker/dealers and their customers.

There are three types of mutual funds:

a. Global funds that can invest in both U.S. and non-U.S. markets.
b. International funds that are restricted by prospectus to investments in non-U.S. markets.
c. Regional funds that are restricted by prospectus to investments in specific countries—also known as country funds.

2. Closed-end investment companies are professionally managed funds listed on stock exchanges. Closed-end investment companies are similar to mutual funds regarding their investment goals—global, international, or regional. The shares of closed-end funds can trade at a premium or discount to the fund's net asset value (NAV). Chapter 2 provides a description of closed-end funds.

Mutual funds and closed-end investment companies are excellent vehicles for participating in foreign markets for investors who don't have the time or the inclination to do their own research. These funds may be suitable investments for IRA, Keogh, 401 (k), and qualified defined benefit/profit sharing plans. Lipper Analytical Services publishes information and performance data on many of the mutual funds.

3. Investors can purchase foreign securities dually traded on a primary foreign exchange and listed in American depository receipts (ADR) form on a U.S. exchange. ADRs on foreign companies may be listed on the New York Stock Exchange, American Stock Exchange, or NASDAQ. For example, Jaguar, the British automobile company, is traded on the London Stock Exchange and on NASDAQ. Currently, many foreign companies are traded in ADR form on U.S. exchanges.

4. Direct investment by an individual, corporation, or institution is the most challenging form of international investment since investors must establish their own criteria, financial objectives, selection of investments, and timing about buying and selling.

Making direct investments in companies listed on foreign exchanges requires a disciplined and knowledgeable approach. We emphasize the following methods for making direct investments to reduce risks and optimize returns:

a. Purchase shares in non-U.S. companies in which the price per share is discounted to book value per share.
b. Special situations in which the price of shares is expected to increase due to significant events.
c. Foreign exchange rate changes that favor purchasing non-U.S. dollar-denominated securities.
d. Purchase securities in which the price-earnings multiples are expected to expand due to changes in micro- or macroeconomic factors.
e. Purchase securities in non-U.S. companies that are leaders in the development of new technology, products, or services.
f. Purchase securities in companies that control natural resources such as strategic metals, oil and gas, forest products, industrial metals, precious metals, and gemstones.

g. Purchase new issues in non-U.S. companies that are privately held but whose managers want to increase capitalization by selling shares to the public. New equity issues are a risky investment, since the companies are usually newer and less mature than companies already listed on the exchanges. In a few cases, well-capitalized companies that have been privately held for hundreds of years are offered to the public for the first time.

AMERICAN DEPOSITORY RECEIPTS (ADRs)

Individual and institutional investors first began trading foreign securities in the form of American depository receipts (ADRs). Companies such as Toyota, Nissan, and Jaguar are well-known names traded as ADRs on U.S. markets.

ADRs are negotiable certificates created by U.S. depository banks to facilitate the trading, clearing, and settlement of a limited number of foreign securities in the United States. ADRs serve as surrogate certificates for foreign shares. They are traded in the United States as if they were domestic shares. ADRs are traded on the New York Stock Exchange (NYSE), the American Stock Exchange (AMEX), or NASDAQ. Usually ADRs represent the common shares of foreign companies; however, a limited number of foreign government bonds are traded as ADRs.

An ADR is created by a U.S. depository bank such as Morgan Guaranty Trust or Citicorp. A U.S. bank appoints a custodian bank, usually one of its correspondents, located in the country that originates the securities. The custodian bank holds the physical securities; the depository bank prints ADR certificates that represent those shares in the United States. Physical shares never leave the country of origin. An ADR certificate may represent 1, 2, 5, 10, or 20 shares of the underlying security.

ADRs are bought and sold on the exchanges through brokerage firms. Either the investor or the broker becomes the registered holder, depending on whether the ADR is held in street name or not. The depository bank, having created the ADR, serves as an intermediary in the process. See Figure 1.3 for the operational structure of an ADR.

FIGURE 1.3

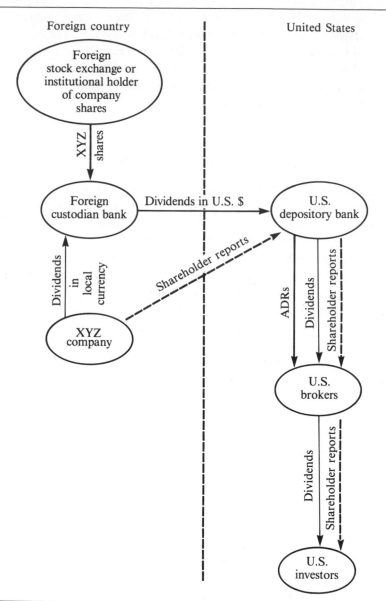

Operational structure of an American Depository Receipt (ADR) for company XYZ as a sponsored account. An ADR may represent one or more shares of the issuing company. The depository bank in the United States is responsible for distribution of dividends, shareholder reports, and other benefits accrued to the investor.

SPONSORED VERSUS UNSPONSORED ADR ACCOUNTS

ADRs can be created from a sponsored or unsponsored account. A foreign company that wants its shares traded in the United States as an ADR will approach a U.S. depository bank to apply for a sponsored account. A sponsored account means that the company is responsible for administrative costs involved in creating and maintaining an ADR, i.e., payment of dividends, transfer costs, adjusting for stock splits, and supplying company reports. A foreign company's motivation in applying for a sponsored ADR is to raise funds in U.S. capital markets. The NYSE and AMEX accept only sponsored ADRs for listing.

Unsponsored ADRs are created when a brokerage firm approaches a depository bank to apply for an unsponsored account. The brokerage firm believes that there will be broad interest by U.S. investors in listing the company. The bank then contacts the company for a "no objection" letter. The company assumes no administrative costs when an unsponsored ADR is created. These costs are passed on to shareholders. Because of listing restrictions, unsponsored ADRs are traded only on the NASDAQ system. Because the company is not financially involved in creating an ADR, shareholders may experience higher costs and reduced benefits for owning unsponsored ADRs.

REGISTRATION AND SALE OF FOREIGN SECURITIES WITHIN THE UNITED STATES

Most securities, options, and futures contracts listed on non-U.S. markets are not registered for sale in the United States. The United States has strict federal and state laws regarding the registration, solicitation, and sale of investment contracts within its borders. Even securities registered for sale in certain states may not be registered for sale in other states. Each state has its own set of blue sky laws, which regulate the registration and sale of securities within the state. In addition, brokers must be registered with a state securities agency before they can transact business with residents of that state.

Registered representatives of U.S. brokerage firms must pass a series of qualifying examinations before they can be licensed to sell securities, options, and futures contracts to U.S. residents. If they solicit the sale of unregistered foreign securities from clients, brokerage representatives risk fines and loss of their licenses. For this reason, registered representatives of U.S. brokerage firms don't study unregistered foreign securities because they can't sell them to clients. Similarly, U.S. brokerge firms produce only limited research reports on foreign equity and debt securities.

Securities of foreign issuers can be registered for sale in the United States if they are listed as regular securities or as American Depository Receipts (ADRs) on an official U.S. exchange. The securities of many Canadian issuers are dually listed on a Canadian stock exchange and a U.S. stock exchange. A limited number of securities of Asian and European issuers are usually listed as American depository receipts (ADRs) on the New York Stock Exchange, the American Stock Exchange, or the NASDAQ system. Legal restrictions on the registration and sale of foreign securities protect investors from illegal and fraudulent schemes. They also promote ignorance from U.S. investors regarding significant investment opportunities existing outside the United States. The equity and debt securities from many of the world's largest public companies are not registered for sale in the United States.

Changes occurring in federal securities laws could facilitate the registration and sale of non-U.S. issuers listed on the primary exchanges of other countries. These changes are necessary for the United States to remain competitive as an international marketplace. The financial markets of certain countries, particularly the United Kingdom, have made structural changes in their regulatory policies to establish a system for trading international securities. The federal and state securities agencies in the United States must make similar changes in regulatory posture to prevent further loss of market share to other countries' capital markets. The market share held by U.S. stock exchanges, as measured by total market capitalization of listed securities, has declined from 75 percent to less than 35 percent in 15 years.

INTERNATIONAL ORGANIZATIONS FOR CLEARING AND SETTLEMENT

Failed deliveries, lost securities, and faulty clearance settlement procedures constitute major risks for investors who make direct investments in foreign markets. Clearance and settlement procedures are not standardized on many foreign exchanges. For example, a transaction settlement may take a few days in West Germany but several months in Italy, Spain, or Austria. U.S. investors accustomed to a five-day settlement avoid investing in countries where clearance and settlement are uncertain. However, the use of automated clearance and settlement systems on the national exchanges is finally changing this unacceptable situation. For these reasons, Euro-clear and CEDEL were created to perform the functions of a service company providing comprehensive services for the safekeeping, administration, and timely settlement of primary and secondary market transactions.

Euro-clear and CEDEL are the world's largest organizations established for clearing and settling international transactions with a single account number in 27 different currencies. Institutional investors who want to participate in international markets must understand the operations of these organizations. In many respects, both organizations are functionally similar, CEDEL and Euro-clear link up with the clearing facilities of stock exchanges in the United States and many European countries. Together they form the structure for an international clearance, settlement, and depository system for cash and securities. Their systems are set up to clear Eurobonds, foreign bonds, domestic bonds, certificates of deposit in tranche form, and selected Euro-equities.

Euro-clear's headquarters is in Brussels, Belgium, and there are branch offices worldwide. It was established in 1968 to clear Eurobond transactions, but it has since expanded to clear Euro-equities and other securities. The company is owned by 124 shareholders including leading banks, brokerage firms, and other financial institutions. Euro-clear has over 1,600 participants. Morgan Guaranty Bank is the lead bank of Euro-clear.

CEDEL's headquarters is Luxembourg, and there are branch offices worldwide. CEDEL is the acronym for Centrale de Livraison de Valeurs Mobilieres; it was established in 1970 to clear Eurobond trades. CEDEL has over 100 shareholders and 1,500 participants. Like Euro-clear, it has expanded services to include clearing Euro-equities and other securities. Citicorp is the lead bank of CEDEL.

CEDEL and Euro-clear provide the following client services to participants:

1. Securities clearance through a book entry system. Physical transfer of securities is eliminated.

2. Custody of securities. These organizations provide safe-keeping facilities. All securities of a particular issue are held by a single depository.
3. Securities lending and borrowing.
4. Money transfer and banking.
5. A worldwide communications network for transmitting and receiving delivery and settlement instructions via mail, telex, or computer terminals.
6. Designated member banks as security depositories.
7. Designated member banks as cash depositories for handling the transfer of funds between participants.
8. These organizations can convert ADRs into ordinary shares through their systems.

In conclusion, CEDEL and Euro-clear are organizations that specialize in clearing and settling international transactions in primary and secondary markets. They are capable of settling transactions in 27 different currencies.

DEVELOPMENT OF ELECTRONIC-TRANSFER BANKING SYSTEM

The expansion of global, electronic-transfer banking will facilitate currency convertibility and the worldwide flow of capital from areas with capital surpluses to areas where capital is needed. The capital markets will benefit immeasurably from these developments. Selected U.S. and foreign securities and commodities exchanges are developing electronic linkages to implement automated order routing and execution and for sharing market information, statistics, and price data. Investors will be able to execute transactions around the world on a 24-hour basis. For example, the New York Stock Exchange will link up with the London Stock Exchange. The Chicago Mercantile Exchange will link up with SIMEX in Singapore. This book describes the linkages and discusses their long-term ramifications. The development of high-speed data processing, interactive computer software, and telecommunication devices permits rapid worldwide dissemination of information on prices, market statistics, and transactions.

International investing encompasses the study of primary and secondary capital markets of Japan, the United Kingdom, Western Europe, Canada, South America, Mexico, Asia, and the Pacific-

Basin countries. Each country may develop primary and secondary markets for securities, options, and futures contracts. For example, the New York Stock Exchange is the primary market for mature, well-capitalized companies in the United States. The Chicago Board Options Exchange (CBOE) is the primary market for options on securities and stock market indexes.

We have been excited about writing on this subject for some time. We wanted to provide readers with an overview of foreign equity and debt securities, options and futures markets, and how they can be combined in appropriate investment strategies. Foreign investments and markets refer to investment opportunities available outside the United States. We have restricted the topics covered to listed equity and debt issues, listed options, and futures markets. Real estate, collectibles, and other investments are not covered.

There are approximately 70 financial markets outside the United States in which shares are traded on publicly held companies. Like the United States, many foreign exchanges are creating options and financial futures markets to accommodate investors who want to speculate or hedge financial risks on a

TABLE 1.2   Ranking of World Capital Markets

Country	Primary Exchange	Official Currency	Market Capitalization ($ billion)
United States	New York	U.S. dollar	$2,231
Japan	Tokyo	Yen	1,314
United Kingdom	London	Sterling	402
West Germany	Frankfurt	Deutsche mark	229
Canada	Toronto	Can. dollar	157
France	Paris	French franc	134
Italy	Milan	Lira	115
Switzerland	Zurich	Swiss franc	102
Australia	Sydney	Aust. dollar	72
Netherlands	Amsterdam	Guilder	61
Sweden	Stockholm	Krona	43
Hong Kong	Hong Kong	HK dollar	41
Spain	Madrid	Peseta	34
Belgium	Brussels	Belgian franc	29
Singapore	Singapore	Sing. dollar	23
Total market capitalization			$4,989

SOURCE: Morgan Stanley Capital International Perspective.

portfolio of securities, commodities, or debt instruments. See Table 1.2 for size comparisons of the major capital markets.

The formation of electronically linked capital and debt markets accomplishes several important capabilities:

1. It facilitates currency convertibility and the settlement of transactions.
2. It disseminates price and statistical information regarding listed securities.
3. It promotes increased efficiency and competition in the world marketplace.
4. It makes capitalism the economic system of choice among developing nations.

WHO SHOULD READ THIS BOOK?

This book is written for corporate treasurers, investment managers, pension/profit sharing managers, individual investors, and business and finance students who want to learn about international investing. We present different strategies for investing to optimize profit potential, to enhance yields, and to reduce portfolio risks using derivative securities such as options and futures contracts.

Why should investors consider investing in foreign markets? These are some reasons for considering investment in the debt and equity securities of foreign companies:

1. Diversification of risk with potentially higher rates of return on capital.
2. Special situations existing in a company or industry.
3. Favorable changes in foreign exchange rates.
4. Risk arbitrage opportunities.
5. Corporate mergers, leveraged buyouts.
6. Investment banking opportunities.
7. Higher potential returns compared to U.S. markets.

THE ROLE OF INFORMATION DISCLOSURE
AND CAPITAL MARKET EFFICIENCY

The Securities and Exchange Commission (SEC) and United States stock exchanges require full disclosure of audited financial information on listed companies. Companies must submit semiannual, annual, 10-K, and supplemental reports to the SEC and stock exchanges to keep them apprised of changes in their financial condition. In addition, SEC regulations prohibit sharing company information with others prior to its public disclosure. This is referred to as "insider information"; investors possessing insider information could profit from prior knowledge of a company's earnings, change in management, and significant announcements. The SEC imposes stiff penalties on company officers who share insider information with prospective investors. SEC and stock exchange officials claim that full disclosure and insider trading regulations make U.S. markets the most efficient in the world. They also believe that these laws are in the best interest of the public investor, since no one has an unfair advantage. In recent years, the great expenses incurred in full disclosure, financial auditing, and listing have encouraged many prominent U.S. companies to list their securities on foreign exchanges, which have substantially lower costs.

Most foreign countries don't have the strict reporting and auditing requirements imposed by U.S. regulatory agencies. Sharing "insider information" isn't prohibited to the extent it is in the United States. Sharing insider information is an accepted practice in making an efficient market in countries that don't require full disclosure of a company's condition.

Listed companies in the United States are covered by security analysts, broker/dealers, and market makers. The efficient flow of information from U.S. capital markets presents advantages and disadvantages to investors. The primary advantage is the easy availability of financial information and price data on a company and comparable statistical data on related industry groups. A disadvantage is that highly efficient markets generally lessen the opportunities for unusual profits.

REASONS FOR NOT INVESTING IN INTERNATIONAL MARKETS

There are reasons for not investing in international markets:

1. Reluctance by senior management to become involved in international markets.
2. Lack of internal international experience in an organization.
3. Inability to evaluate and take foreign currency risks.

4. Inability to evaluate political, economic, and credit risks associated with foreign countries.

After reading this book and other references, readers will be better judges about investing any amount of money in international markets.

HOW TO GET STARTED

International investing begins with an educational process that continues for life. Even if an investor chooses professional management of funds through an investment manager, mutual fund, or investment company, intelligent decisions can only be made with careful selection of the countries, currencies, companies, and financial instruments needed for investment. Knowledge and experience separate amateurs from professionals.

Reading *Barron's, Euromoney, The Economist, The Asian Wall Street Journal, The Wall Street Journal,* and *Financial Times* is an excellent way to get started. Public and university libraries have books and publications on international investing. Full-service stock brokerage firms have international departments that provide research reports and recommendations to clients.

For investors with access to computers, Dow Jones News Retrieval, Telerate, Standard & Poor's, Chase Econometrics, and Euromoney have computer-readable databases for accessing news events, market information, and statistical data on foreign economies, business activities, and financial markets. Some of these services are inexpensive; others are very expensive depending on who uses them, what time of day they are used, and the extent of usage.

WHAT IS THE ROLE OF CAPITAL AND FINANCIAL MARKETS?

During the past 500 years, capitalism has evolved from a system of barter and trade between cities into a system of global electronic-transfer banking, automated clearing and settlement of transactions, and multinational ownership of corporate equity and debt securities. Advances in banking, automation of transaction settlements, information dissemination, and telecommunication technologies have made this possible.

"Capital market" refers to a centralized organization where the ownership of equity and debt capital can be transferred through the exchange of certificates of listed companies. "Financial market" refers to a centralized organization where derivative instruments are traded for risk management purposes. Financial futures and options contracts on stock indexes, debt securities, and currencies allow their holders to transfer ownership or price risk to investors who want to speculate on price changes. Financial futures and options contracts do not represent ownership of equity or debt capital. Capital and financial markets can be either regulated or left unregulated by government or industry agencies depending upon which country's securities are issued.

Primary capital markets allow the creation of wealth by issuing new capital shares and debt obligations. Secondary capital markets allow convenient transfer of ownership between buyers and sellers. Financial markets perform the function of risk transference; the risks of ownership are transferred through the exchange of derivative instruments.

We forecast that within the next 10 years, capital and financial markets will be linked electronically through a network of depository and custodian banks and centralized clearing organizations to create a Global capital and financial system for clearing and settling transactions. The exchange of securities and derivative instruments will occur as book entries and journaled credits and debits. Physical securities and their transfer will be eliminated. Securities will be registered at a Global registry and depository trust. Universal banks and multinational brokerage firms will execute orders and perform record-keeping procedures for their clients as usual. The difference will be that clients can trade listed securities, options, and financial futures contracts on any world exchange from their primary exchange—whether it be New York, London, Paris, or Toronto.

CAPITALISM VERSUS SOCIALISM AND COMMUNISM

Capitalism as an economic system is distinguished from socialism and communism in that privately owned organizations such as corporations, partnerships, and sole proprietorships control the production and distribution of goods and services in a national economy. Governments and political parties that encourage private enterprise also foster the growth of capital formation and capital markets.

Socialist and communist economic systems rely on government agencies and central planning committees to make decisions regarding economic production and the allocation of goods and services. These agencies decide what will be produced, who will produce it, where production will occur, and how the product will be distributed in domestic and international economies. Socialist and communist governments legislate the transfer of capital from the private sector to the public sector, which harms the growth and efficiency of capital markets and their overall national economies.

The installation of socialist or communist governments poses a major risk to investors because these governments can legislate policies to confiscate privately owned assets without compensation to shareholders. These governments enact anticompetitive labor policies that stifle economic productivity. Furthermore, communist governments can renege on their debt obligations, which causes foreign investors to lose their entire principal.

A country's political philosophies and systems largely determine the type of economic system that prevails. We distinguish between two types of governments:

1. Governments dedicated to centralized planning, allocation, and control of material resources, technology, management, and labor. They promote nationalization of private enterprises.
2. Governments dedicated to decentralized planning, allocation, and control of material resources, technology, management, and labor. They promote privatization of state-owned enterprises.

Governments that allow institutions to promote the creation and maintenance of capital markets generally represent the democratic societies of the world. These governments recognize the need for formation of private capital and decentralized decision making in fostering economic growth and productivity.

Investors buy debt or equity securities in companies to provide them with the necessary capital to purchase labor, resources, equipment, and management personnel to sell products and related services for a profit. The creation of profits allows companies to retain a portion of their earnings for growth and to distribute the remainder either to shareholders in the form of dividends or to debt holders in the form of interest payments.

In recent years, conservative governments that have replaced socialist governments are trying to make their economic systems more efficient and responsive to the populace. France, Italy, the United Kingdom, and Spain are embarking on privatization programs to transfer ownership of state-owned enterprises to private shareholders. They hope the enterprises will operate more efficiently and cease being financial burdens on national treasuries.

ORGANIZATION OF THE BOOK

We have organized this book in two parts. Part One includes chapters on international mutual funds and portfolio and risk management strategies for equity and debt securities. Foreign currency risks, opportunities for making investment gains, and material on international investment banking are discussed.

Part Two provides an overview of the history, geography, demographics, and trends for various national economies including a presentation of the political and economic systems within each country. These chapters also describe the specifics of primary markets in each country.

CHAPTER TWO

How to Invest in International Mutual and Closed-End Funds

International mutual and closed-end funds offer investors the opportunity to participate in foreign economies' growth through investment in professionally managed portfolios of equity and debt securities. Mutual and closed-end funds offer shares in which investors can invest from $500 to several million dollars. Their shares are quoted in U.S. dollars; dividends and capital gains are distributed in U.S. dollars. See Example 2.1.

International funds invest in the debt and equity securities from countries other than the United States. As an example, fund managers can invest in companies located in Europe, Asia, Latin America, or Canada. In recent years, many international funds have significantly outperformed domestic mutual funds.

Regional funds are a special class of international funds in that they invest in companies from a specific country or geographic region. For example, the Korea Fund invests in South Korean-based companies. Fund managers specialize in analyzing the South Korean economy and focus investments in companies that will benefit from trends in the South Korean economy.

Mutual funds can issue new shares continually. Mutual fund shares are neither listed nor traded on a stock exchange. Shares are issued and redeemed by the management company through a custodial agent. The price of a fund's shares are usually valued once a day, and they reflect the net asset value (NAV) of the portfolio of securities. A fund's NAV is computed by taking the total value of its securities at market prices divided by the number

---

EXAMPLE 2.1 Creation of a Portfolio of Country Funds

A manager of a corporate pension plan with $1 million in assets decides to diversify into the international markets. He wants to invest 10 percent of the plan's assets ($100,000) in country funds listed on the New York and American Stock Exchanges. He allocates the $100,000 by country:

Country Fund	Percentage Allocation	Price per Share	Dollar Amount	Shares Purchased
Japan	30%	$16.50	$ 30,000	1,818
Germany	20	10.38	20,000	1,926
Italy	20	10.75	20,000	1,860
France	10	9.50	10,000	1,052
Australia	10	8.25	10,000	1,212
Korea	5	38.75	5,000	129
Mexico	5	3.25	5,000	1,538
Totals	100%		$100,000	9,535

This example shows how convenient it is to create a portfolio of securities by investing in country funds. The portfolio's allocation can be changed by establishing different percentages for each country. For example, the plan manager may want to sell shares in the Japan fund and buy more shares of the Korea fund at a future date. Because share prices for each fund are listed in the newspaper, the manager can monitor the performance of his holdings daily.

---

of shares outstanding. For example, if a fund has $90 million worth of securities with 10 million shares outstanding, its NAV would be $9 per share. A customer can redeem shares at the net asset value minus redemption charges.

Closed-end funds (also referred to as regulated investment companies) issue a limited number of shares. Shares are traded on a stock exchange. The share price changes with the supply and demand for the fund's shares, and it may not reflect the actual value of securities in the portfolio. Share prices can trade for a significant discount or premium to the net asset value of the fund's securities. This fact has provided opportunities for majority shareholders to convert a closed-end fund to a mutual fund at a handsome profit. The conversion of a closed-end fund to a mutual fund is known as "open ending."

As the capital needs of both mature and less-developed countries increase, we will see tremendous growth in the popularity and asset size of international and regional funds. These funds serve as pools of capital for allocation in different areas of the private and public sectors.

The infusion of capital can be used to: build public works projects, replace depreciated plants and equipment, finance research and development projects, stimulate production of goods and services, and reduce unemployment. Capital raised by international funds can provide tremendous social benefits to developing nations. Italy legalized domestic mutual funds in 1983. The infusion of new capital into Italian stock markets was phenomenal. The Milan Indice Generale increased dramatically from 1984 to 1986.

Investors are learning quickly that the United States doesn't have a monopoly on productive ideas, inventions, new technologies, products, or services. Many non-U.S. companies are world leaders in computer technology, biotechnology, optical lasers, and alternative energy—areas where the United States once had the leading edge.

U.S. capital markets are highly efficient in raising investment and venture capital to finance the research and development (R&D), production, and marketing of new products and services. U.S. economic and political systems provide sources and networks for raising and distributing capital where it is needed.

The "mutual fund" concept has been popular in the United States for decades. It has been instrumental in raising billions of dollars to stimulate and maintain high levels of economic prosperity and entrepreneurial opportunities. The creation of individual retirement accounts and qualified pension and profit-sharing plans provides tax incentives and source of money for investment in U.S. mutual funds. These tax-deferred monies are invested in equity and debt securities of corporations to foster industrial growth.

In recent years, there has been a trend in the United States to invest in mutual funds with portfolios of U.S. Treasury and government agency securities. In effect, investors subsidized deficit financing of the U.S. Treasury. Real interest rates were quite high compared to inflation levels. This spread provided an opportunity to earn a high rate of return without credit risk.

Regional funds specialize in analyzing companies from a specific country. They may appeal to the expatriates of a country who want to use professional management to invest in that country. A person with Korean ancestry may want to invest in the Korea Fund (KF). The Korea Fund is the only way for nonresidents to invest in a rapidly growing South Korean economy. The Korea Fund was offered at $12 per share in May 1984, and it has traded as high as $35 per share in 1986—reflecting the increased valuation of South Korean companies.

U.S. securities laws require that a management company use a prospectus to disclose a fund's investment selection criteria, risks, management costs, administrative fees, sales charges, and other information. In addition, management companies must distribute quarterly and annual accounting reports detailing the portfolio of securities, distribution of capital gains, cash dividends, and any changes in management and goals relevant to an investor. A fund's prospectus contains a wealth of information about the country, securities markets, and types of issues that the fund managers intend to invest in. Prospective investors should read and understand a fund's prospectus before buying. Independent reporting services such as Standard & Poor's, Moody's, and Lipper Analytical Services provide third-party information on funds.

Even though the asset size of international funds appears substantial, there is a sizable shortfall of capital needed for industrial and economic growth in most countries. In addition, fund managers often focus on and invest in only companies with the largest capitalization that have an adequate supply of tradable stock. Newer and more innovative companies are overlooked because they lack either a track record in earnings and management experience or liquidity in the marketplace. Investment bankers and fund underwriters concentrate their efforts on raising capital for large companies rather than emerging companies since large companies have a longer record of earnings and experienced management. International funds provide a conduit for transfer of pooled funds from areas of the world with capital surpluses to areas with deficits. Before describing the various available funds, here is a summary of the advantages and disadvantages of investing in these funds:

The advantages of investing in these funds are:

1. Active, daily, and professional management of assets. An investor doesn't have to decide about selecting countries, industries, companies, or foreign currencies to invest in.
2. Broad diversification and allocation of assets by industry and companies.
3. Convenience in buying and selling shares. No problems with

failed delivery, delayed settlements, or compliance with foreign securities laws.

4. Easy access to information about fund performance, companies invested in, and data from quarterly reports.
5. Flow of cash dividends and capital gains to investors as required by the Investment Company Act of 1940. Dividends and capital gains paid in U.S. dollars.
6. A convenient way to diversify holdings among different countries and foreign currencies as a hedge against a declining U.S. dollar.
7. In some cases, funds are the only way to invest in foreign markets because of restrictions on the types of investments made by nonresidents.
8. Most mutual funds allow the transfer of money from one fund to another for a small charge. They usually have an automatic reinvestment option to buy shares at net asset value.

The main disadvantages are:

1. Sales charges and advisory, administrative, and management fees.
2. Diversification tends to limit potential capital appreciation and risks.
3. Closed-end funds can sell at a discount to the market value of the underlying assets—the net asset value (NAV).
4. The management team's performance record may underperform foreign market indexes.
5. An investor relinquishes control of assets to fund managers.

The rest of this chapter describes some regional funds that invest in securities of specific countries. More background information on these countries is presented in Chapters 8 to 19.

ASA LIMITED

NYSE Symbol ASA

As of this writing, the Republic of South Africa is undergoing political and economic turmoil due to its apartheid policy. Only if racial reconciliation and peace occur will South Africa regain its stability and positive image in the world. South Africa is a primary producer of diamonds, gold, platinum, and certain strategic metals essential to making defense equipment. Threats of economic sanctions against the government have caused a sharp devaluation of the rand, which is the official South African currency. The dramatic drop in the rand has hurt the prices of South African gold stocks traded on the Johannesburg Exchange and on other stock exchanges with dual listing of South African shares.

ASA Limited is a closed-end, nonregulated investment company that must keep at least 50 percent of its assets in South African gold shares. Up to 20 percent of the fund's assets can be invested outside South Africa. In the South African gold stock portfolio, it concentrates on long-life mines with high-grade ore. The fund retains a portion of its dividend receipts as a reserve to offset the depletion of mines. The dividend payouts (and yields) are usually lower than payouts obtained from individual mining shares.

During times of high inflation, gold prices tend to rise with the inflation rate—outperforming stocks and bonds. This usually creates a strong demand for South African gold shares. Likewise, during times of disinflation, gold prices fall due to weakened demand for gold bullion and mining shares. Gold prices have fallen dramatically from 1980—when their value rose above $800 an ounce. A combination of tight monetary and credit policies, high interest rates, and declining crude oil prices triggered the gold price collapse.

South Africa's social and political unrest have put a cloud of uncertainty over the investment quality of South African securities. Many U.S. investment managers are divesting their holdings in South African stocks to protest apartheid policies. An investment in South African gold shares might be attractive if the country's political and economic problems are resolved.

THE FIRST AUSTRALIA FUND

AMEX Symbol IAF

The Commonwealth of Australia is a huge continent (2,967 million square miles) with a population of less than 16 million people. Australia was a British penal colony in the 1800s. It is rich in natural resources—bauxite, gold, iron ore, coal, gemstones, oil, and gas. Australia exports a large percentage of its grain and livestock commodities.

The people of Australia are well educated and enjoy a high standard of living. The Australian capital market is the ninth largest market in the world with $72 billion of the total world market capitalization.

The First Australia Fund was formed as a closed-end investment company in December 1985. The First Australia Fund issued 3.5 million shares at $10 per share. The fund's assets are invested in Australian equities and debt securities. Its objective is to achieve long-term capital appreciation by investing in Australian industries. Australian industry is heavily concentrated in natural resources production, mining, agricultural commodities, and energy resources. The Australian economy prospers during times of rising commodity prices, but it falters during times of declining prices. The First Australia Fund is managed by Equitilink International Management, Ltd. The Prudential Insurance Company of America acts as the investment consultant.

THE FIRST AUSTRALIA PRIME INCOME FUND

AMEX Symbol FAI

The First Australia Prime Income Fund is a closed-end regulated investment company with 75 million shares outstanding. Unlike the First Australia Fund, the Prime Income Fund is limited to investing in Australian and New Zealand debt securities rated A or higher by independent credit rating agencies. The securities are government or corporate debt issues. The Prime Income Fund is the largest issue traded on the American Stock Exchange. At the offering, 75 million shares were issued at $10 per share in April 1986.

When this fund came to market in the United States, interest rates on short-term maturity debt issues yielded 15 to 20 percent in Australia and New Zealand—which provided an opportunity for a high rate of real return since the Australian inflation rate was about 10 percent. Comparable interest rates in the United States ranged from 6 to 8 percent.

THE MEXICO FUND

NYSE Symbol MXF

Mexico has faced tough economic decisions since the late 1970s. The country has accumulated a large national debt that was borrowed to finance development of oil and mining industries as well as new industry. Mexico has experienced high levels of inflation and unemployment. The Mexican peso, which was once pegged at 8 pesos to the dollar, devalued sharply against the dollar in 1981. Mexico exports oil, natural gas, industrial metals, produce, and consumer beverages to the United States. For investors wanting to invest in Mexican companies, the Mexico Fund offers an opportunity to invest in a rapidly developing economy.

The Mexico Fund is a diversified, closed-end investment company with an investment objective of long-term capital appreciation. Holdings are diversified over a broad spectrum of the Mexican economy. Certain sectors of the economy, such as oil, gas, electricity, and railroads are state-owned enterprises, and equity investments in those sectors are not permitted. Mexico nationalized its banks in 1982. The fund commenced its investment program in Mexican equity securities in June 1981. The fund is required by law to invest at least 70 percent of its assets in equity securities—primarily securities listed on the Bolsa Mexicana de Valores S.A. de C.V. (the Mexican Stock Exchange). There are 20 million shares outstanding; 10 percent of these shares are held by institutions. Impulsora del Fondo Mexico, S.A. de C.V. is the investment advisor to the fund.

THE JAPAN FUND

NYSE Symbol JPN

Japan has experienced tremendous economic growth with low unemployment since the end of World War II. The economy has been restructured, and the country has become a major exporter of durable and consumer goods. Japanese companies manufacture machinery, chemicals, automobiles, optical equipment, and electronic components for the world marketplace. The United States is Japan's largest customer for exported goods. Because of the great difference between what Japan exports to the United States and what it imports, Japan has accumulated a large balance of payments surplus with the United States in recent years. Japan's capital markets are the second largest in the world; they comprise $1.314 billion of total world market capitalization.

Japan is a major importer of natural resources, since it has few natural resources of its own. In the 1970s, Japan experienced a sudden jolt in economic growth when crude oil prices rose dramatically. Japan imports nearly all of its crude oil.

The Japan Fund is a publicly traded investment company with a principal investment objective of capital appreciation. The general policy of the fund is to invest at least 80 percent of its assets in Japanese Securities, primarily common stocks of Japanese companies, with no more than 25 percent of the total assets in one industry.

Asia Management Corporation is the investment advisor to the Japan Fund. Asia Management is an affiliate of Scudder, Stevens & Clark. Nikko Research provides investment advice to Asia Management. There are 23.184 million shares outstanding with institutions holding approximately 5.3 percent. At the annual meeting in April 1985, shareholders voted to increase authorized common shares to 40 million from 25 million. The additional shares will be used in future years for dividends and capital gains distributions.

THE KOREA FUND

NYSE Symbol KF

Since the end of military conflict between North and South Korea in 1953, South Korea's economy has grown steadily. In recent years, the economy has blossomed to become a leading exporter of durable and consumer goods to the United States, Asia, and Europe. Like Japan, Korean companies export automobiles, electronic components, and textiles.

The Korea Fund was formed in May 1984 as the first U.S. investment company organized to invest in Korean securities. The fund's objective is long-term capital appreciation through investment of at least 80 percent of net assets in the securities of companies listed on the Korean Stock Exchange. Investment in the securities of Korean companies and the Korean government involves special considerations including restrictions on foreign investment and repatriation of capital invested in Korea and restrictions and costs associated with the conversion of investment principal from nondenominated to dollar-denominated securities. As of this writing, nonresidents of Korea can't make direct investments on the Korean Stock Exchange. The Korea Fund is exempt from this restriction.

The Korea Fund is managed by Scudder, Stevens & Clark. A subsidiary of Daewoo Securities Co., Ltd., acts as investment advisor to the fund. There are 5 million shares outstanding; 35 percent of the shares are held by institutions.

THE ITALY FUND

NYSE Symbol ITA

The Italian economy has developed rapidly since World War II. Italy is considered a private enterprise economy with the state participating in significant areas of the economy including banking, shipping, transportation, and communications. In 1984, Italy was the sixth largest economy among countries comprising the Organization for Economic Cooperation and Development (OECD). Italy has a gross domestic product (GDP) of $348 billion. Italy has primarily a service and industry oriented economy. The principal industries are chemicals, food processing, furniture, leather goods, automobiles, and textiles. Italy has the seventh largest capital markets with $115 billion in total world market capitalization.

The Italy Fund was issued at $12 per share in March 1986. It is a diversified, closed-end management investment company that seeks long-term capital appreciation through investing at least 65 percent of its assets in Italian debt and equity securities. American Express Asset Management S.A. acts as the fund's investment advisor.

SCANDINAVIA FUND

AMEX Symbol SCF

Scandinavia is the region in northern Europe that includes Sweden, Denmark, Norway, and Finland. Finland borders the Soviet Union, and it is influenced strongly by Soviet economic policies. Norway, due to its location on the North Sea, has substantial oil production. Sweden is the largest of the Scandinavian countries with a population of over 8 million people. The Kingdom of Denmark is the southernmost country in Scandinavia with a population of 5 million. The price of crude oil and foreign trade are important factors in the economy of each Scandinavian country. Sweden's stock market is the largest of the Scandinavian countries, and it is the 11th largest market in the world with total market capitalization of $43 billion.

The Scandinavia Fund is a closed-end investment company with a primary objective of capital gains through investment in Swedish, Danish, Norwegian, and Finnish equities. The fund was brought public in June 1986 with an initial offering of 6.5 million shares at $10 per share. The fund is managed by Aktiv Placering. Aktiv Placering is a wholly owned subsidiary of Skandinaviska Enskilda Banken (S-E-Banken). S-E-Banken is the largest commercial bank in Scandinavia.

FRANCE FUND

NYSE Symbol FRN

France is the largest country and the biggest European food producer except for the USSR. France is known for its wines, automobiles, fine fashions, and perfumes. France has achieved steady economic growth following World War II. The worldwide recession in 1974, caused by sharp increases in crude oil prices, affected economic growth negatively.

France's economic and political environment changed dramatically after the election of President Francois Mitterrand in 1981. Mitterrand's Socialist government nationalized many large French industries and financial institutions. Following the elections in March 1986, the Socialist Party was replaced as the majority party in France by an alliance of conservative parties. Jacques Chirac was appointed prime minister, and the new government decided to eliminate price controls, deregulate companies, and denationalize many state-owned enterprises over a five-year period. France's capital markets are the sixth largest markets in the world with a total market capitalization of $134 billion.

The France Fund was formed in May 1986 as a diversified closed-end investment company. The initial offering was 7.5 million shares at $12 per share. The fund is managed by Dillion, Read International Asset Management. Its objective is to achieve long-term capital appreciation by investing its assets in French equity and debt securities. The fund can invest in debt issues of the French Government and in ECU-denominated securities.

The fund can invest in denationalized French companies as they become available through France's privatization program. The fund is limited to investing no more than 10 percent of its total assets in a single corporate issuer and no more than 25 percent of the assets in one industry. The fund's managers can trade option and financial futures contracts to hedge portfolio and foreign exchange risks; however, the managers are limited to five percent of the total assets for options and futures-related transactions. The France Fund receives income in francs and makes distributions in U.S. dollars. The fund may be subject to withholding taxes up to 15 percent on dividends from French securities.

THE GERMANY FUND

NYSE Symbol GER

Germany was divided into East and West Germany after World War II. East Germany is politically aligned with the USSR, whereas West Germany is a democratic and independent country. West Germany experienced steady economic growth following World War II. West Germany is the world's largest trading country. It is a major exporter of chemicals, machinery, automobiles, and electrical equipment. West Germany permits universal banking, which allows banks to perform many financial services that U.S. banks can't perform. German banking law allows banks to act as securities brokers/dealers, investment advisers, asset managers, and underwriters. The three largest commercial banks are Deutsche Bank, Commerzbank, and Dresdner Bank. They are members of the German Stock Exchange, and they manage mutual funds through subsidiaries. West German capital markets are the fourth largest in the world with total market capitalization of $229 billion.

The Germany Fund went public in July 1986 with an offering of 7.5 million shares at $10 per share. It is incorporated as a closed-end investment company that can invest 65 percent of its assets in the equity-linked securities of German companies. Deutsche Bank Capital Corporation, a subsidiary of Deutsche Bank, is the fund's manager. The Germany Fund is authorized to invest in privately owned and state-owned German equity and debt securities. Fund managers can hedge foreign currency risks in the interbank market if fund managers believe that the deutsche mark will decline against the U.S. dollar.

GLOBAL YIELD FUND

NYSE Symbol PGY

The Global Yield Fund was incorporated as a closed-end investment company. It went public in June 1986 in an offering of 57 million shares at $10 per share. The Prudential Insurance Company of America is the fund's manager. It plans to invest its assets in the debt securities of countries that offer an opportunity for high current yield relative to current yields available from dollar-denominated debt securities. The fund can achieve capital appreciation during periods of declining interest rates. The fund may invest in the debt securities of Canada, the United States, Australia, Hong Kong, Japan, New Zealand, Singapore, and 14 European countries.

SIMMS GLOBAL FUND

The Simms Global Fund is an open-end management investment company whose shares were first offered to the public on January 12, 1987, at a price of $9.50 per share. As an open-end fund, shares are continuously available through investment dealers and the principal underwriter at a price equal to their net asset value plus a sales charge.

The fund's investment objective is capital appreciation through investment in a globally diversified portfolio consisting primarily of equity securities. The fund normally invests at least 65 percent of its assets outside the United States, although the percentage fluctuates depending on the judgment of the investment adviser, Simms Capital Management, Ltd. Currently, the investment adviser plans to invest at least 90 percent of the fund's assets in developed countries of the Far East (Japan, Hong Kong, and Singapore), Western Europe (the United Kingdom, Germany, Holland, France, Switzerland, Italy, Belgium, Norway, Sweden, and Spain), Australia, Canada, and the United States.

The investment advisor utilizes various techniques, including foreign exchange and index options contracts, to hedge foreign currency exposure and equity market exposure. In addition, the investment advisor can write call options on individual securities it holds (with certain restrictions) when this action helps achieve the fund's investment objective.

SUMMARY AND CONCLUSION

Mutual and closed-end funds offer investors an opportunity for professional management, diversification into international markets, and liquidity of market shares. Investment companies furnish a supply of needed capital for listed foreign companies. We believe that mutual fund management companies will offer more funds that specialize in third-world country investing. These countries have the greatest growth potential in domestic economies and export markets, but they also entail the greatest danger in foreign exchange risks, political stability, maturity of capital markets, and the strength of balance sheets for listed companies.

The market price of closed-end funds may trade at a discount to the net asset value (NAV). Purchasing closed-end funds at a substantial discount to their NAV reduces the risk of investing in them compared to mutual funds that must be offered at their NAV. Information on the NAV of closed-end funds is available in *Barron's* and in *The Wall Street Journal*. See Table 2.1.

TABLE 2.1   Comparison of Listed Country Funds as of October 17, 1986

Country Fund	Net Asset Value	Fund Price	Percent Difference
ASA Ltd.	74.74	37.00	−50.50
First Australia Equity Fund	10.71	8.75	−18.30
First Australia Prime Income	8.50	8.25	−2.9
France Fund	13.10	10.00	−23.66
Germany Fund	10.13	9.88	−2.50
Italy Fund	14.44	10.50	−27.30
Japan Fund	22.50	16.50	−26.70
Korea Fund	22.02	35.00	58.90
Mexico Fund	4.41	3.25	−26.30
Scandinavia Fund	9.46	7.00	−26.00
Global Yield Fund	10.25	9.50	−7.32

SOURCE: *Barron's*, October 17, 1986.

LISTING OF CLOSED-END REGIONAL MANAGEMENT INVESTMENT COMPANIES

ASA Limited
PO Box 39
Chatham, NJ 07928

First Australia Fund
One Seaport Plaza
New York, NY 10292

France Fund
535 Madison Ave.
New York, NY 10022

Korea Fund
345 Park Ave.
New York, NY 10154

Mexico Fund
477 Madison Ave.
New York, NY 10020

Scandinavia Fund
755 New York Ave.
Huntington, NY 11743

First Australia Prime Income
One Seaport Plaza
New York, NY 10292

Italy Fund
Two World Trade Center, 106th floor
New York, NY 10048

Japan Fund
345 Park Ave.
New York, NY 10154

Germany Fund
40 Wall Street
New York, NY 10005

Global Yield Fund
One Seaport Plaza
New York, NY 10292

LIST OF GLOBAL AND INTERNATIONAL MUTUAL FUNDS

This is a partial list of global and international mutual funds. Many of these funds make it convenient for investors to set up IRA, Keogh, and 401 (k) plans. Some funds charge a front-end load; others are no-load. Performance varies widely among the funds because of differences in their approach to market timing and valuation.

Prospective investors must read the prospectus thoroughly to understand the objectives, restrictions, and fees associated with each fund. In addition, investors may want to consult independent advisory services for assistance in choosing the most appropriate fund for their financial objectives.

Nomura Pacific Basin Fund
Nomura Securities International, Inc.
The Continental Center
180 Maiden Lane
New York, NY 10038

Fidelity Overseas Fund
Fidelity Distributors
P.O. Box 660603
Dallas, TX 75266

Scudder Global Fund
Scudder Fund Distributors
175 Federal Street, Dept 784
Boston, MA 02110

T. Rowe Price International Bond Fund
T. Rowe Price International Stock Fund
T. Rowe Price
100 East Pratt Street
Baltimore, MD 21202

GT Global Growth Funds
GT Capital Management
601 Montgomery Street, Suite 1400
San Francisco, CA 94111

EuroPacific Growth Fund
Capital Research and Management Company
333 South Hope Street
Los Angeles, CA 90071

Templeton World Fund
Templeton Foreign Fund
Securities Fund Investors
P.O. Box 3942
St. Petersburg, FL 33731

Transatlantic Fund, Inc.
Kleinwort Benson International Investment, Ltd.
100 Wall Street
New York, NY 10005

Keystone International Fund
Keystone Custodian Funds
99 High Street
Boston, MA 02110

CHAPTER THREE

Portfolio and Risk Management Strategies for the International Equities Markets

The objective of investing in foreign equities markets is to earn a high return by purchasing undervalued securities denominated in undervalued currencies. An investor must also plan to sell securities when they become fairly valued to the market or to liquidate a position through stop-loss protection. A 15 percent stop-loss protection is recommended to conserve capital.

An equities investor should also have a longer-term investment horizon than an investor in debt securities. Unlike debt issues, which have a defined maturity date, common and preferred shares are perpetual unless terminated by bankruptcy or merger. Research has confirmed that a diversified portfolio of equities significantly outperforms a portfolio of straight debt securities over a 10-year period. See Table 3.1.

VALUATION OF COMMON SHARES

What constitutes an undervalued common share? Valuation of a company's shares depends on (1) future earnings, (2) cash flow, (3) actual book value, or (4) special situations that may alter the earnings or net asset value, such as a new patent, discovery of natural resources, or technological breakthroughs. These are the germane factors that securities analysts uncover and present to clients.

TABLE 3.1   Performance of Equity and Bond Market Total Returns

The following statistics represent an average of total percentage returns from equity and bond markets from 1975 to 1984. The data reveal that total returns of the world's nine largest equity markets significantly outperformed bond markets.

Country	Equity Market Total Return	Bond Market Total Return
United States	14.8%	7.2%
Japan	16.8	11.6
United Kingdom	22.7	11.1
Canada	12.1	4.9
Germany	7.9	6.9
Australia	12.6	2.7
Switzerland	9.7	6.1
France	10.4	2.4
Netherlands	18.0	5.6

SOURCE: *Euromoney Yearbook 1985* (London: Euromoney Publications).

VALUATION OF A CURRENCY

What constitutes an undervalued currency? Another country's currency is undervalued to the U.S. dollar if that country's real growth in GDP/GNP, trade account, surplus account, capital account, balance of payments, and real returns on bond yields and interest rates favor the purchase of its currency and the sale of U.S. dollars. This subject is covered more thoroughly in Chapter 5, which describes the revaluation and devaluation processes of foreign exchange rates.

THE PRINCIPAL APPROACHES TO INVESTING IN EQUITIES

The total return of a common stock can consist of (1) appreciation in price of a security, (2) dividends paid in cash or stock, and (3) revaluation of a country's currency versus the U.S. dollar. There are three basic approaches to investing in the international equities market:

1. Selection of individual securities with expectations that total returns will outperform a stock market index. For example, XYZ listed on the London Stock Exchange gained 35 percent in price,

while the FT-SE 100 index gained 20 percent. XYZ outperformed the market by a margin of 15 percent.

2. Selection of securities that comprise a stock market index with expectations that this group (basket) will match the index performance. For example, the basket of listed securities on the London Stock Exchange gained 21 percent, while the FT-SE 100 index rose 20 percent.

3. Selection of a group (basket) of securities that comprise a stock market index, which also has a corresponding futures index or options market for hedging portfolio risks. For example, a basket of securities listed on the London Stock Exchange hedged with FT-SE 100 index futures yielded an annualized return of 12 percent compared to UK short gilts yielding 10%.

These approaches, with differing objectives and outcomes, have been used by money managers investing large sums of money in U.S. stock markets.

THE PRINCIPAL RISKS OF INVESTING
IN THE INTERNATIONAL EQUITY MARKETS

An investment's degree of risk is measured by its variability of return. A high degree of risk implies a potentially high profit or loss. Certain risks defy quantitative evaluation. Selection of either individual securities or a basket of securities requires evaluating the following risks:

1. Country risks—unfavorable changes in the governing political cal party, the credit rating of the country's debt obligations, taxation policies, or the government's nationalization of private businesses.
2. Industry risks—unfavorable changes in an industry or sector such as demand for products and/or services, labor costs, changes in technology, high interest rates, import/export restrictions, and/or commodity prices.
3. Company risks—unfavorable changes in a company's management, balance sheet, earnings, or credit rating.
4. Currency risks—unfavorable changes in a currency's exchange rate versus the U.S. dollar. A currency could experience a sharp devaluation to the U.S. dollar, which might eliminate any profit in a transaction.

Investors should consider the effects of estimated risks versus returns and the amount of time allocated for research and idea development and translating these ideas into actual transactions. Besides the broader risks associated with a country, industry, company, or currency, investment in foreign securities entails specific risks:

1. Lack of available information and price data on companies, sectors of the economy, and industry groups.
2. Illiquidity—the inability to instate or liquidate a position in the market due to a lack of market makers.
3. Auditing, financial, and tax accounting procedures that don't conform to generally accepted accounting practices.
4. Incomplete disclosure of a company's balance sheet, income statement, business operations, and management changes as required by the Securities and Exchange Commission (SEC) for companies listed on U.S. stock exchanges.
5. Clearance and settlement risks—certain foreign exchanges haven't installed systems for timely clearance and settlement of transactions; in some cases, transaction settlements and delivery of securities can take months.
6. "Insider trading" and unfair market practices deemed illegal by the SEC in the United States may be permitted in other countries.

GUIDELINES FOR DEVELOPING INVESTMENT CRITERIA AND MEASURING REAL RATES OF RETURNS

Inflation-adjusted returns on U.S. Treasury bills are considered the benchmark for U.S. investments. Because U.S. Treasury bills are considered a riskless investment, their yields are used to measure different types of investments compared to the U.S. economy's inflation rate.

If U.S. Treasury bills yield 8 percent and the inflation rate is 4 percent, then the inflation-adjusted return is 4 percent in real terms. However, if the Treasury bill rate is 8 percent and the inflation rate is 8 percent, then the real return is zero. If inflation-adjusted returns are close to zero or negative, investors will seek alternative investments to preserve purchasing power—investments whose potential returns are greater than the inflation rate. Investors' funds flow in and out of financial markets based on comparable yields, risks, and capital appreciation.

The investment horizon must also be considered before investing in foreign securities. An investment horizon is the time commitment an investor is willing to make for holding a security. For example, if an investor wants to commit funds for less than one year, investing in the equities market may be inappropriate.

INVESTMENT STRATEGIES FOR SELECTION OF INDIVIDUAL EQUITIES

Investors can utilize one or more of the following approaches in selecting an equity security. These strategies are used for selecting individual securities that could outperform the stock market averages.

1. **Asset valuation model**—A fundamental approach for determining a company's actual market value regarding its price to book value, price to earnings, or price to cash flow. For example, if XYZ Plc were trading on the London Stock Exchange at 350 pence per share, and its estimated book value were 425 pence, its price to book value would be at a 21 percent discount. XYZ might be a candidate for a leveraged buyout that would realize full shareholder values of the company. Appraisal of a company's assets requires an in-depth analysis of its business operations, cash flow, proprietary patents, asset base, management capability, and earnings. A major problem with the asset valuation approach is the great discrepancies in accounting practices permitted in foreign countries. For example, West German companies employ ultraconservative accounting practices that overstate liabilities and understate cash flow, earnings, and book value.

2. **Market timing model**—This approach uses technical analysis tools for buying and selling securities. Technical analysis uses defined chart patterns, volumetric studies, series of moving averages, and other indicators as buy and sell signals without regard for a company's fundamentals.

3. **Dollar-cost averaging model**—Fixed amounts of money are committed to purchase a security at periodic times to achieve an

---

EXAMPLE 3.1   Dollar-Cost Averaging Approach

A U.S. investor wants to accumulate a position in XYZ Plc using the dollar-cost averaging method. XYZ is a U.K. beverage company listed on the London Stock Exchange. The investor decides to invest $1,000 each quarter for two years regardless of share price and exchange rates. The investor will buy various amounts of shares depending on the exchange rate between the U.S. dollar and the British pound and the price of shares. One BP = 100 pence (p).

Quarter	US$	US$/BP	Share Price	Number of Shares
1	$1,000	$1.25	500p	160
2	1,000	1.30	525p	146
3	1,000	1.35	470p	158
4	1,000	1.40	480p	149
5	1,000	1.45	490p	141
6	1,000	1.50	500p	133
7	1,000	1.55	535p	121
8	1,000	1.60	540p	116
Totals	$8,000			1,124

In this example, the investor's average price per share is $7.12, or 445 pence at the exchange rate of $1.60. The market value is computed by multiplying the total number of shares owned by the share price and the exchange rate. The market value of XYZ is $9,711.36—a gain of $1,711.36.

---

average of high and low prices for a company's shares. An investor's goal is achieving a lower average price than the future selling price. Dollar-cost averaging is an appropriate method for investors who want to accumulate long-term positions in the shares of a company, in the units of an investment trust, or in a mutual fund. See Example 3.1.

4. **Risk arbitrage model**—An investor buys shares in a company with an announced buyout (tender offer) at a specified price. For example, XYZ Plc company announces a tender offer for the shares of ABC Plc at 825 pence. Prior to the announcement, ABC was trading at 550 pence. This strategy is for sophisticated investors with substantial capital who understand the risks of leveraged buyouts, mergers, and acquisitions.

5. **New issues**—An investor buys shares in a company on an initial public offering (IPO). New issues are risky investments if an investor hasn't done any homework because IPO's are generally less mature companies issuing stock for the first time. A special case for using this approach would be purchasing the shares of privatized companies. Many foreign governments are privatizing

state-owned enterprises by offering their shares to the public. In many cases, these shares are priced attractively in relation to their actual market value. Refer to Chapter 7 for more information on investing in privatizated companies.

Examples of these five investment strategies are presented to compare their benefits. We have developed a computer-assisted investment model that considers the numerous factors present in making an investment decision. The model allows investors to make qualitative assessments and to convert them into quantitative statements regarding the degrees of risk and the rewards associated with these investments. Computer programs can facilitate the storage, retrieval, and processing of voluminous data in creating a database of companies for screening investment opportunities.

The investment process begins with defining one's objectives and desired outcomes. An investor can choose from one or more of these objectives in selecting a security:

1. Current yield from cash dividends.
2. Safety of principal as measured by assets to liabilities, cash flow, and ability to service debt.
3. Stability in net asset value.
4. Price to current and future earnings.
5. Price to estimated book value.
6. Price to estimated cash flow.
7. Potential for revaluation in the denominated currency of a security.

DESCRIPTION OF PORTFOLIO
MANAGEMENT STRATEGIES

Portfolio management involves procedures for selecting, allocating, and deciding when to buy and sell securities. Portfolio management requires extensive quantitative evaluation of risks and returns associated with the different types of investment instruments, allocation of assets, investment strategies, and portfolio composition. A portfolio's characteristics can be quite different than the sum of the risks for individual securities.

Quantitative evaluation of portfolio risks and returns is a complex task that utilizes computers to perform accounting functions, graphic displays, and financial analyses. A basic list of risk evaluation and management techniques includes:

1. Diversifying by country, sector, company, and denominated currency.
2. Creating an asset-mixed portfolio of equities, debt securities, convertible issues, and derivative instruments such as stock index futures and options on the indexes.
3. Creating a portfolio of securities related to an index. This is a passive management technique.
4. Creating a portfolio of securities related to an index hedged with stock index futures or index option contracts.
5. Modifying securities portfolios related to an index by using options on stock indexes to hedge risks and increase income.
6. Purchasing stock index futures or index options contracts as derivative instruments in lieu of purchasing the underlying securities.

THE ROLE OF STOCK MARKET INDEXES

Before presenting investment strategies that utilize indexed portfolios of common stocks, we will provide background information for understanding the evolution and importance of these approaches in current portfolio management theory and practice.

The idea of formulating an index for measuring the activity of business cycles originated with Charles H. Dow (1851–1902). After Dow's death, William P. Hamilton, who succeeded Dow as editor of *The Wall Street Journal,* formulated the tenets of Dow Theory.

Dow recognized that the price movement of certain leading securities seemed to foretell future trends in the U.S. economy. The price movement of railroad and mining stocks appeared to forecast, months in advance, upturns or downturns in the U.S. economy. Dow Theory has been an important component of stock market theory for over a century.

Over the years, newer and broader-based indexes have evolved to measure and forecast economic trends and business cycles. The Standard & Poor's 500 is one of 15 leading economic indicators used to forecast trends in the U.S. economy. The U.S. Department of Commerce uses the S&P 500 Index as the benchmark index to measure U.S. capital market activities compared to other countries.

An index is useful in comparing historical and contemporary data, even though the base values and composition of an index are revised to reflect the additions or deletions of companies. Stock market indexes also mirror investor sentiments, attitudes, and behavior prior to actual changes in economic fundamentals. In recent years, public and private statistical reporting has become commonplace. Foreign exchanges have developed their own representative market indexes and market indicators to record and compare changes over time.

THE CREATION OF NATIONAL, INTERNATIONAL, AND WORLD STOCK INDEXES

Three types of stock market indexes are employed to monitor economic activity and investor psychology nationally and internationally:

1. **National Stock Index**–This index is composed of companies that represent the composite sectors of a national economy, such as the FT SE-100 index on the London Stock Exchange and the Nikkei Stock Averages on the Tokyo Exchange. It includes subindexes such as industrials, transportation, financial, and utilities.
2. **International Stock Index**–This index is composed of companies representing the composite sectors of several national economies, such as the E.A.F.E. Index—which includes the stock markets of Europe, Australia, and the Far East.
3. **World Stock Index**–This index is composed of companies representing composite sectors of the United States and other countries that comprise the largest percentage of total world market capitalization, such as the Euromoney/First Boston World Index, which is comprised of 1,700 stocks.

Stock market indexes are derived in two ways; index reporting services maintain proprietary formulas for computing an index. An index can be either price-weighted or capitalization-weighted. A

TABLE 3.2   List of Foreign Stock Market Indexes

Country	*Index Name*
Japan	Nikkei Dow Jones Average
United Kingdom	Financial Times 100
Canada	Toronto Stock Exchange 300
West Germany	Frankfurter Allgemeine Zeitung
Italy	Milan General Indice
Australia	All Ordinaries Share Price
Switzerland	Swiss Bank Corporation
France	Compagnie De Agents De Change
Netherlands	A.N.P.-C.B.S. Beursindex
Hong Kong	Hang Seng
Singapore	Stock Exchange of Singapore
World	Morgan Stanley Capital International
	Euromoney-First Boston
	Financial Times

---

price-weighted index gives equal value to each index issue regardless of total shares outstanding. A capitalization-weighted index give a higher value to issues that have a larger number of shares outstanding. Most indexes are capitalization-weighted.

Other countries have developed indexes for measuring their capital market activities; however, these indexes vary in computation methods and don't provide a basis for comparison. Table 3.2 lists the primary world stock market indexes.

Market indexes are usually computed and maintained by financial reporting services, foreign banks, and national exchanges. Morgan Stanley Capital International (MSCIP) has standardized reporting of national stock indexes to make comparisons among the markets easier for analysts and investors. MSCIP has a representative index for most capital markets. These indexes are published daily in financial publications.

High-speed computers collect continuous price information from the trading floor and calculate the value of an index. Index values are updated at one-minute intervals throughout the trading day. The creation and maintenance of market indexes has led to the development of new investing approaches such as indexing and index arbitrage.

INDEXING AS A PORTFOLIO MANAGEMENT STRATEGY FOR EQUITIES

What is indexing? Indexing is an approach to managing funds through purchasing a basket of securities whose price movement replicates a specified index, such as, the Financial Times-SE 100 (FT-SE 100) Index. Creating indexed portfolios has become popular in managing large fiduciary accounts.

Growth of indexed portfolios stems from research done on the performance of investment managers. Investment managers are paid management fees to outperform the market. Research has indicated that most money managers underperform stock indexes over a period of years. The diminished results are due largely to brokerage commissions and management and administrative fees associated with active management. Clients therefore wonder why they should pay large commissions and fees for funds that aren't outperforming the market averages.

The concept of creating indexed portfolios was promulgated as a way to match the performance of a standard market index. Indexing results in significantly reduced costs because large blocks of stocks comprising an index can be purchased at reduced commissions.

The objective of investment research is to discover undervalued stocks before others do in the hopes that the marketplace will fairly value the security at a future date. Indexing eliminates the need to pay for expensive research since the goal of an indexed portfolio is to match but not outperform market index.

INDEX ARBITRAGE AS AN INVESTMENT MANAGEMENT STRATEGY

Straight indexing entails portfolio risks because an index on the market can fluctuate significantly from month to month. Some years, an index can rise or fall by as much as 20 percent. Many investment managers prefer not to take that risk. Index arbitrage was developed to reduce portfolio risk while achieving returns several percentage points higher than the risk-free rate. Index arbitrage is commonly called "program trading" because it is an actively managed program utilizing index futures or option contracts on an index.

TABLE 3.3   Listing of Foreign Stock Market Indexes with Futures Contracts

---

Stock Index	*Exchange*
Nikkei Stock Average	SIMEX
FT SE-100	LIFFE
Hang Seng	Hong Kong Futures
Toronto 300	Toronto Futures
All ordinary shares	Sydney Futures

SIMEX—Singapore International Monetary Exchange.
LIFFE—London International Financial Futures Exchange.

The objective of program trading is to enhance yields while hedging portfolio risks. Program trading occurs when a specified number of shares of preselected issues are bought through an automated order entry system proprietary to stock exchange members. Stock index futures contracts are sold against a basket of securities.

Program trading is commonly used by investment managers of pension funds in the United States for achieving high real returns without taking portfolio risks. Several countries have permitted the establishment of index futures and options exchanges that correspond with indexes on their stock markets. Table 3.3 shows several foreign stock markets with index futures and options contracts.

The concept of program trading is easy to understand. Execution of trades in an index arbitrage program, however, is more difficult. Before showing how index arbitrage works, we reiterate several assumptions:

1. Prior to the expiration of a futures or options contract, the difference between the theoretical and actual values of index futures can change significantly. The difference is called basis. Basis provides an opportunity to buy an underlying index of securities and sell the corresponding index futures with no risk if they are held until expiration. See Figure 3.1.

2. At expiration, the actual index value becomes equal to the theoretical value. In other words, the value of the index futures equals the value of the underlying index.

3. The difference between when the arbitrage was initiated and

---

FIGURE 3.1 **Difference between the Theoretical and Actual Values of the Index Futures Price**

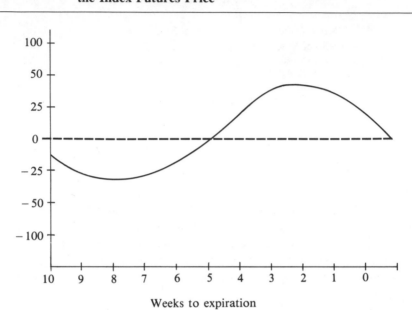

Weeks to expiration

This graph shows the differences between the theoretical and actual values of the index futures prices plotted over time. The theoretical value of an index futures price represents the spot index value plus unpaid dividends and the cost of financing a basket of securities. The variance between theoretical and actual values is due to the differing expectations that investors have about trends in stock index prices.

---

when it was taken off is the profit. In efficient markets, this profit can range from 2 to 4 percentage points higher than the risk-free rate. For example, if the risk-free rate is 8 percent, then an index arbitrage program should yield 10 to 12 percent.

CALCULATION OF THE THEORETICAL VALUE AND BASIS DIFFERENTIALS

The theoretical value (price) of an index futures contract is the sum of an index's spot price, the risk-free return, and unpaid dividends until contract expiration. The spot price of an index is the actual index value calculated at the most recent interval during a trading session.

The basis is the difference between the spot index price and the index futures price. Changes in the basis reflect changing investor expectations about future events in the market. The price of an index futures contract is subject to inefficient market forces that cause prices to deviate from the theoretical value, which provides opportunities for arbitrage and riskless profits. The following formulas illustrate these relationships.

$$TV = IND + RFR + UD$$
$$BASIS = IND - INF$$
$$D = INF - TV$$

Legend:
TV = Theoretical value
IND = Spot value of index
INF = Value of index futures
RFR = Risk-free rate of return
UD = Unpaid dividends

When $D = 0$, the index futures price is fairly valued to the spot index, providing no opportunities for profit. If D is negative, the index futures price is valued at a discount to the spot index. If the value of D becomes highly positive, the index futures price is valued at a premium to the index, which provides arbitrage opportunities for riskless profits depending on the amount of the futures price premium to the theoretical value. Figure 3.2 shows changes in the basis.

Program trading variations are done with put and call options on the indexes. Conversion strategies involve purchasing a basket of stocks, selling an index call, and purchasing an index put to lock in a specified yield. There are times when put and call option premiums deviate from their theoretical values, which allows opportunities for a riskless profit. The four basic strategies are:

1. Buy the underlying basket of securities (the index) and sell index futures at a premium to the theoretical value.
2. Sell the underlying basket of securities (the index) and buy index futures at a discount to the theoretical value.
3. Buy the underlying basket of securities. Sell index calls at a premium. Buy index puts at a discount. This is a conversion strategy.

FIGURE 3.2   Basis Graph

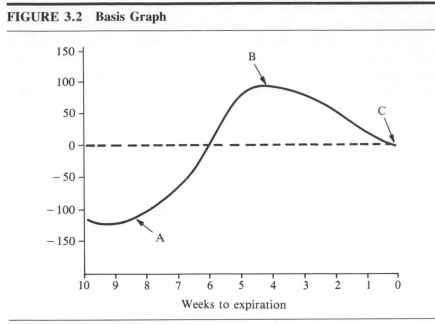

Weeks to expiration

A basis graph shows the relationship between the spot index price and the corresponding index futures price.

Basis = Spot price − Index futures price

A—Index futures are at a premium to the spot index. This provides an opportunity to purchase a basket of stock representing the spot index and to sell the corresponding index futures contract to lock in a risk-free rate of return.

B—Index futures are at a discount to the spot index. This provides an opportunity to sell short a basket of stocks representing the spot index and to purchase the corresponding index futures contract to lock in a risk-free rate of return.

C—The convergence of index futures and spot index prices when the futures contract expires.

4. Sell the underlying basket of securities. Buy index calls. Sell index puts. This is a reverse conversion strategy.

The success of program trading as an investment strategy depends on the ability to buy blocks of securities and sell index futures contracts at price differentials needed to achieve a specified rate of return.

The New York Stock Exchange, the American Stock Exchange, and certain foreign stock exchanges have installed automated order entry programs for executing a programmed sequence of buy or sell transactions at limit prices on a specified number of shares of certain companies. The NYSE's proprietary system is called Designated Order Turnaround (DOT). The DOT system executes orders on any group of NYSE-listed securities with a limit of 2,099 shares or less. Index futures on the NYSE, S&P 100, or S&P 500 can then be sold to establish a hedge against the basket of purchased securities.

HOW TO USE STOCK INDEX FUTURES AND OPTIONS ON THE INDEXES AS DERIVATIVE SECURITIES

Many foreign exchanges are introducing stock index futures and options on their primary market indexes. Stock index futures and options markets provide investors with instruments for managing portfolio risk and allow numerous combinations for enhancing a portfolio's current yield.

Index futures and option contracts are derivative securities because they represent an underlying basket of securities. These instruments are a complement to selecting securities, not a permanent substitute for them. We recommend using these instruments as risk management tools and not for speculating on the market's direction. Trading index futures and options contracts as a speculation can be very risky because of the contracts' brief life, the high degree of price volatility, and the leverage involved. Unlike long option contracts, which are fully paid for, futures and short option contracts entail a high risk because they are traded in margin accounts. Because margin accounts may have a customer's funds representing less than 20 percent of the total market value of contracts on deposit, brokers calculate variation margin requirements daily to prevent default on contracts.

Reasons why investors should consider trading these instruments are:

1. Buying index futures contracts is a market timing tool for entering the market quickly; it is a temporary substitute for purchasing a basket of stocks. Buying index futures and options contracts is considerably less expensive than buying a portfolio of stocks.

2. Selling index futures is used to adjust the relative characteristics of a portfolio—its duration and the implied volatility (beta) of a portfolio—in line with market expectations.
3. Writing index call options and option straddles can add premium income to a portfolio.
4. Buying index put options can protect the downside value of the portfolio without limiting the upside potential.
5. Synthetic option strategies can provide unique opportunities for managing risks. Synthetic positions involve a combination of an option and a basket of securities.

Investors usually construct portfolios within the context of an investment philosophy guided by certain parameters of safety, quality, estimated risks, and expected total returns. For example, investors who seek high growth in earnings with no dividends through aggressive management of biotechnology stocks use different parameters than investors selecting stocks based on quality, safety, and dividends. Investment objectives requiring current yield with the average growth in earnings imply the selection of mature companies with dividend payouts such as utility companies.

Before the arrival of stock index futures and options, investors were in a quandary about changing portfolio compositions to enhance performance in a cost-effective manner. During periods of rising index prices (bull markets), investors want to own high-beta stocks that usually outperform the market. Likewise, during periods of declining index prices (bear markets), investors want to hold low-beta stocks or be in cash. These instruments provide an immediate and cost-effective way to adjust the duration and implied variability of a portfolio in line with market conditions. See Examples 3.2, 3.3, 3.4, and 3.5 to clarify these points.

EXAMPLE 3.2

Scenario: A U.S. mutual fund manager believes that London's Financial Times Index will rise over 10 percent during the next two months. The manager wants to invest in a broad base of equity securities traded on the London Stock Exchange without making individual stock selections. He decides to buy one December FT-SE 100 Index futures at 165. The contract is traded on the London International Financial Futures Exchange (LIFFE). The actual index is 1,620. Quotation of the spot index = FT-SE Index ÷ 10.

Market Data:	Initial	Final
FT-SE 100 Index	1,620	1,750
FT-SE 100 Spot Index	162.00	175.00
FT-SE 100 Index futures	165.00	175.00
Basis	−3.00	0
U.S.$/British £	$1.40	$1.40

Contract Specifications:		
One index point	£25.00	$ 35.00
Index value	£40,500	$56,700
Margin per contract	£750	$ 1,050

The fund manager decides to sell the contract in December when the index futures price is $175. He made a profit of 10 index points of £2,500 or $3,500. The profit on this transaction could be affected by the exchange rate at the time of sale. His gain would have been greater had the British pound revalued to the U.S. dollars.

EXAMPLE 3.3

Scenario: A U.S. pension fund owns British stocks. The investment manager believes FT-SE 100 will decline 10 percent during the next two months. He wants to protect the current value of the portfolio without selling stocks. He sells one December FT-SE 100 Index futures contract at 170. The actual index is 1,670. Quotation of the spot index = FT-SE Index ÷ 10.

Market Data:	Initial	Final
FT-SE 100 Index	1,670	1,600
FT-SE 100 Spot Index	167.00	160.00
FT-SE 100 Index futures	170.00	161.00
Basis	−3.00	−1.00
U.S.$/British £	$1.40	$1.40

Contract Specifications:		
One index point	£25.00	$ 35.00
Index value	£40,500	$56,700
Margin per contract	£750	$ 1,050

The manager buys back the contract in December when the futures price is 161. A profit of 9 index points was made amounting to £2,250 or $3,150. The profit on this transaction can be used to offset the unrealized losses taken on the portfolio. The profitability of this transaction could be affected by the exchange rate. The gain would have been greater if the British pound had revalued to the U.S. dollar.

EXAMPLE 3.4

Scenario: An investor holds British securities worth £64,000 on which options are not listed. She feels that their prices may remain stable or decline. She wants to protect her investment and obtain additional income by writing index call options against the portfolio. With the index standing at 1,620, she decides to sell December 1,625 index calls for a premium of 50 pence. If, at expiration, the index stands at 1,625 or less, the call options are then valueless, and she can retain the entire premium of £500 or $700 per contract. Put and call options on the FT-SE 100 Index are traded on the Stock Exchange of London and not on the LIFFE. Quotation of the spot index = FT-SE Index × £10.

Market Data:	*Initial*	*Final*
FT-SE 100 Index	1,620	1,600
FT-SE 100 Index, 1,625 calls	£.50	0
U.S.$/British £	$1.40	$1.40
Contract Specifications:		
One index point	£10.00	$ 14.00
Index value	£16,200	$22,680
Margin per contract	£2,025	$ 2,835

She buys back her contract in December when the index futures price is 1,600. She made a profit of £500 per contract or $700. The profit on this transaction compensates for the small decline in the index price. The investor actually received additional income of £500 during the holding period. The profitability could be affected by the exchange rate at time of sale. Her gain would have been greater if the British pound revalued to the U.S. dollar.

EXAMPLE 3.5

Scenario: An investor holds British securities worth £64,000 on which options are not listed. He feels their prices will decline by 20 percent. He wants to protect his investment by buying index puts as portfolio insurance. With the index standing at 1,620, he decides to buy December 1,600 index puts for a premium of 50 pence. If, at expiration, the index stands at 1,600 or higher, the put options will be valueless and he will forfeit the entire premium of £500 or $700 per contract. Quotation of the spot index = FT-SE Index × £10.

Market Data:	Initial	Final
FT-SE 100 Index	1,620	1,500
FT-SE 100 Index 1,600 puts	50p	100p
U.S.$/British £	$1.40	$1.40
Contract Specifications:		
One index point	£10.00	$ 14.00
Index value	£16,200	$22,680
Premium per contract	£500	$ 700

He sells the contract in December when the index futures price is 1,500. He made a gross profit of £1,000 per contract or $1,400. The gross profit on this transaction partially compensates for the 100-point decline in the index price. The net profit, however, is reduced to £500 or $700 because the option premium must be subtracted from the proceeds. The profitability could be affected by the exchange rate at time of sale. His gain would have been greater if the British pound had revalued to the U.S. dollar.

CHAPTER FOUR.

Portfolio and Risk Management of International Debt Securities

Debt securities are obligations issued by a government agency, municipality, or corporation. With the exception of zero-coupon issues, an issuer of debt securities promises to make periodic interest payments and repay the principal at maturity. Debt obligations can be issued in fixed rate, floating rate, or convertible issues. An issuer may specify provisions in the indenture of a security by which it may call a security prior to maturity date.

The objectives for investing in foreign debt securities are:

1. To earn a higher yield on foreign currency denominated issues than comparable U.S. dollar-denominated securities.
2. To purchase undervalued debt issues denominated in under-valued currencies for a higher total return.
3. To purchase debt issues denominated in a currency as a substitute for owning that currency.

VALUATION OF DEBT SECURITIES

What constitutes an undervalued debt security? The price of a debt security is inversely related to its yield components. When interest rates rise, prices on low coupon issues decline to match the current yield of high coupon issues. Rising interest rates can cause a loss of principal on low coupon issues. Likewise, when interest rates decline, the prices of high-coupon debt securities rise, which results in capital gains for an investor.

Valuation of a debt security is a function of (1) investor demand for an issue, (2) the issuer's credit rating, (3) the issue's credit rating, (4) tax treatment of principal and interest payments, and (5) price and yield components compared to issues with a similar maturity, coupon, and credit rating.

VALUATION OF A CURRENCY

What constitutes an undervalued currency? Another country's currency can be undervalued to the U.S. dollar if that country's real growth in GDP/GNP, trade account, surplus account, capital account, balance of payments, and real returns on bond yields and interest rates favor purchasing its currency versus U.S. dollars. This subject is covered more thoroughly in Chapter 5, which describes the revaluation and devaluation processes for foreign exchange rates.

THE PRINCIPAL APPROACHES TO INVESTING IN DEBT SECURITIES

There are four approaches to investing in foreign securities:

1. Purchasing individual issues that fit specific parameters set by an investor. An investor can select securities based on credit rating, frequency of coupon payments, maturity, type of issuer, discount to par value, current yield, and the yield-to-maturity rate.

2. Purchasing debt securities denominated in a currency to substitute for buying that currency in foreign exchange markets.

3. Purchasing a portfolio of debt securities that match an index such as the Salomon Bond Index, that is, creating an indexed portfolio of securities designed to match the performance of a standard index.

4. Purchasing debt issues that can be hedged with interest rate futures and/or option contracts. Usually this strategy is limited to purchasing selected government obligations and selling interest rate futures or options against them.

HOW DEBT SECURITIES DIFFER FROM EQUITIES

Debt securities differ from equities in the following ways:

1. They are senior to equity shares in case of default, that is, the bankruptcy of an issuer. Holders of debt have senior claim to

the assets of an issuer compared to common and preferred share-holders.

2. Debt securities carry no voting privileges or other benefits of equity ownership unless they are issued with rights or warrants convertible to shares.

3. Debt issues have a maturity date for redemption at a spec-ified price.

4. Interest payments are usually taxed as income and not as dividends. In some countries, share dividends receive preferential tax treatment. Certain governments exempt holders of their obliga-tions from taxation.

5. Debt issues are generally priced with respect to the yield curve of comparable issues, and the credit ratings of issue and issuer.

THE TOTAL RETURN ON DEBT SECURITIES

Total return on a foreign debt security is comprised of (1) interest payments, (2) changes in the price of the security, and (3) gains and losses on foreign exchanges. The largest buyers of foreign debt obligations are corporate and public pension funds, insurance com-

TABLE 4.1 Domestic Government Bonds Historical Performance Annualized Returns and Standard Deviations, 1975–1985

Country	U.S. Dollar Adjusted		Local Currency	
	Average Return	Standard Deviation	Average Return	Standard Deviation
Japan	12.85	18.53	9.93	7.58
Denmark	12.14	17.77	18.14	15.86
United Kingdom	10.54	19.16	16.38	14.19
Foreign Bond Index	9.65	11.79	11.13	7.02
Germany	9.63	15.97	10.53	9.54
Switzerland	9.45	19.34	6.55	7.12
Netherlands	9.06	16.65	10.91	11.24
United States	8.58	11.25	—	—
Ireland	8.14	18.32	16.06	13.86
ECU	8.07	13.16	12.15	8.07
Canada	6.86	11.35	10.04	10.83
France	6.21	15.14	12.20	9.28
Belgium	5.54	13.64	9.47	7.74
Italy	3.15	18.02	13.22	14.38
Australia	2.50	11.66	8.74	10.58

SOURCE: Morgan Guaranty *World Financial Markets* (based on 129 monthly observa-tions) and OECD *Financial Statistics Monthly*.

FIGURE 4.1

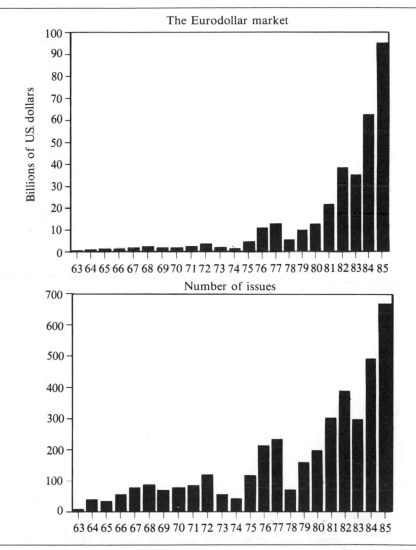

The Eurodollar market

Number of issues

panies, banks, investment trusts, and mutual funds. (See Table 4.1.)

Financial institutions own a portfolio of debt securities to match assets with liabilities. For example, insurance companies want safe, high-yielding assets such as bills, notes, and bonds to pay off current and future liabilities of policyholders. Pension fund

FIGURE 4.2

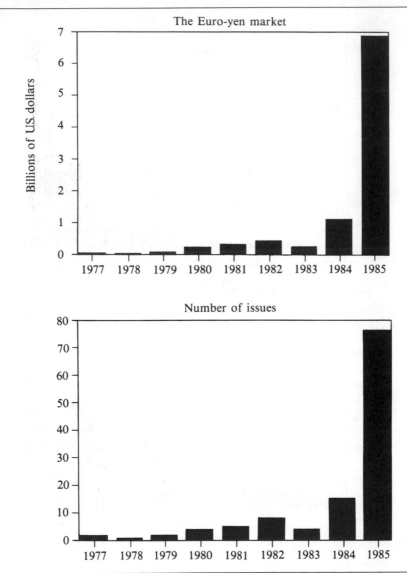

The Euro-yen market

Number of issues

managers must accumulate assets to meet the contingent liabilities of employee disability and retirement claims. For this reason, institutions purchase debt obligations with specific maturities.

Outside the United States, there is a large demand for debt securities. In European countries, the supply and volume of trad-

FIGURE 4.3

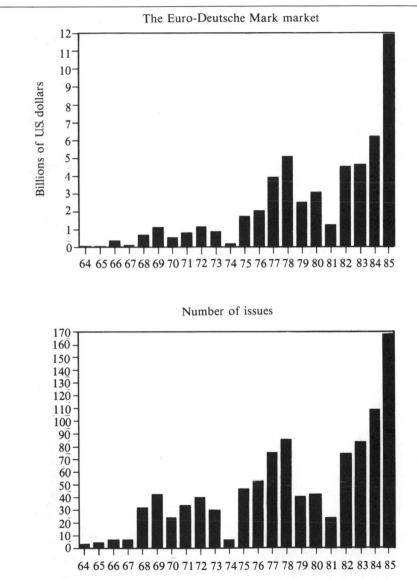

The Euro-Deutsche Mark market

Number of issues

FIGURE 4.4

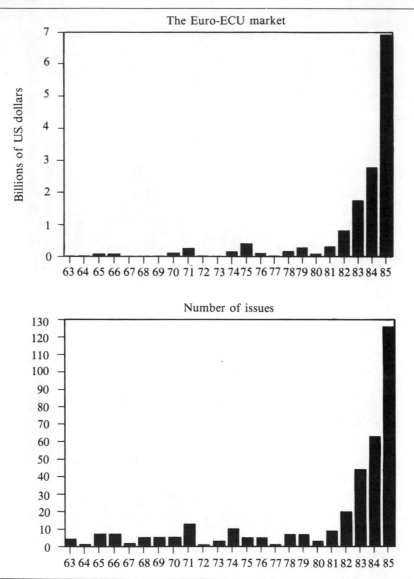

The Euro-ECU market

Number of issues

FIGURE 4.5

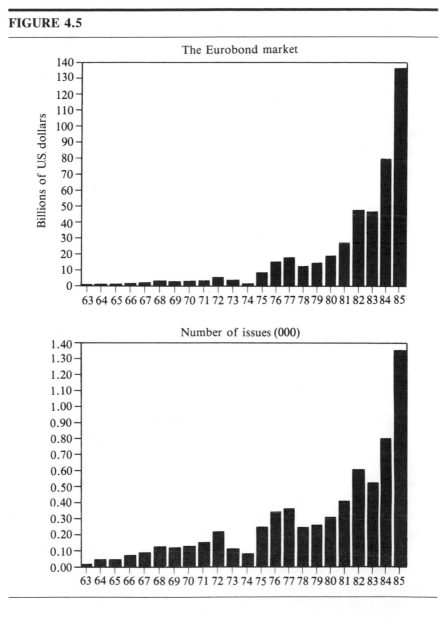

The Eurobond market

The Eurobond market
Billions of US dollars

63 64 65 66 67 68 69 70 71 72 73 74 75 76 77 78 79 80 81 82 83 84 85

Number of issues (000)

63 64 65 66 67 68 69 70 71 72 73 74 75 76 77 78 79 80 81 82 83 84 85

ing in Eurobonds is four to five times that of Euro-equities. Foreign currency denominated debt securities offer U.S. investors the benefits of higher current yields, capital gains, and potential gains in foreign exchange rates. Likewise, adverse changes in exchange rates can negate the benefits of owning non-U.S. dollar-denominated debt issues. See Figures 4.1 through 4.5, which show historical growth in foreign currency denominated debt issues.

THE INTERNATIONAL MARKET FOR JUNK BONDS

Debt securities are purchased in substantial quantities by employee retirement funds, corporate pension plans, insurance companies, banks, and other institutions that require guaranteed interest payments and safety of principal. In the past, financial institutions were restricted to owning investment-grade issues. In recent years, there has been a growing demand worldwide for low-quality corporate debt issues called "junk bonds."

Junk bonds are rated either below investment grade or not rated at all by credit agencies. Junk bonds have higher yields to compensate owners for assuming additional credit risks. Under certain conditions, specific issues of low-rated bonds can be significantly undervalued. For example, the value of a low-rated bond can increase if a credit agency raises its rating on a particular issuer. An investor could realize a substantial capital gain if the credit rating of a low-rated bond is upgraded. New issues of junk bonds have financed corporate restructuring, leveraged buyouts (LBOs), and mergers and acquisitions (M&A).

INTEREST RATE FUTURES AND OPTIONS MARKETS

The Chicago Board of Trade and Chicago Mercantile Exchanges pioneered development and marketing of interest rate futures and option contracts nearly a decade ago. In recent years, the creation of interest rate futures and options markets has become more common on foreign exchanges. The financial centers of the United Kingdom, the Netherlands, France, Japan, and Singapore have had growing, active markets in interest rate contracts. Usually these instruments are limited to selected government securities because they have standardized specifications regarding credit rating, size, and delivery.

Interest rate futures and options contracts provide hedging instruments to manage price risks and enhance yields on underlying securities. Financial futures and options contracts can be incorporated into an overall portfolio strategy to enhance performance. Managers of debt securities can utilize interest rate contracts (1) to immunize a bond portfolio against price variability, (2) to reduce reinvestment risks, (3) to achieve additional income, and (4) to alter the duration of the securities.

CONCEPTS AND TERMINOLOGY

Before discussing how to invest in international debt securities markets, certain basic concepts and terminology must be understood:

Principal. The full amount of monies borrowed by an issuer denominated in a local currency. For example, a West German corporation issues 10-year bonds in units with a par value of DM 1,000. In 10 years, the issuer promises to repay the principal amount of DM 1,000 to the investor.

Maturity. The date when the security is redeemed by an issuer. For example, Federal Republic of Germany 6 percent bonds mature on June 15, 1990.

Par Value. The value imprinted on a certificate that provides the basis for interest payments and the amount to be repaid to a holder at maturity.

Coupon Yield. The specified percentage yield of a security.

Zero Coupon. Securities that pay principal and all interest payments at maturity; they pay no (hence, zero) coupon payments during the holding period.

Current Yield. The percentage return currently paid to holders that can be higher or lower than the coupon yield.

Yield-to-Maturity. Total percentage return resulting from capital gains and interest payments of a security if held to maturity.

Interest Payments. Amount of money paid to the holder periodically. Payments can be made monthly, quarterly, semiannually, or annually.

Fixed-Rate Issue. A debt security that promises to pay a fixed return (coupon rate) at periodic intervals until maturity.

Floating-Rate Issue. A debt security that promises to pay a variable rate based on a benchmark rate (LIBOR, 90-day Treasury bill) at periodic intervals until maturity.

Bills. Debt securities with maturities up to one year; bills are purchased at a discount and redeemed at par on maturity.

Notes. Debt securities with maturities from 1 to 10 years.

Bonds. Debt securities secured by the specific assets of an issuer with maturities from 10 to 30 years.

FIGURE 4.6   Normal Yield Curve

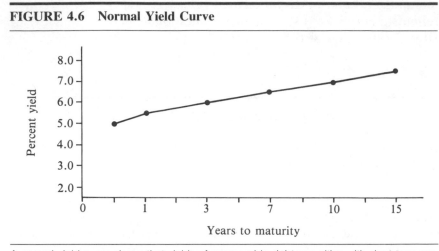

A normal yield curve shows that yields of comparable debt securities with short-term maturities are lower than yields of securities with long-term maturities. A normal yield curve
represents a situation of adequate liquidity in the banking system. The demand for credit
matches the availability of loanable funds.

Eurobond.   Debt security whose principal and interest are denominated
in a currency other than the country of origin, for example, when a Swiss
corporation issues 10-year bonds denominated in deutsche marks.

Dual-Currency Bonds.   A debt security with a principal denominated in
one currency and interest denominated in another currency, such as when
a U.K. corporation issues 10 bonds with the principal denominated in
pounds sterling and the interest payments denominated in U.S. dollars.

Debenture.   Debt securities secured by the general assets of an issuer
with maturities from 10 to 30 years.

Convertible Debenture.   Debt securities issued by a corporation convertible to equity shares at a specified price.

Risk-Free Rate Of Return.   The current yield of a 90-day government bill;
a 90-day U.S. Treasury bill is considered the safest debt instrument in the
world and, therefore, a benchmark for comparing other debt and equity
securities.

Call Feature.   The conditions stated in an indenture whereby securities
can be called for redemption prior to maturity.

Indenture.   The legal contract between an issuer and holder that specifies their contractual provisions, restrictions, and responsibilities.

Credit Rating.   The estimate of an issue or issuer's credit worthiness,
given by an independent rating agency such as Standard & Poor's or

FIGURE 4.7   Inverted Yield Curve—Disintermediation of Interest Rates

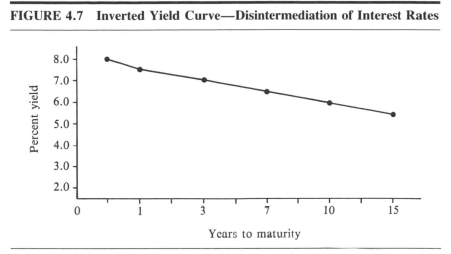

An inverted yield curve shows that the yields of comparable debt securities with short-term maturities are higher than yields of securities with long-term maturities. An inverted yield curve represents disintermediation of interest rates caused by a shortage of liquidity in the banking system. The demand for credit exceeds the supply of loanable funds.

Moody's.   The ratings are usually designated by a series of letters and/or numbers such as ABB/B22.

Yield Curve.   A graphic representation of current yields for specific securities plotted against maturity dates. See Figure 4.6.

Disintermediation.   A condition in which yields on debt securities with short-term maturities are higher than yields with long-term maturities. See Figure 4.7.

Real Rate of Return.   The total return minus the current inflation rate; also referred to as an inflation-adjusted return.

Stock versus Bond Yields.   The difference between the expected yields on common stocks and bonds.

Interest Rate Futures.   The financial futures contracts that correspond to specific debt instruments such as government bills, notes, or bonds.

Options on Interest Rate Futures.   Put and call options that can be exercised into interest rate futures contracts by the holder.

Interest Rate Options.   Put and call options that can be exercised into specific debt instruments such as government bills, notes, or bonds.

Sinking Fund.   A fund accumulated to pay off corporate or public debt. U.S. insurance companies are large buyers of sinking fund bonds for asset/liability management.

ECONOMIC AND POLITICAL FACTORS
THAT AFFECT INTEREST RATES, PRICES,
AND YIELDS ON DEBT SECURITIES

Prices and yields of debt securities are sensitive to the general level of interest rates in the economy. The general level of rates responds to changes in the demand for credit by government, commercial banks, corporations, and consumers. The extension of credit allows government, businesses, and consumers to build plants, to pay salaries and wages, and to buy capital goods and services immediately with money not yet received.

The level of interest rates is an important barometer to the degree of liquidity in the banking system and credit markets. A rising level of interest rates indicates increased credit demand and a shortage of available funds to finance borrowing. Declining interest rates indicates an adequate supply of funds for borrowers.

Government policymakers use interest rates as a monetary tool to implement temporary changes in the national economy through the central bank. Economic planners, who subscribe to monetarist theories, propose intervention by the central bank to adjust the level of interest rates in the economy to achieve socially desired goals. They believe intervention can cause changes in national productivity, unemployment, inflation, and capital investment. For example, if policymakers want to slow business expansion, a central bank can implement a restrictive credit policy through the commercial banking system. Likewise, a central bank can be more accommodating toward credit if policymakers want to stimulate the economy. These changes can occur by raising or lowering the discount rate. The discount rate is the interest that a commercial bank pays the central bank when it borrows funds—using government bonds or other eligible securities as collateral. The federal funds rate is the lending rate between banks charged daily on funds borrowed to meet their reserve requirements.

The level of real interest rates and yields on debt securities result from a composite of variables interacting in different sectors of an economy. Future expectations about the level of interest rates play an important role in maintaining the current level. For example, if policymakers believe that a decline in interest rates below a certain level will result in double-digit inflation, interest rates can be artificially maintained at higher levels until market forces drive them down. The following is a partial list of macroeconomic factors that shape present and future expectations about interest rates:

1. Real rate of growth in the GDP/GNP. The real rate of growth is the nominal rate minus the inflation rate. A rising GDP/GNP generally produces lower interest rates because foreign investment provides additional liquidity.
2. Rates of growth and velocity in the money supply (M-2). Nominal interest rates increase with an expansion in the money supply.
3. Rates of inflation in wages and producer and wholesale prices. A rising inflation rate causes rising interest rates in an unregulated economy.
4. Level of unemployment—a high unemployment level generally causes central banks to lower interest rates to stimulate the economy so that unemployment will decline as businesses hire new people.
5. Capacity utilization—the level at which industry utilizes plants and equipment.
6. Real rate of return on government securities, such as inflation-adjusted yields on government bills, notes, and bonds.
7. Level of real interest rates in other countries. For example, real interest rates might be 7.5 percent in the United States, 5 percent in Japan, 5 percent in West Germany, and 10 percent in the United Kingdom.

Interest rate changes demonstrate a cyclical pattern that can help forecast trends in foreign exchange rates, stock index prices, and yields on debt securities. Accurate forecasts of interest rates and the inflation rate are essential to managing portfolio risks and in formulating profitable investment strategies.

FORMULATING INVESTMENT STRATEGIES FOR DEBT SECURITIES

The selection process for debt securities differs from equities. Investors in debt securities usually work within specific parameters regarding the type of issue, yield components, frequency of coupon payments, securing of the principal, maturity, and credit ratings.

Investors purchase equities to participate in long-term growth in corporate earnings and profits through dividend increases and the price appreciation of capital shares. Corporate earnings generally increase in relationship to the growth in a country's real GDP/GNP. Unlike equity investors, buyers of foreign debt obligations prioritize selecting issues regarding the type of issuer, the currency denomination of issue, the safety of principal, the maturity dates of obligations, and the yield derivatives.

Governments, government agencies, and multinational corporations issue currency-denominated bonds to take advantage of yield spreads between countries. As borrowers, they want to pay the lowest interest rates. Lenders, which include investment managers, pension funds, and corporate treasurers, purchase currency-denominated bonds to obtain higher yields and potential gains from foreign exchange rates.

Investors must consider the following guidelines and questions in purchasing foreign debt obligations:

1. Type of issuer; government, government agency, municipality, or corporation.
2. Credit rating of the issue and the issuer.
3. Maturity of an issue.
4. Foreign currency risks.
5. Political and economic risks of the country where an issuer is domiciled.
6. Provisions in the indenture for early call or other special features.
7. Is the issue secured by specific assets or the general credit worthiness of an issuer?
8. What is the current yield, yield to call, and yield to maturity?
9. Is the issue priced fairly in relation to comparable issues?
10. What is the minimal acceptable current yield?
11. What is the objective for capital gains? Deep discount or zero-coupon bonds are purchased if capital appreciation is the primary goal.
12. What are the systems for clearing and settling a transaction and safekeeping the securities once a purchase has been made from a primary issuer or in the secondary market?

THE RISKS OF PURCHASING DEBT SECURITIES

Purchase of debt obligations entails the following risks to the investor:

1. Risk of inflation where the inflation rate surpasses the expected yield. This is known as purchasing power risk.
2. Risk of rising competitive interest rates that cause prices to fall. Bond yields and prices are inversely related. A sharp rise in interest rates can cause a sharp decline in prices, which results in the loss of principal.
3. Reinvestment risk where interest payments are invested at a lower rate than the issue's coupon rate.
4. Credit risks of the issue and issuer. The issuer may default on paying interest or default on the principal at maturity.
5. Credit risk of the country where the issuer is domiciled. A radical change in government, such as a change from conservative to socialist or communist. A change in central bank policies can cause an issuer to default or delay interest and principal payments.
6. Foreign exchange risks due to fluctuating currency values versus the U.S. dollar.
7. Risks of failed delivery, delayed settlement, or loss of securities due to faulty clearing and settlement systems.

THE ASSIGNMENT OF CREDIT RATINGS

When an investment banker underwrites a new debt issue, a credit rating is applied for from an independent credit agency such as Standard & Poor's, Moody's, or Fitch. Many countries have independent rating agencies that evaluate domestic debt issues. A rating agency establishes criteria for evaluating an issuer's ability to meet interest and principal obligations until maturity. The agency assigns applicable ratings to issues based on the issuer's credit history, net worth, current assets to liabilities, and the ability to service its total outstanding debt. If an investor is unfamiliar with a rating agency, further investigation is warranted regarding the criteria and assumptions made in assigning a rating. The highest credit rating is AAA. A high credit rating facilitates placing an issue with prospective clients. It is much easier for investment bankers to place a high-quality issue with clients because the assumed default risk is less than for lower quality issues.

A specific debt security can become undervalued for many reasons, such as a downgrade in its credit rating or lack of investor interest in the issue. Opportunities for purchasing undervalued debt issues occur when an investor anticipates an upgraded credit rating or an increased demand for a particular issue. Professional investors closely monitor potentially undervalued issues and purchase them before their true value is realized in the market.

COMPARATIVE ANALYSIS OF THE YIELD CURVE

The value of a debt issue is a function of its credit rating, credit worthiness of the issuer, current yield, yield-to-call, yield-to-maturity, and special features and benefits that may accrue to the holder. A yield curve is a graph of percentage yields for selected debt issues plotted against different maturities. The maturities range from one month to 30 years. It is a useful analytical tool for comparing relative values of debt securities with different yields, prices, coupons, maturities, and credit ratings. Comparison of relative values helps determine which issues might be undervalued and thus suitable for purchase. In addition, the yield curve's shape assists an investor in selecting which issues to purchase, sell, or swap. Before investing in the debt issues of other countries, an investor must evaluate yield curves of comparable issues selected from different countries to make an appropriate selection based on value.

A yield curve's shape reveals information about the present credit and monetary conditions in a country. A yield curve can be normal, inverted, or flat. A normal yield curve exists when yields on short-term issues are lower than long-term issues. A normal yield curve suggests sufficient availability of credit and liquidity in the economy to meet borrowers' needs. A flat yield curve exists when the yields for short-term issues equal yields for long-term issues. An inverted curve exists when yields for short-term issues are higher than long-term issues. For example, if yields for short-term issues are higher than long-term issues, this indicates a tight credit situation and a lack of liquidity in the economy. An inverted

TABLE 4.2   Comparison of Selected Government Obligations

	Yields in Percentage			
Maturity in Years	United States	United Kingdom	Australia	West Germany
1	7.5%	13.0%	17.0%	6.0%
3	8.3	12.6	16.5	6.2
5	8.5	12.4	16.2	6.4
10	8.7	12.2	15.5	6.7
15	9.0	12.0	15.0	7.0
20	9.2	11.6	14.7	7.2
30	9.4	11.4	14.3	7.4

yield curve suggests gross distortions in the credit markets and the general economy because investors are unwilling to assume the risks of making long-term commitments to borrowers. Investors can receive a higher return by lending funds on a short-term basis.

Table 4.2 presents simplified yield curve data that compare U.S. Treasury obligations against government obligations issued by the United Kingdom, Australia, and West Germany. The yield curves for the United Kingdom and Australia are inverted; the yield curves for the United States and West Germany are normal.

EXAMPLES OF SELECTION OF DEBT SECURITIES

This chapter concludes with examples illustrating the process of selecting debt securities offered in international markets. Before selecting debt securities, an investor must know the assumptions made by a credit agency in assigning an issue's rating. In addition, an investor should review historical and current trends in macroeconomic data of the countries and see how the trends affect interest rates in local currencies. See Table 4.3. The shape of the yield curve provides useful insight into current monetary conditions of a country. The yield curves of different types of debt instruments, such as corporate bonds and government obligations, should be compared to find undervalued securities that have been overlooked in the market.

TABLE 4.3 Macroeconomic Indicators

Indicators	United States	United Kingdom	Australia	West Germany
Real growth in GDP/GNP (percent)	3.0	3.0	1.0	7.0
15-year bond yield (percent)	9.0	12.0	15.0	7.0
Inflation rate (percent)	4.0	9.0	8.0	1.0
Real rate of return (percent)	5.0	3.0	7.0	6.0
Exchange rate (U.S.)	$1.00	$1.40	$0.63	$0.40

EXAMPLE 4.1

Scenario: A corporate treasurer with $1 million to invest believes that the deutsche mark will revalue against the U.S. dollar. His company will purchase electronic equipment from a West German manufacturer in one year. Rather than buy deutsche marks in the interbank market, he purchases West German government obligations with a 5 percent coupon maturing in three years. He buys DM 2.5 million worth of German bonds. The exchange rate at the time of purchase is U.S. $ = DM 2.50. He holds the bonds for one year and sells them at the same price. However, the deutsche mark has revalued to U.S.$ = DM 2.00 or 50 cents for a net gain of 10 cents. These are the net gains made on principal and interest in deutsche marks and U.S. dollars:

	Principal	Interest	U.S.$/DM	Principal	Interest
Initial	DM 2,500,000	DM 125,000	0.40	$1,000,000	$50,000
Final	DM 2,500,000	DM 125,000	0.50	$1,250,000	$62,500
Net gain	–0–	–0–	0.10	$ 250,000	$12,500

As the example shows, he made $262,500 ($250,000 + $12,500) in currency gains when the principal and interest were converted from deutsche marks to U.S. dollars. This is an annualized return of 26.25 percent in terms of U.S. dollars. Because the inflation rate in Germany was 1 percent, his real rate of return was 4 percent in the local currency.

EXAMPLE 4.2

Scenario: A pension fund manager with $1 million to invest wants to earn high current yields in A-rated paper. U.S. corporate bonds yield only 9 percent. Her investment horizon is at least five years. She decides to buy fixed-rate Commonwealth Bank of Australia bonds with a 14 percent coupon due February 1, 1991. The bonds are rated Aaa/AAA and denominated in Australian dollars (A$). The current yield is 14 percent. The exchange rate at purchase time is U.S.$ = A$ .63. She holds the bonds until maturity and sells them at the same price. However, the Australian dollar has revalued to U.S.$ = A$ .70 for a net gain of 7 cents. These are the end results of her positions:

	Principal	Interest	U.S.$/A$	Principal	Interest
Initial	A$ 1,587,301	A$ 222,222	0.63	$1,000,000	$140,000
Final	A$ 1,587,301	A$ 222,222	0.70	$1,111,111	$150,555
Net gain	–0–	–0–	0.10	$ 111,111	$ 10,555

As the example shows, her transaction gained $111,111 on the principal and $10,555 on interest when Australian dollars were converted to U.S. dollars.

EXAMPLE 4.3

Scenario: A bond fund manager owns £1 million of long gilts with a coupon of 10 percent maturing in 2005. Current yield on long gilts is 12 percent. He believes that interest rates may rise in the United Kingdom and wants to protect his principal against rising interest rates by hedging with long gilt futures contracts. He decides to sell short 20 contracts of the long gilt futures. Long gilt futures contracts are listed on the London International Financial Futures Exchange (LIFFE). The contract standard is £50,000 nominal value national gilt with a 12 percent coupon. The initial margins are £1,000 per contract. He deposits £20,000 with his broker to make the transaction. His objective is to lock in a yield spread while reducing the risk of capital losses. The exchange rate remains stable at US$ = £1.40. Six months later, he buys 20 contracts to close out his hedged position. The table below shows net gains made on hedging the transaction.

	Principal	Interest	Contracts	Gilt Price	Gilt Value
Initial	£1,000,000	BP 100,000	SOLD 20	101-00	£1,010,000
Final	£950,000	BP 100,000	BUY 20	97-00	£970,000
Net gain	£ – 50,000	–0–		+ 4-00	£ + 40,000

As the table shows, he lost £50,000 on his portfolio due to a rise in interest rates, but he recovered £40,000 of the loss through hedging with long gilt futures. His net loss was £10,000 versus a possible loss of £50,000 if he had not hedged.

EXAMPLE 4.4

Scenario: XYZ Corporation buys electronic parts from suppliers in England, France, Germany, and Italy. The company will owe these suppliers the equivalent of $1 million in one year for purchases. The company treasurer believes that the U.S. dollar will decline against the major European currencies due to trade imbalances with the European Economic Community (EEC). To protect himself, he decides to buy $1 million in bonds issued by Credit Foncier denominated in ECUs. The ECU is a composite currency representing currencies of member nations of the EEC. Credit Foncier's bonds are rated Aaa/AAA with a coupon of 9.75 percent maturing in 1995. The exchange rate at purchase time is ECU = $1.05. He holds the bonds for one year and sells them at the same price. However, the ECU mark has revalued to ECU = $1.15 for a net gain of 10 cents. The table below shows net gains made on principal and interest.

	Principal	Interest	U.S.$/ECU	Principal	Interest
Initial	ECU 952,381	ECU 92,857	1.05	$1,000,000	$ 97,500
Final	ECU 952,381	ECU 92,857	1.15	$1,095,238	$106,786
Net gain	–0–	–0–	+0.10	+$95,238	+$9,286

The multinational company hedged its foreign currency exposure by buying ECU-denominated bonds. Chapter 5 describes how to evaluate foreign currency risks and how to hedge against them to protect an investment's value.

CHAPTER FIVE.

The Evaluation and Hedging of Foreign Currency Exchange Rate Risks

Fluctuations in foreign exchange rates create risks and opportunities for profits of international investors. Before investing funds in the financial markets of another country, an investor must know the political, economic, and interest rate risks that affect the value of its currency. The objectives of determining a currency's value are:

1. To determine when a currency is undervalued relative to the U.S. dollar and, therefore, gains in value (revaluation). An investor's goal should be to buy securities denominated in an undervalued currency.
2. To develop hedging strategies for protection if a currency should face a loss in value (devaluation).

Since the breakdown of stable foreign exchange rates during the Nixon administration in 1973, exchange rates have floated freely between the U.S. dollar and other currencies—based on supply and demand for a currency. They haven't been arbitrarily fixed by the International Monetary Fund (IMF).

THE EUROPEAN MONETARY SYSTEM

Members of the European Economic Community (EEC) established a formalized exchange rate system called the European Monetary System (EMS). The EMS fosters close monetary coop-

TABLE 5.1   Composition of the ECU

The ECU is presently defined as the sum of the following components as of December 1985:

Member Country	Currency	Number of Units of Currency	Percent of ECU Value
West Germany	Deutsche mark	0.719	32.4%
United Kingdom	Pound sterling	0.0878	14.9
France	French franc	1.31	19.2
Italy	Italian lira	140.00	9.6
Netherlands	Dutch guilder	0.256	10.2
Belgium	Belgian franc	3.71	8.2
Luxembourg	Luxembourg franc	0.14	0.3
Denmark	Danish krone	0.219	2.7
Ireland	Irish pound	0.00871	1.2
Greece	Greek drachma	1.15	1.3

FIGURE 5.1   The U.S. Dollar versus the ECU

eration among member states, making the EEC a zone of monetary stability.

The EMS sets fixed exchange rates within narrow bands among its 10-member organization. The European Currency Unit (ECU) is a composite currency recognized by EMS members. The ECU is comprised of specific, fixed amounts of each EEC member state's currency based on the relative individual GNP contribution made to the EEC. The ECU is the third most important currency used for denominating international debt issues behind the U.S. dollar and the deutsche mark. Because the United States is not a member of the EMS, the U.S. dollar floats freely against the ECU. See Table 5.1 and Figure 5.1 for further details.

Foreign exchange rates are negotiated on a bid/asked basis between buyers and sellers. Buyers of currency purchase it at the asked price from banks. Sellers of currency sell it at the bid price. There are no daily price limits set on exchange rates. For example, the value of the British pound versus the U.S. dollar can change significantly by the hour if supply and demand conditions for the currency warrant.

FACTORS THAT AFFECT CURRENCY VALUES

Supply and demand components of foreign exchange involve the simultaneous interaction of both fundamental and technical conditions in the market.

Factors that affect a currency's supply are:

1. Exchange controls—formal rules and regulations governing the flow of funds in and out of countries; also, within each country, banks' official rules for foreign exchange transactions. Foreign exchange transactions must be cleared through the central bank in countries that impose exchange controls and restrictive policies on their currencies.

2. Quantity of currency outstanding available for foreign exchange transactions, that is, floating a country's currency in the interbank markets.

3. Growth in the domestic money supply—the growth rate in the money supply within a country; the growth rate is monitored and regulated by a country's central bank.

Factors that affect the demand for a currency are:

1. Comparative value of exchange rates—commercial banks and dealers buy currencies of countries with undervalued exchange rates and sell overvalued currencies. The objective is to achieve trading profits. Surplus foreign exchange earnings due to more export sales than import purchases can increase the value of a country's currency.

2. Interest rate differentials—currency dealers tend to buy currencies of countries with higher real interest rates and sell currencies of countries with lower rates. The objective is a higher real return on invested funds.

3. Relative rates of inflation—currency dealers tend to buy currencies of countries with low inflation rates and sell currencies of countries with high inflation rates. High inflation rates lower the comparative value of a country's currency due to the risks associated with volatility and uncertainty.

4. Real rates of return on government obligations—capital flows into countries that have high real rates of return on their government obligations, thus creating a demand for a country's currency.

5. Central bank intervention—official buying, by a central bank, of domestic currency versus the sale of other currencies, or vice versa, in the open exchange market to maintain desired exchange rate relationships with other currencies.

6. Confidence in government—investors prefer to buy currencies of a country with a strong and stable government whose political leaders are unlikely to make unexpected and dramatic changes in monetary and fiscal policies.

After the sharp rise in world crude oil prices in 1973, the U.S. dollar's value experienced extreme volatility. From 1973 to 1980, the U.S. dollar experienced successive devaluations against the deutsche mark, Swiss franc, and Japanese yen. During President Reagan's administration, from 1980 until March 1985, the U.S. dollar regained its prominence as the strongest currency in the world. The strength of a nation's currency depends on the (1) growth in real GDP/GNP, (2) real yields on government obligations, (3) perception of confidence in government and political leadership, (4) surplus in balance of trade payments, and (5) low levels of wage and price inflation.

THE ABANDONMENT OF FIXED EXCHANGE RATES

The present international monetary system of floating exchange rates began in 1973 with the demise of the Bretton Woods and Smithsonian agreements. Prior to 1973, foreign exchange rates of selected currencies were stable because they were pegged against the U.S. dollar within a narrow band of variance. The Bretton Woods agreement, signed in 1944 by representatives of 44 Western nations, allowed for a band of ± 1 percent par value parameter. That is, the exchange rate was allowed to vary only within limits of ± 1 percent value as determined by the International Monetary Fund (IMF). The Bretton Woods agreement created the IMF to oversee and maintain the fixed-rate system. After World War II, the United States enjoyed a high level of economic growth and prosperity that resulted in large government and private debts and mounting balance of trade deficits. The huge national debt resulted from excessive government spending to finance World War II and the Korean and Vietnam wars.

The Bretton Woods agreement lasted for 27 years. In 1971, it gave way to the Smithsonian agreement, which widened the band to ± 2.25 percent of par value. The worsening U.S. balance of trade deficits resulted in consecutive devaluations of the dollar.

The abandonment of the flexible fixed-rate system in 1973 created opportunities for currency dealers and investors to profit from buying undervalued currencies and selling overvalued currencies. Floating exchange rates were problematic for governments and corporations that hadn't adapted to the consequences of unstable and unpredictable changes in currency values. In effect, foreign exchange markets had become deregulated and subject to the changing expectations of supply and demand.

THE INTERBANK MARKET FOR FOREIGN EXCHANGE TRANSACTIONS

Foreign currency transactions occur among a network of commercial banks and their correspondents. Transactions are processed as book entries between banks, and they are settled daily. Commercial banks act as dealers for their own accounts and customers. This is known as the interbank market; banks buy, sell, or swap currencies at negotiated prices.

Customers in the interbank market are multinational entities that conduct business in several countries and therefore need the currency trading and settlement facilities of a commercial bank with an extensive network of correspondent banks. The correspondent banks are located in each country to finance business operations quickly. In the interbank market, currency transactions of $3 to $5 million are normal-sized transactions.

Three types of negotiated foreign exchange transactions comprise the interbank market's facilitation of the quotation, buying, and selling of currencies.

1. **Spot transaction**—currencies are bought and sold for immediate delivery. For example, 1 million U.S. dollars buys 2.25 million deutsche marks (DM) for immediate delivery at an exchange rate of DM 2.25 per U.S. dollar. Spot currency prices are usually quoted in terms of another currency: how many units of one currency it takes to buy a unit of another currency.

2. **Forward transaction**—currencies are bought and sold for delivery at a future date. Quotations are usually for 30-, 90-, and 180-day periods. For example, 1 million U.S. dollars buys 1.176 million Canadian dollars (CD$) for delivery in 90 days at an exchange rate of CD$ 1.176 per U.S. dollar. Forward exchange rates can be quoted at a premium or discount to the spot rate.

3. **Swap transaction**—simultaneous purchasing and selling of currencies for different maturities at different prices. For example, transactions involving the purchase of 30-day forward 5.1 million deutsche marks are swapped for the sale of 90-day forward 1.607 million British pounds in the interbank market.

QUOTATIONS OF FOREIGN CURRENCIES

In countries with restrictions on foreign exchange transactions, there are two systems for quoting rates: commercial and financial rates. In addition, the country's central bank must approve and process all transactions between parties to monitor and control capital flows in and out of the country.

Quotations for spot and forward currency prices, currency futures, and options prices can be obtained daily from *The Wall Street Journal,* Telerate, ADP Comtrend, Reuters, Bunker Ramo, and Quotron provide real-time display services for monitoring cur-

TABLE 5.2   Examples of Foreign Exchange Rates versus
            the U.S. Dollar

All exchange rates are quoted as U.S. dollars per one unit of foreign currency as
of December 1985.

Country	Currency	Exchange Rate (U.S.$)
Australia	A$ dollar	$0.68
Canada	C$ dollar	0.72
France	French franc	0.13
Hong Kong	HK$ dollar	0.13
Italy	Lira	0.0006
Japan	Yen	0.0049
Netherlands	Guilder	0.36
West Germany	Deutsche mark	0.41
Sweden	Krona	0.13
Singapore	S$ dollar	0.48
Switzerland	Swiss franc	0.48
United Kingdom	Pound	1.45
European Currency Unit	ECU	1.13

rency prices and news events that affect markets. Table 5.2 lists
foreign exchange rates by country compared to the U.S. dollar.

Spot market quotations in the interbank market are in the
inverse form, that is, units of a foreign currency to the dollar. For
example, an interbank quote of 2.50 deutsche marks to the dollar
can be converted to U.S. dollars by taking the reciprocal value:

$$\text{U.S.\$} = \frac{1}{\text{DM } 2.50} = \$0.40 = 40 \text{ cents}$$

Currencies of several commonwealth countries are quoted in U.S.
dollars. British pounds, Australian dollars, and New Zealand dollars are quoted as U.S. dollars to the currency.

THE EUROPEAN CURRENCY UNIT (ECU)

The European Currency Unit is a composite currency of specified
amounts from each currency of the 10 member countries of the
European Economic Community (EEC). Spain and Portugal joined
the EEC in 1986. The Spanish peseta and the Portuguese escudo
should be included in the revised ECU after September 1989.

In recent years, European countries and corporations have issued debt securities denominated in ECUs. Financial institutions of the Benelux countries make an active secondary market in ECUs and ECU-denominated securities. ECU-denominated bonds allow investors such as pension funds, insurance companies, and corporate treasurers to match future liabilities in foreign currencies with a foreign currency denominated asset.

THE EFFECTS OF CHANGES IN FOREIGN EXCHANGE RATES ON AN INVESTMENT

Changes in foreign exchange rates can turn an unprofitable investment into a profitable one or vice versa. Assuming the price of an underlying security denominated in a currency remains unchanged, revaluation of that currency against the U.S. dollar increases the security's value; likewise, devaluation of that currency reduces its value. Examples 5.1 and 5.2 show these relationships.

EXAMPLE 5.1

A U.S. investor buys 1,000 shares of Beechams, which is listed on the London Stock Exchange. Beechams is quoted at 400 pence (p) (400 p = BP 4.00). The exchange rate is U.S.$/BP = $1.30.

Problem: What would the investment be worth in U.S. dollars, if the British pound appreciated to $1.50, but the price of stock remained unchanged?

Solution: 1,000 shares are worth $5,200 at US$/Bp = 1.30. With the exchange rate at $1.50, the value of the shares increases to $6,000—a profit of $800.

EXAMPLE 5.2

A U.S. investor buys 1,000 shares of Hitachi, which is listed on the Tokyo Stock Exchange. Hitachi is quoted at 1,050 yen. The exchange rate is: yen/US$ = 180 yen.

Problem: What would the investment be worth in U.S. dollars if the value of the yen per U.S. dollar declined to 220 and the price of the Hitachi remained unchanged?

Solution: The initial value of the investment is $5,833. If the exchange rate declines to yen/U.S.$ = 200, the investment declines in value to $5,250—a loss of $583.

Since abandoning fixed exchange rates, the risk of foreign exchange transactions has increased considerably. Interbank forward, foreign currency futures, and options contracts can be used to hedge some of the risk of owning foreign currency denominated securities. Example 5.3 shows the mechanics of hedging.

Spreadsheet programs for personal computers such as Visi-Calc® and Lotus 1-2-3® are useful in analyzing the effect of foreign exchange rate changes. A spreadsheet program can determine the various values of a security as a function of changing exchange rates.

EXAMPLE 5.3

A U.S. corporate treasurer owns DM 1.25 million of West German government bonds 8 percent maturing in 1995. He believes that the deutsche mark (DM) will devalue by 25 percent versus the U.S. dollar during the next three months. He expects the DM to devalue from 2.00 to 2.50. He wants to protect principal and interest on his bonds. He examines three possible strategies to obtain the best insurance against devaluation of the deutsche mark.

Market Data	Deutsche marks	U.S. dollars
Principal	DM 1,250,000	$625,000
Annual interest payment (8%)	100,000	50,000
Quarterly interest payment (2%)	25,000	12,500
Present exchange rate	2.00	.050
Expected exchange rate	2.50	0.40
June DM futures contact size	125,000	62,500
Initial margins		2,000
June DM call option premium		2,875
June DM put option premium		1,875

Strategy 1: He sells 10 June DM currency futures contracts traded on the Chicago Mercantile Exchange at an exchange rate of 50 cents. He deposits $20,000 in initial margins with a futures broker to effect the transaction. Three months later he repurchases 10 contracts at 40 cents. The transaction appears as follows:

	DM/U.S.$	Bond Value	Interest	Futures
Initial	2.00	$625,000	$12,500	$0.50
Final	2.50	$500,000	$10,000	$0.40
Gain/loss		−$125,000	−$ 2,500	+$0.10

In this strategy, the loss of $127,500 in principal and interest from currency devaluation is offset by a 10 cent gain per contract in the currency hedge. A 10 cent gain equals a $125,000 gain, which is applied against the $127,500 loss.

EXAMPLE 5.3 (concluded)

Strategy 2: He buys 10 June DM currency put options traded on the Chicago Board Options Exchange (CBOE) at a strike price of 50 cents. She pays a premium of $1,875 per contract. The total premium debited to his cash account is $18,750. Three months later, he sells 10 contracts at 40 cents. The transaction appears as follows:

	DM/U.S.$	Bond Value	Interest	Put Premium
Initial	2.00	$625,000	$12,500	−$ 18,750
Final	2.50	$500,000	$10,000	+$125,000
Gain/loss		−$125,000	−$ 2,500	+$106,250

In this strategy, the loss of $127,500 in principal and interest from currency devaluation is offset by a net gain of $106,250 in the put option hedge. The gain of $106,250 is applied against the loss of $127,500 for a net loss of $21,250.

Strategy 3: He sells 10 June DM currency call options traded on the Chicago Board Options Exchange (CBOE) at a strike price of 50 cents. He receives a premium of $2,875 per contract. The total premium credited to his margin account is $28,750. Three months later he buys back 10 contracts at 40 cents. The transaction appears as follows:

	DM/U.S.$	Bond Value	Interest	Call Premium
Initial	2.00	625,000	$12,500	+$28,750
Final	2.50	500,000	$10,000	−0−
Gain/loss		−$125,000	−$ 2,500	+$28,750

In this strategy, the loss of $127,500 in principal and interest from currency devaluation is partially offset by a net gain of $28,750 in the call option hedge. The gain of $28,750 is applied against the loss of $127,500 for a net loss of $98,750.

HEDGING FOREIGN EXCHANGE RISKS WITH FOREIGN CURRENCY FUTURES AND OPTIONS CONTRACTS

Currency futures and option contracts are derivative instruments; they represent and may substitute for actual currencies. Futures and options markets provide centralized trading, clearing, and settlement facilities on national exchanges for both hedgers and speculative traders in the currency markets. The exchanges allow buyers and sellers to trade currency contracts on margin. Contracts are standardized as to size, delivery, and price reporting. In addition, exchanges have installed clearinghouses that guarantee performance of contracts in case of default.

Hedging is purchasing or selling a derivative instrument to temporarily substitute for a future spot transaction or offset an opposite transaction or position in the spot market. In making the transaction, any loss in one transaction hopefully will be offset by a gain in the other transaction, and thus loss through price change will be significantly reduced.

A hedge protects investment profits and dividend and interest income from a currency devaluation; the hedger's purpose is not to profit from price movement. It is important to know recent trends in various currencies. The spot, forward, and futures prices are affected by the same fundamental factors. The essence of effective hedging is the basis and its movement. The basis, in this context, is the difference between the spot exchange and futures exchange rates. The basis is identical to the difference between spot and forward exchange rates for the same period.

$$\text{Basis} = \text{Spot rate} - \text{Futures rate}$$

The basis tends toward zero as the delivery day for the futures contract approaches because a futures delivery becomes a spot delivery. They become perfect substitutes for each other, hence, they should have equal value.

In foreign exchange, the basis reflects the interest rate differential between countries. If there are no restrictions for trade and capital flows, forward rates will vary inversely with the interest rate differentials between two countries. For example, if interest rates are 4 percent higher in the United Kingdom than in the United States, the forward price for British pounds should be at a 4 percent discount on an annual basis in terms of U.S. dollars. This is known as interest rate parity.

HEDGING FOREIGN CURRENCY RISKS WITH CURRENCY FUTURES AND OPTIONS CONTRACTS

An investor doesn't usually want to enter into an investment to hedge currency risks. The primary purpose of purchasing securities denominated in undervalued currencies is to profit from a revaluation in the currency's value. Hedging is contrary to this investing approach because it limits an investor's potential gains.

Hedging foreign currency risks becomes important when an unexpected change in market sentiment occurs and an investor wants insurance against a loss of principal due to a devaluation in currency. Three types of hedging strategies are:

1. Sell a currency futures contract to protect against price decline.
2. Buy a put option on a currency to protect against a decline in principal.
3. Sell a covered call option against a position. Selling covered calls provides only limited protection. This strategy is used to enhance yields on debt obligations.

These strategies are best illustrated in Example 5.3 on page 91. As Example 5.3 illustrates, a short sale of currency futures contracts and the purchase of put options provide the optimal insurance against a major devaluation. A covered call strategy is best if only a minor devaluation is expected. Naturally, there are benefits and disadvantages to each strategy. The investor must first analyze all alternatives and then select the optimal strategy for achieving best results.

FUNDAMENTAL AND TECHNICAL ANALYSIS IN FORECASTING FOREIGN EXCHANGE RATES

Methods of forecasting foreign exchange rates range from thorough study of macroeconomics and monetary policies to interpretation of graphs and moving averages. Fundamental and technical analysis tools complement each other in forecasting changes in exchange rates. The objectives for using these techniques are: *(a)* to purchase undervalued securities denominated in undervalued currencies, *(b)* to sell undervalued securities when they become fairly valued, or *(c)* to obtain portfolio insurance by hedging with financial instruments. As a corollary, constructing a portfolio of securities denominated in undervalued currencies reduces the overall risk of a portfolio.

FUNDAMENTAL ANALYSIS

Fundamental analysis involves the study of government, monetary policies, and macroeconomic variables as to how they affect the supply of and demand for a country's currency. Revaluation is the strengthening of a country's currency in relation to another currency's value or the price of gold. Revaluation results from an increased demand for currency relative to its supply.

Devaluation is the reduction of a currency's value as to another currency or the price of gold. Devaluation can be caused by a reduced demand for a currency or an increased supply through monetary expansion. Devaluation usually results from a lack of investor confidence in a government's ability to control an expanding money supply through the central bank and provide incentives to increase productivity.

Hyperinflation is the worst scenario for countries with dramatically devalued currencies. Mexico's economic crises and subsequent devaluation of the peso provide an excellent illustration of hyperinflation at its worst. In the early 1970s, the peso was pegged at 8 pesos to $1 U.S. In 1987, the exchange rate became 1,450 pesos to $1 U.S., resulting from a sharp drop in crude oil prices and the Mexican government's technical default on its foreign loans.

Hard currencies are issued by governments that permit the convertibility of their currencies into gold bullion. The governments and central banks of most countries prohibit the convertibility of their currencies into gold. The U.S. dollar remains the world's reserve currency because of the superior credit rating held by the United States for paying off its debt obligations, the large gold stocks held by the government, and the huge circulation of U.S. dollars in the interbank market.

The following is a description of primary variables that affect exchange rates:

1. Confidence in government and its political leaders in developing the private sector. Foreign investors are attracted to countries with governments that promulgate economic growth in the private sector, privatization of state-owned enterprises, anti-inflationary policies, low tax rates on capital gains, corporate earnings and dividends, competitive labor conditions, and cost containment of social welfare programs. The influx of foreign capital creates a demand for a country's currency, and its value rises.

2. A strong rise in the real GDP/GNP increases a currency's value. Real GDP/GNP is the nominal GDP/GNP minus the inflation rate. A strong growth economy, as measured by real GDP/GNP,

TABLE 5.3 Comparisons of Real GDP/GNP for Selected Countries

Country	1981	1982	1983	1984	1985
United States	2.2	−2.5	3.5	6.5	2.3
Japan	5.5	3.1	3.2	5.1	4.6
United Kingdom	−1.1	1.2	3.7	1.7	3.3
Canada	3.3	−4.4	3.3	5.0	4.5
France	0.5	1.8	0.7	1.6	1.3
Singapore	9.9	6.3	7.9	8.2	−1.8

SOURCE: Economist Intelligence Unit, Country Reports 1986.

attracts foreign investment and creates a demand for a currency. See Table 5.3 for comparisons of the real GDP/GNP for selected countries.

The real growth in GDP/GNP for Japan and Singapore outpaced other countries. With the exception of 1985, when Singapore experienced a dramatic slowdown in exports, Singapore's economic growth was two to three times as large as European and North American countries.

3. A rise in real interest rates and yields on government obligations can increase the value of a country's currency. Real interest rates and yields are adjusted for the inflation rate. Commercial lenders make loans in countries where they can receive high interest rates on borrowed monies. Likewise, financial institutions invest in the government obligations of countries where they can earn high real rates of return with a low credit risk. The U.S. dollar strengthened dramatically against other currencies from 1980 to 1985 due to superior yields on U.S. Treasury obligations. When the real return of U.S. Treasury securities yielded more than 5 percent, foreign investment capital flowed into the United States to finance the huge federal budget deficits.

4. Countries that earn more from export sales than they spend on imports produce a balance of payments surplus. A surplus of foreign exchange earnings strengthens a country's currency. Japan has pursued this policy for 15 years, resulting in a major revaluation of the yen to the U.S. dollar.

Research and interpretation of macroeconomic data requires a substantial amount of work in reading monetary reports issued by central banks, commercial banks, government agencies, financial periodicals, and private research organizations. The data are available, but they may be incomprehensible to people who lack academic training in international economics and finance. For this reason, many individual and institutional investors prefer to use technical analysis to form an opinion about exchange rates.

TECHNICAL ANALYSIS

Technical analysis involves studying incremental changes in exchange rates illustrated in bar graphs, point-and-figure charts, and moving averages. Pure technical analysis disregards fundamentals and focuses on graphic interpretation of price series, trading volume, chart patterns, trend lines, support, resistance, and channel zones. Graphic presentation of historical changes in prices and volume assists investors in visualizing the direction and extent of a trend. Technical analysts utilize this method to forecast the direction and magnitude of change in exchange rates.

Technical analysis presumes the compilation of accurate data about exchange rates and volume. Because most currency transactions occur in the interbank market and aren't publicly disclosed, accurate data are nearly impossible to obtain. Foreign currency futures and options exchanges provide the most reliable sources of information where public disclosure of prices, volume, and transaction size is mandatory. Computer databases can now retrieve historical and current data on currency prices and volume.

Volumetric analysis is the study of volume statistics regarding changes in market sentiment. Volume of trading in a currency associated with currency price changes can provide important information. For example, if a price rises or declines on low volume, this is a weak move and probably should be disregarded. If, however, a price rises or declines on heavy volume, a possible change in market sentiment may have occurred.

Space limitations preclude a thorough presentation of technical analysis. Excellent references are available that describe technical analysis in greater detail. Refer to Martin Pring's *Technical Analysis Explained* (McGraw-Hill, 1981) for more information.

We believe that technical analysis is an incomplete discipline alone, but it becomes extremely powerful as an analytical method when combined with fundamental analysis. Understanding the fundamental reasons for change in a currency's valuation helps the

FIGURE 5.2 Pivotal Points for Trend Change, Exchange Rate for the British Pound

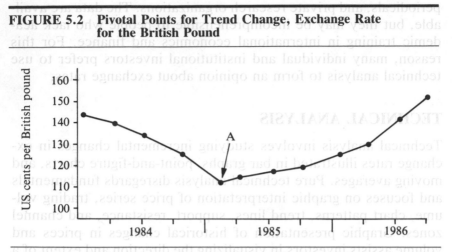

Point A shows the change in trend for the British pound from a declining trend to a rising one.

investor to anticipate changes in the expected direction of exchange rates. Technical analysis can be used to confirm the expected results of fundamental analysis, to improve market timing of purchases and sales, and to evaluate risk/reward parameters.

For the investor in foreign equities and debt securities, technical analysis of foreign exchange rates can be simplified by asking these questions (see Figure 5.2):

1. What is the current direction of a currency's price versus the U.S. dollar? Is the exchange rate rising, declining, or moving sideways (consolidation) without a trend?

2. What are the pivotal points that signify a change in direction? When is the exchange rate perceived to have changed direction?

Our purpose in using technical analysis is not to trade short-term currency fluctuations but to recognize when a currency begins a long-term rise or decline in value relative to the U.S. dollar. For example, a corporate treasurer wants to buy 1 million deutsche marks worth of West German 10-year government bonds. He believes that the mark is 20 percent undervalued to the U.S. dollar based on fundamentals. Before making a purchase, he reviews a chart of the deutsche mark to determine the optimal time for buying bonds at a favorable exchange rate. See Figure 5.3.

FIGURE 5.3 Exchange Rate for the Deutsche Mark

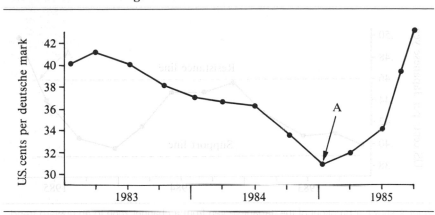

Point A shows the change in trend for the deutsche mark from a declining trend to a rising trend. This point would signal a buy point for securities denominated in deutsche marks.

Another example is an investment manager who owns a portfolio of Swiss shares worth 10 million Swiss francs. Her cost basis was seven million Swiss franc before the Swiss franc experienced a dramatic revaluation to the U.S. dollar. She believes that the Swiss franc is overvalued to the U.S. dollar and vulnerable to a devaluation. She wants to take profits on her shares, and she

FIGURE 5.4 Exchange Rate for the Swiss Franc

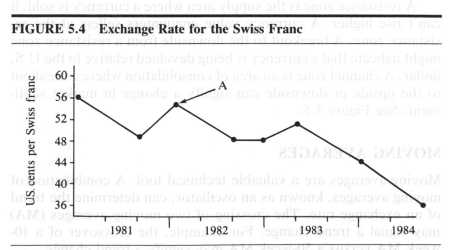

Point A shows the change in trend for the Swiss franc from a rising trend to a declining trend. This point would signal a selling time for securities denominated in Swiss francs.

FIGURE 5.5   Channel Zone, Exchange Rate for the Japanese Yen

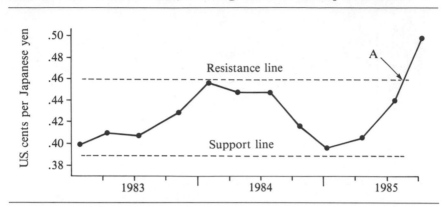

Point A shows a breakout of the Japanese yen from a channel zone to an upward trend.

reviews a chart on the Swiss franc to determine an optimal time to begin selling securities. See Figure 5.4.

Three zones of a graph that should be identified are: (1) the support zone, (2) the resistance zone, and (3) the channel zone. A support zone is the demand area in which a currency is bought. A currency's value is supported by buyers at the support level; the value does not decrease. A breakout to the upside from a support level can mean that a currency is being revalued relative to the U.S. dollar.

A resistance zone is the supply area where a currency is sold; it can't rise higher. A currency value encounters sellers at the resistance zone. A breakout to the downside from a resistance zone might indicate that a currency is being devalued relative to the U.S. dollar. A channel zone is an area of consolidation where a breakout to the upside or downside can signify a change in market sentiment. See Figure 5.5.

MOVING AVERAGES

Moving averages are a valuable technical tool. A combination of moving averages, known as an oscillator, can determine the trend of an exchange rate. The crossing of two moving averages (MA) may signal a trend change. For example, the crossover of a 10-week MA versus a 50-week MA may signify a trend change.

To construct a 10-week moving average for any currency, basis the closing rate, take the sum of the previous 10 weeks' closes and divide by 10. This number can be plotted on a graph to illustrate the 10-week trend. A 50-week moving average changes more slowly than the 10-week MA, and it filters out aberrations of short-term changes. When the 10-week moving average crosses the 50-week moving average, a trend change could occur; in that case, an investor might decide to buy or sell a currency-denominated security. Moving averages overlaid on bar graphs can provide a clearer picture of major support and resistance levels coupled with trend changes.

In conclusion, moving averages, bar graphs, and volumetric analysis can all be used as analytical tools in deciding when to buy or sell currency-denominated securities. An investor's objective should be to determine the major trend in a currency's price-to-profit ratio due to a revaluation against the U.S. dollar.

INTERNATIONAL EXCHANGES THAT LIST FOREIGN CURRENCY FUTURES AND OPTIONS CONTRACTS

The following is a list of exchanges that make active markets in foreign currency futures, options on futures, and options on currencies. The New York Cotton Exchange makes a market in futures on the European currency unit (ECU). The contract size is 100,000 ECUs. At this time, the ECU futures contract isn't actively traded. More information about contracts and operations for each exchange can be obtained from its Public Information department.

Exchange: Philadelphia Stock Exchange (PHLX)
Location: Philadelphia, Pennsylvania
Primary instruments: Options on currencies

Currency Contract	Contract Size
Australian dollar	50,000
British pound	12,500
Canadian dollar	50,000
Deutsche mark	62,500
Japanese yen	6,250,000
Swiss franc	62,500
ECU	62,500

Exchange: Chicago Mercantile Exchange (CME)
Location: Chicago, Illinois
Primary instruments: Currency futures and options on futures

Currency Contract	Contract Size
Australian dollar	100,000
British pound	25,000
Canadian dollar	100,000
Deutsche mark	125,000
Japanese yen	12,500,000
Swiss franc	125,000

Exchange: Chicago Board Options Exchange (CBOE)
Location: Chicago, Illinois
Primary instruments: Options on currencies

Currency Contract	Contract Size
Australian dollar	50,000
British pound	25,000
Canadian dollar	100,000
Deutsche mark	125,000
Japanese yen	12,500,000
Swiss franc	125,000

Exchange: London International Financial Futures Exchange (LIFFE)
Location: London, England
Primary instruments: Currency futures and options on futures

Currency Contract	Contract Size
U.S. dollar/deutsche mark	50,000
British pound	25,000
Deutsche mark	125,000
Japanese yen	12,500,000
Swiss franc	125,000

Exchange: Singapore International Monetary Exchange (SIMEX)
Location: Singapore
Primary instruments: Currency futures and options on futures

Currency Contract	Contract Size
British pound	25,000
Canadian dollar	100,000
Deutsche mark	125,000
Japanese yen	12,500,000
Swiss franc	125,000

SIMEX has a mutual offset clearing arrangement with the Chicago Mercantile Exchange that allows for the expansion of trading hours.

Exchange: European Options Exchange (EOE)
Location: Amsterdam, Netherlands
Primary instruments: Options on currencies

Currency Contract	Contract Size
British pounds in guilders	10,000
U.S. dollars in guilders	10,000
U.S. dollars in deutsche marks	10,000
ECU in U.S. dollars	10,000

British pounds are also traded on the Montreal Exchange in Canada. An agreement allows trading of these options for 16 hours a day.

CHAPTER SIX

How to Develop a Computer-Assisted Model for the Evaluation of Foreign Equity and Debt Securities

The primary objective of investing in international markets is to achieve the highest total returns with a defined risk. The creation and management of international portfolios requires evaluating risks and opportunities in the following categories:

1. Selection of country.
2. Selection of currency in which a security is denominated.
3. Selection of economic sectors.
4. Selection of an issuer's security, that is, common shares, preferred shares, and convertible or straight debt issues.
5. Allocation of assets by country, currency, sector, and issuer.
6. Asset mixture—equity versus debt securities.
7. Market timing of purchases and sales.

There are numerous foreign equity and debt securities available to an investor. As many as 13,000 companies are publicly traded. Presently, most securities research firms maintain a current database on the world's 2,000 largest companies. Access to these databases is the only way for an investor to research a large number of securities. For example, a portfolio manager may impose stringent selection criteria regarding a company's market capitalization, dividend yield, net worth, and earnings growth, which would significantly narrow the list of appropriate companies.

With the advent of computer technology, investors can retrieve fundamental and technical data for the analysis of foreign securities and currencies. Advanced software programs help investors establish selection screens that automatically search a database for securities that meet specified criteria.

Valuable insights about a company's management and operations can be obtained from securities analysts who specialize in selected industry groups. These are important analysts' reports to read because they give information not revealed in a company's financial statements. Such reports may reveal unusual situations and opportunities not yet published about a company.

As presented in Chapters 3 and 4, there are several basic approaches to investing in international markets:

1. Purchase undervalued equity or debt securities denominated in undervalued currencies.
2. Purchase an indexed portfolio of equity or debt securities.
3. Purchase an indexed portfolio of securities and hedge them with future and/or option contracts. This is known as a hedged portfolio.

MEASUREMENT OF INVESTMENT PERFORMANCE AND VARIABILITIES OF RETURN

Portfolio investment performance can be measured against two benchmarks: (1) the return on risk-free securities, such as 90-day U.S. Treasury bills, and (2) a recognized index, such as the S&P 500 Stock Index. Ninety-day U.S. Treasury bills are considered risk-free because they are issued at a discount and redeemed at par value with no risk of principal to an investor. At maturity, the investor realizes a nominal return on capital. When the nominal return is adjusted for inflation, the real rate of return could be negligible or negative.

The total return on an indexed portfolio of equity or debt securities can exhibit a high degree of variability due to the cyclical nature of the markets. The total return on an index of equities could vary as much as 70 percent or more from year to year. Many investors with fiduciary responsibilities won't assume the systematic risks of the market even though, in the long run, total returns should be higher than the risk-free rate.

Many institutional investors prefer to hedge their portfolios with stock index contracts to achieve more consistent rates of return without the large variability in a portfolio's value. The application of stock index futures and options contracts allows investors to obtain portfolio insurance against dramatic changes in value. The total return on a hedged portfolio should show returns of 2 to 4 percentage points over the 90-day Treasury bill rate. Because hedging techniques reduce the variability of return, opportunities to make large percentage gains in the market are eliminated.

We have found that earning superior returns while reducing market risks creates a portfolio of undervalued securities denominated in undervalued currencies. This approach requires extensive research and active management. An investor must research a large database of securities to select undervalued securities denominated in an undervalued currency. There are more than 13,000 publicly traded foreign companies. Presently, most financial databases can provide information on 2,000 of these companies. The number of listed companies will increase as institutional and retail investors internationalize their portfolios.

SEARCHING FOR VALUE IN THE INTERNATIONAL MARKETS

Equity and debt securities of publicly traded companies become undervalued for a variety of reasons. Changes in business, credit, and market cycles affect investor psychology, which affects how investors value financial assets. During times of pessimism, investors convert financial assets to cash, reducing asset values. During times of optimism, investors convert cash to financial assets.

Our purpose is to describe the qualitative factors that tend to undervalue securities and therefore present opportunities for profit. The common and preferred shares of a company can be undervalued regarding their market price to earnings, cash flow, and/or book value. The debt securities of an issuer can be undervalued regarding the credit rating, yields, prices, and maturities of comparable issues.

Undervaluation is caused by shareholders' misperception of a company's potential value in earnings or assets. This misperception can result from a lack of knowledge, a change of sentiment toward the company, and the general economy. The accounting practices of countries differ widely and may encourage the undervaluation of corporate assets. In certain countries such as West Germany, Switzerland, and Austria, a company's earnings and assets are deliberately understated because of high tax rates and strong labor unions that discourage management from reporting profits. In Japan, real estate may be carried on the company books at the purchase price but not the current market value. For example, an office building in downtown Tokyo may be valued on a company's balance sheet at 100 million yen but have a current market value of 1 billion yen.

In developing a systematic approach to analyzing foreign securities and their local currencies as monetary instruments, investors need to have a clear understanding of their investment objectives, evaluation of risks, selection criteria, portfolio management, tax considerations, and reliable information sources.

The same principles that govern domestic investment decisions can apply to foreign markets. A sound approach to selecting undervalued securities denominated in undervalued currencies must include a combination of fundamental and technical analysis for both the security and the currency. The following lists of questions and statements will help in analyzing foreign investments in securities and currencies.

Investment Objectives

1. Capital gains—to achieve price appreciation of underlying assets.
2. Yield—to obtain the desired yield derived from interest or dividend payments.
3. Safety—to preserve principal by selecting issues with a high credit rating for the issue or issuer.
4. Reduce tax liabilities—to lower tax payments owed to local, state, or federal taxing authorities.
5. Diversification—To reduce risks by allocating assets to different types of investments. We recommend that no more than 3 to 5 percent of the total portfolio value be committed to any one security.

Evaluation of Risks

1. What is the minimum credit rating of an issue? Should I consider only investment-grade issues?
2. What is the investment horizon? How long do I want to hold this investment?
3. What percentage of capital should be risked? Where should I set a stop-loss point to liquidate a losing position?
4. What percentage of capital should be allocated to each category of investments that I consider?

Selection Criteria

1. What instruments should I consider—common or preferred shares, corporate bonds, straight debt securities, convertibles, options, or futures contracts?
2. Choice of country.
3. Choice of currency denomination.
4. Credit rating of the issue.
5. Current yield of the issue.
6. Market capitalization and liquidity.
7. Years in business.
8. Status of balance sheet and income statement.
9. Cash flow per share.
10. Book value compared to market price.
11. Debt to equity ratio.

Portfolio Management Techniques

1. Establish stop-loss points.
2. Establish target price to take profits.
3. The amount of portfolio turnover.
4. The number of issues in a portfolio.
5. Use of financial instruments for hedging risks.
6. Market timing methods.
7. Allocation of assets in portfolio.

HOW TO FORMAT INFORMATION FOR COMPARATIVE ANALYSIS

We have developed a fundamental and technical data assessment format to help investors analyze investment opportunities—a comparative analysis of fundamental and technical data on relative values and price levels for both the securities and the currencies they are denominated in. The quantitative information can then be transferred to a spreadsheet program for investment analysis.

The objective is to obtain data on a security and the currency to estimate target prices for both. A stop-loss price should be calculated to cut losses on a losing position. A stop-loss point representing a 15 percent decline from the purchase price is set to cut losses. For example, an investor selects XYZ listed on the Frankfurt Exchange. XYZ's current price is DM 50. Based on his analysis, the investor estimates that the share price is worth DM 70. The deutsche mark is currently priced at DM 2.50 or 40 cents. The analysis indicates that the deutsche mark should be valued at DM 2.00 or 50 cents within one year. He sets a stop-loss at DM 42.50, a point where the investor will sell XYZ for a loss. The following table is a summary:

	Share Price	U.S.$/DM	Principal
Initial	DM 50	$0.40	$20.00
Final	DM 70	$0.50	$35.00
Net gain	DM 20	$0.10	$15.00

The table shows that the selection of XYZ resulted in a gain of 20 deutsche marks in the security and a 10 cent gain in the currency for a total gain of $15 per share or a 75 percent annualized return.

The next section presents a fundamental and technical assessment format for evaluating the relative risks and profit potential of selected securities.

I. FUNDAMENTAL AND TECHNICAL DATA ASSESSMENT FORMAT

Name of Issuer:
Type of Issue:
Denominated Currency:
Country of Origin:
Primary Exchange Security Is Listed on:

A. Evaluation of Country and Currency Risks

1. What is the probability that the government will impose exchange controls on currency exchanges? (0 to 100 percent)

2. What is the probability that the government will nationalize the issuer without compensation to shareholders or debt holders? (0 to 100 percent)
3. What are the withholding tax rates on:
    a. Dividends (0 to 100 percent)
    b. Capital gains (0 to 100 percent)
    c. Coupon payments (0 to 100 percent)

B. Evaluation of Currency Valuation

1. What is the probability that the currency will revalue against the U.S. dollar? (0 to 100 percent)
2. What is the estimated percentage of revaluation? (0 to 300 percent)
3. What is the support level of the currency?
4. What is the resistance level of the currency?

II. FUNDAMENTAL AND TECHNICAL ANALYSIS OF AN EQUITY SECURITY

Five-Year History of Balance Sheet and Income Statement Data

		1-Year	2-Year	3-Year	4-Year	Present
1.	Share price					
2.	Earnings/share					
3.	Book value/share					
4.	Cash flow/share					
5.	Dividend/share					
6.	Dividend yield					
7.	Price/earnings					
8.	Price/book value					
9.	Price/cash flow					
10.	Current assets/ current liabilities					
11.	Total debt/ total assets					
12.	Number of shares outstanding					

Technical Analysis

1. What is the support level?
2. What is the resistance level?
3. What is the 20-week moving average?
4. What is the 50-week moving average?
5. What are the recognizable chart formations?

Target Prices and Stop-Loss Points

1. What is the estimated target price of the security in the local currency?
2. What is the estimated target price of the currency?
3. What is the stop-loss point in local currency?
4. What is the estimated total return in U.S. dollars?

III. FUNDAMENTAL ANALYSIS OF A DEBT SECURITY

1. Credit rating of the issuer
2. Credit rating of the issue
3. Name of rating agency
4. Coupon yield
5. Maturity date
6. Frequency of coupon payments
7. Current price
8. Current yield
9. Yield-to-call
10. Yield-to-maturity
11. Special call provisions
12. Special features such as attached warrants and conversion privileges

ROLE OF COMPUTER AND TELECOMMUNICATIONS TECHNOLOGIES IN INTERNATIONAL INVESTING

Computer and telecommunications technologies will play an increasingly important role in the electronic linkage of primary and secondary financial markets worldwide. Computers and telecommunications permit the rapid compilation and dissemination of information and transaction data through high-speed computers and communication satellites. The new technologies pose problems for the linkage of primary markets, such as information security and the reliability and validity of data transmittal.

In the future, companies may be required to file reports electronically on their balance sheets, income statements, and changes in business operations and management to a central computer that will permit access by auditors, regulatory agencies, and shareholders. These reports could be updated periodically for review by interested parties. The United States has already implemented such a system called *Disclosure*. Private information vendors may compile information on companies and industry groups which they, in turn, make available to subscribers in a computer-readable format. Information services are available in the United States that compile information about nearly 7,000 companies on a time-sharing basis. Application software programs have been written to set up decision screens that allow users to set specific criteria for selecting stocks.

In the future, all securities may be registered electronically with a global depository organization to keep records of registered owners and the number of shares issued. Certificates will be completely eliminated and transactions will be journaled electronically with confirmations and statements mailed to customers. Options and futures contracts will be cleared and settled through a central organization.

One of the benefits of electronic miniaturization and cellular technology is the creation of a product line with state-of-the-art technology. For example, Telemet America has developed Pocket Quote, which allows subscribers to receive quotes on listed stocks, options, and futures from a wireless, hand-held terminal. Computer companies are marketing low-priced, portable computers that can be taken on business trips and connected to any telephone.

Dow Jones News Retrieval, CompUserve, Telerate, and The Source are database services that allow subscribers to receive timely market information displayed on a personal computer via telephone.

HOW TO USE PERSONAL COMPUTERS FOR INTERNATIONAL INVESTING

The evolution and growth of computer and information technologies over the past 50 years has been phenomenal. Computers were invented originally to perform tedious computations with a high degree of accuracy for the military. With the development of wafer-thin microprocessor chips, computer size has diminished and computational powers have increased. Personal computers now have thousands of times the computational power that military mainframe computers had in the 1960s.

During the last decade, personal computers (PCs) were designed as information storage and retrieval devices. Most recently, personal computers have performed transactional tasks. Subscribers to consumer information services can use a PC to purchase consumer items, do home banking, or buy and sell securities over a telephone network system. These transactions can be performed at home with considerable savings and convenience for the customer.

Investors use personal computers for the following functions:

1. To obtain and store fundamental information on companies, industry groups, national economies, and domestic and foreign financial markets.
2. To obtain and store technical information such as price histories and trading volume, and to display price and trendline charts over time.
3. To analyze fundamental and technical information from on-line databases to assist in investment decisions.
4. To screen a list of securities for those that meet certain criteria. The screen automatically rejects securities that do not meet minimal criteria.
5. To enter purchase or sell transactions for securities through a broker affiliated with a subscriber service.

TYPES OF FUNDAMENTAL INFORMATION AVAILABLE FROM INVESTOR INFORMATION SERVICES

The following information is available to subscribers of certain investor information services. Examples that follow illustrate the usefulness of this information in making decisions.

1. Current news items from domestic or international sources that affect a country, industry, or company.
2. Description of a company's primary business, price, and earnings histories. Presentation of itemized balance sheets, income statements, listing of corporate directors, officers, and major shareholders of publicly held corporations.
3. Reports from investment analysts that cover companies with respect to their long-term outlook, current earnings, changes in management, product development, mergers and acquisitions, and other timely information.
4. Information on foreign currency and interest rate markets, and news events that impact foreign exchange markets.

TYPES OF TECHNICAL INFORMATION AVAILABLE FROM ON-LINE INFORMATION SERVICES

1. Historical prices presented in tabular form or displayed graphically.
2. Volume of trading data; the number of shares, bonds, and units traded daily, weekly, and monthly.
3. Computation of moving averages to plot trendlines against prices.
4. Graphic price data display in bar charts or point-and-figure graphs to visualize patterns of support, resistance, breakout points, price channels, cycle patterns, and other technical formations such as head-and-shoulder, flags, and pennants.

HOW TO SET UP SCREENS FOR SELECTION

Personal computers can assist investors in screening securities that do not fit certain user-defined criteria. This is a selection process where criteria are defined and used to screen out issues that wouldn't interest an investor. Selection criteria must be quantifiable parameters that can be expressed as a range of numbers.

User-defined criteria can be viewed as a set of filters employed to eliminate unqualified issues. A computer search has severe limitations in that many variables important for evaluating a company's performance can't be quantitatively defined; for example, a company's management experience and performance in gaining market share or containing labor and production costs. These factors are known as qualitative variables. Research reports written by company analysts are essential in providing this type of insightful information.

There are thousands of common stocks, corporate bonds, and government securities listed and traded on U.S. exchanges alone, and the plethora of securities listed on foreign exchanges increases the total. How do you sort through thousands of securities to select a few issues to focus on for investment?

There are several preliminary steps to take before using a personal computer in the selection process. They are:

1. Establish specific written criteria to define parameters for selection.
2. Before subscribing to a database, evaluate it according to your informational and screening requirements; determine whether the types of issues you are interested in are included; evaluate the degree of selectivity in setting up screens.
3. Gain experience with the database on a trial basis by using sample companies with known criteria as a test for selectivity, sorting speed, and accuracy.
4. Add further selection criteria or narrow the definition of the parameters, if needed, to reduce the number of issues sorted out for review.

The next section provides examples for specifying user-defined criteria and setting up sample screens in selecting a small number of companies to focus on.

AN EXAMPLE OF HOW TO DEFINE CRITERIA AND SET UP SCREENS

An investor believes that crude oil prices will decline over the next two to three years. She wants to invest in companies that will benefit from lower oil prices. She believes that selected chemical companies will be major beneficiaries in this scenario, since their profit margins will be greater due to lower production costs. Therefore, she wants to conduct a computer search for companies that satisfy the following criteria:

1. Companies in the industrial chemical manufacturing business.
2. Companies that paid a cash dividend for the last five years.
3. A current dividend yield of at least 3 percent.
4. Common shares held by at least 20 percent institutional shareholders.
5. The market value of stock sells at a discount to the book value by at least 15 percent or more.
6. The five-year compounded growth of the stock is at least 10 percent per year.
7. The equity to debt ratio is at least 2:1 or higher.
8. The company's market capitalization is at least $200 million.

After the computer has printed out a list of companies that satisfy the eight criteria, an investor must then evaluate a company's management, ability to gain market share, and future prospects to increase sales and contain labor and production costs. These are qualitative evaluations that a computer search can't perform. A computer search is helpful in reducing the potential candidates in the chemical industry to a manageable number.

CONCLUSION

This chapter has concentrated on securities traded in the secondary market because they have acquired a history of earnings and dividends. Securities issued in the primary market lack historical information because of their newness. The lack of information makes them riskier investments because they are more difficult to assess. However, as explained in Chapter 7, many undervalued securities can be purchased in the primary market due to the privatization of state-owned enterprises.

CHAPTER SEVEN

Corporate and Public Finance in International Markets

Deregulation of the world's financial markets will cause a transfer of capital and the creation of new wealth across national borders. Because deregulation is in its infancy, most countries still have barriers impeding the flow of capital. These barriers can be: (1) exchange controls, (2) trade barriers, (3) withholding taxes, (4) tariffs and import quotas, or (5) laws restricting or prohibiting direct foreign investment. Most countries have laws that restrict movement of capital across their boundaries to prevent domestically owned capital from seeking safer and higher returns in other countries, to prohibit foreign investors from gaining control of businesses, and to better control foreign exchange rates.

Investment capital is raised by two distinct types of organizations: (1) securities broker/dealers operating as investment bankers and (2) universal banks allowed to underwrite and syndicate issues. In many cases, investment bankers and universal banks will cooperatively manage a syndicate to underwrite and place new issues.

International electronic-transfer banking has facilitated currency conversion, clearing transactions for customer accounts, and the flow of capital in the form of cash equivalent funds, shares of capital stock, and debt issues (notes, bonds, syndicated loans, and interest rate and currency swaps). Electronic-transfer banking permits the rapid transfer and conversion of funds from a bank in one country to a bank in another country through the central banking and clearing system. Prior to electronic-transfer banking, it took weeks to transfer funds between international banks.

Supranational organizations such as CEDEL and Euro-clear comprised of participating agent banks, were established to provide centralized clearing and administrative services for the burgeoning Euro-equity and Eurobond markets.[1] These organizations originally were formed to clear and settle Eurobond transactions, but, in recent years, they have expanded to include selected Euro-equities. They provide participants with a range of custodial, financing, bond lending and borrowing, and depository services for primary and secondary transactions. In addition, their clearing facilities link up with many national stock exchanges.

THE ROLE OF UNIVERSAL BANKS IN INTERNATIONAL UNDERWRITING AND SYNDICATIONS

Universal banks such as Citicorp, Morgan Guaranty Trust, Deutsche Bank, and Credit Suisse-First Boston play a prominent role in underwriting equity and debt issues in international markets. Universal banking laws permit commercial banks to function as securities underwriters, syndicators, and broker/dealers for customers. Most countries permit universal banking. Notable exceptions are the United States, Canada, and Japan.

Universal banking has inherent conflicts of interest because banks operate as commercial lenders and securities underwriters for the same customers—usually large multinational corporations. Universal banking is prohibited in the United States, Canada, and Japan to protect public investors from the abuses of banks and their clients sharing insider information and engaging in unfair trading practices. Universal banking also favors underwriting debt and equity issues for mature, well-capitalized companies that have been privately held. Unlike securities brokers, universal banks tend to reject underwriting companies that are less mature with small capitalizations.

---

[1] CEDEL, located in Luxembourg, is a clearing organization of over 100 agent banks and 1,500 participants. Citicorp is the lead bank for CEDEL. CEDEL is an acronym for Centrale de Livraison de Valeurs Mobilières. Euro-clear, located in Brussels, Belgium, is a clearing and service organization consisting of several hundred agent banks and several thousand participants. Morgan Guaranty Trust is the lead bank for Euro-clear.

TABLE 7.1   Ten Largest Banking Concerns in the World

Company Name	Headquarters by City	Assets (U.S.$ millions)	Capital (U.S.$ millions)
Citicorp	New York	$173,597	$26,020
Banque Nationale	Paris	123,074	10,117
Dai-Ichi Kangyo	Tokyo	122,895	4,170
Credit Agricole	Paris	122,884	18,347
Fuji Bank	Tokyo	121,384	9,195
BankAmerica	San Francisco	118,541	9,935
Sumitomo Bank	Osaka, Japan	113,985	5,860
Credit Lyonnais	Paris	111,452	8,314
Mitsubishi Bank	Tokyo	105,819	14,651
National Westminster	London	104,677	8,223

SOURCES: Worldscope, Wright Investors' Service and Center for International Financial Analysis & Research, 1986.

An example of a preferred underwriting occurred when Deutsche Bank underwrote and syndicated an offering on West German auto manufacturer Daimler-Benz in 1983. The floatation was 5 million shares with an offering price of DM 800 ($300). The Daimler-Benz issue was placed with institutional accounts. Another example was the privatization of British Telecom in 1984. Kleinwort, Benson sold 100 million shares valued at £10.50 billion to investors throughout the world at an attractive discount to the market price. Table 7.1 ranks the 10 largest banking concerns in the world by assets and capital.

Universal banks have committed capital and personnel to underwrite primary issues for brokerage firms that lack the necessary capital. Unlike universal banks, brokerage firms have highly motivated sales and marketing organizations. In this manner, the underwriting and syndication activities of universal banks and securities brokers complement each other in financing and placing primary and secondary issues.

The Glass-Steagall Act (1933) prohibits U.S. banks from underwriting issues in the United States. The Glass-Steagall Act doesn't prevent U.S. banks from underwriting issues in countries where it is legal. The trend toward universal banking is increasing throughout the world despite its inherent problems. There is a need for substantial capital commitment and expertise from underwriters to syndicate the deals and place them with retail and institutional clients. Universal banks are in a better position than most brokerage firms to manage these deals because of their expertise, relationships with customers, and huge capital resources.

As businesses become larger and more diversified, substantial amounts of capital are needed to fund the company's daily operations and expansion needs. The capital markets are a source for a permanent supply of capital through equity and debt issues. The capital raising and distribution function of international markets must be structured to meet the financing needs of the issuer and the profit incentives of the investor.

HOW TO RAISE CAPITAL
IN THE INTERNATIONAL MARKETS

The Selection of an Investment Banker

When an issuer wants to raise capital in the international markets, there are many important considerations. A primary item is selection of an investment banker. An investment banker can be either a securities broker/dealer or a universal bank capable of underwriting and placing an issue. An issuer hires an investment banker to help achieve its financial goals. An investment banking firm must determine if it wants to be retained by the client or if the client's needs might better be served by another relationship.

An investment banking firm is the lead manager and underwriter in placing an issue with customer accounts. The lead manager invites other investment bankers to form a syndicate. They participate in distributing an issue and in underwriting risks and fees. Syndication fees are divided among the corporate finance department, syndicate members, and the sales force. The syndicate agrees to place an issue on a firm commitment or on a best-efforts basis. Under an arrangement of a firm commitment, syndicate members agree to purchase unsold shares for their accounts.

A lead manager is responsible for hiring legal counsel to register a security with all regulatory agencies and to prepare all legal documents, including a prospectus. In addition, the lead manager organizes the selling process, negotiates the allocation of an issue among syndicate members, determines the spread, and prices the issue for the public. International investment banking is further complicated in that an issue must be registered for sale with the regulatory agencies and stock exchanges in several countries. The registration process may take months, especially if an issuer has had no prior securities registrations. The lead manager places tombstone ads in financial publications to notify the public of the impending sale.

An issuer can be a foreign government, a multinational corporation, or a small biotechnology company. The investment banking needs of a multinational company are quite different in scope and size than the needs of a smaller company. Investment bankers specialize in arranging financing for their clients. For example, some investment bankers specialize in foreign currency denominated bonds; others specialize in underwriting specific industry issues. An investment banker must evaluate the financial condition, management team, and future prospects of an issuer before taking it on as a potential client. The underwriter has a reputation to consider. The results of a poorly managed underwriting could hurt an investment banker's image and business. An investment banker's salespeople present the details of a new issue to persuade clients to purchase the issue on the offering if it has been properly cleared for registration and issuance.

Certain issuers may hire several investment bankers to manage a deal. An investment banker can advise its client on the following items:

1. The stated objectives of the offering.
2. The use of offering proceeds.
3. The types of securities offered—equity, debt, convertible.
4. Special features of the issue such as convertibility, call dates, warrants, rights, and maturity date.
5. With what types of investors the securities will be placed— retail clients, institutional clients, existing shareholders, or private placements.
6. Exchanges on which listing will occur—the Tokyo Stock Exchange, the London Stock Exchange, the NASDAQ, and/or the unlisted market.
7. Research reports written by the underwriter to keep clients informed of a company's financial condition.
8. Corporate finance follow-up work to ensure proper registration, placement, and other details.

ACTIVITIES OF INVESTMENT BANKERS

Investment bankers are involved in a wide range of activities including: mergers and acquisitions, new issue underwritings, private placements, privatization of nationalized companies, and advising clients on corporate restructuring and fending off hostile takeovers. In response to increased competition, investment banking firms have created innovative financial instruments to meet a client's needs. The issuance of low-rated corporate bonds known as "junk bonds" was spearheaded by Drexel, Burnham, Lambert to raise capital for companies that couldn't obtain financing from conventional sources.

Considerations of Investors

Investors who purchase non-U.S. debt or equity issues from an underwriter should consider certain items regarding the investment's merits. In the United States, the Securities and Exchange Commission (SEC) requires that full details of a new issue be disclosed in a prospectus. A prospectus provides substantial information regarding the company's use of offering proceeds, financial history, directors, officers, management team, products, balance sheet, earnings, and investment risks. A preliminary prospectus, known as a "red herring," is given to prospective buyers to assist in making a decision. A final prospectus is given to investors after completion of the offering. The reason for strict SEC information requirements for new issues is the concern that U.S. markets be fair for all investors.

The legal and administrative costs of registering a new issue has encouraged many U.S. companies to seek financing outside the United States, where underwriting costs are significantly reduced. Many large foreign companies, which normally are attracted to U.S. capital markets, have preferred to become listed on non-U.S. exchanges because of the stringent financial and disclosure requirements imposed by the SEC.

Outside the United States, underwriters aren't usually required to provide investors with large amounts of information on a primary or secondary offering. In many cases, only a brief offering memorandum is given to prospective investors. Most international investment banking firms only deal with professional and institutional investors. They exclude the public investor from subscribing to primary and secondary issues. In this way, the need for full disclosure is greatly reduced because investors are presumed to know about the risks.

Underwriters place the securities with institutional accounts that may have their own research staffs for evaluating a new issue's merits without a lengthy document. With the growing retail interest in foreign markets, federal and state regulatory agencies are reviewing their policies regarding dissemination of written information prior to an offering. Specifically, these agencies may require full disclosure on a new issue regarding the following items:

1. The financial rating of the issue and the rating agency.
2. Background history of the company—products, services, patents, and market position.
3. Background information on the directors, officers, and management team.
4. Listing of major shareholders.
5. Strength of the balance sheet.
6. Cash flow and earnings per share.
7. Detail disclosure in the company's prospectus.
8. Use of offering proceeds.
9. A presentation of political and economic risks in the issuer's country of origin.
10. Description of foreign currency fluctuation risks.
11. Problems with settling and clearing transactions between buyers and sellers regarding delayed settlement, designated currency, instructions for delivery of certificates, insurance against loss of securities, safekeeping, and recordkeeping.

THE INITIAL PRICING
OF FIXED-INTEREST SECURITIES

Investment bankers receive input from retail and institutional clients regarding the types of fixed-interest securities they want to purchase, such as straight bonds, convertible bonds, currency-denominated bonds, or bonds with warrants. In our experience, investment parameters for institutional clients are usually well defined and restricted by internal investment policies to achieve specific goals. In contrast, investment goals for retail clients tend to change with popular trends.

The goal of investment bankers is to match the types of securities that investment clients want to own with the financing needs of corporate finance clients. For example, if an investment banking firm has client relationships with life insurance companies, their investment managers may want to own a portfolio of high-rated sinking fund bonds to fund future liabilities incurred by their policies. The investment banking firm will specialize in underwriting sinking fund bonds for corporate finance clients if it fits the client's financial objectives.

Investors purchase new issues on an initial public offering (IPO) hopeful that the issues are fairly valued to the current market environment and undervalued as to future earnings. In a global market, the initial pricing of a new security is highly competitive and requires the expertise of experienced investment bankers. Occasionally, investment bankers misprice a new issue, and the market values it differently than was expected. In some cases, investors put a premium on the new issue, and it rises significantly in price in after-market trading. In other cases, investors sell their holdings after the offering and depress the price in the after-market. Investor psychology can be unpredictable and may not correspond to realities of the new issue. The following passages provide some guidelines for pricing new issues of debt, equity, and convertible issues.

Ownership of debt securities represents a senior lien of investors over an issuer's assets. Investors buy fixed-income securities expecting to make a total return on their investment of interest payments plus price appreciation of the underlying security. Debt buyers do well when interest rates decline because the price of a debt security appreciates in value to give an equivalent yield.

Pricing of debt securities is a function of current yield, the obligation's maturity, perceived credit worthiness of an issuer, and the credit rating assigned to the issue. Debt issues are priced competitively to the yields of comparable issues with similar maturity and quality. Debt issues are priced to yield a current return to potential investors for a specific issue. Zero-coupon bonds are priced to yield at maturity because they don't pay a current return. Buyers of debt securities are concerned about both preserving

TABLE 7.2   Ranking of Top Ten Lead Managers in Eurobond Market

Name of Manager	Amount (U.S.$ millions)	Number of Issues
Credit Suisse-First Boston	$13,170	90
Morgan Guaranty	6,107	40
Deutsche Bank	5,850	62
Morgan Stanley International	5,090	55
Salomon Brothers	4,779	37
Merrill Lynch	4,296	29
Nomura Securities	2,648	36
Goldman Sachs	2,468	27
S.G. Warburg	1,937	24
Banque Nationale de Paris	1,758	10
Total	$48,104	410

SOURCE: Euromoney Bondware.

principal and an issuer's ability to make interest payments. The indenture of a debt security states the issuer's obligations and any special arrangements that an investor should be aware of, such as call features, redemption, and the assets backing an issue. The variables to consider in pricing straight debt issues are:

1. Current level of interest rates as reflected by the yield curve of comparable issues traded on the market.
2. Credit rating of the issue and the issuer as evaluated by an independent rating agency such as Standard & Poor's or Moody's.
3. The yield-to-call and yield-to-maturity.
4. Tax treatment of issue—subject to tax-exempt status and withholding taxes.

From its inception in the 1960s, the Eurobond market has constituted a primary market for international investors both in number of issues and dollar volume. In 1984, lead managers issued over 576 Eurobond issues comprising 61 billion dollars. The procedures for underwriting, issuance, and clearing and settling transactions are well-standardized compared to other debt markets. Table 7.2 ranks the top 10 lead managers in the Eurobond market in 1984.

INITIAL PRICING OF EQUITY ISSUES

Investment bankers bring new equity issues to market to satisfy investor needs for participating in the long-term growth of national economies and the earnings of publicly held companies. Underwriting firms are responsible for providing maintenance research on companies that they bring to the public. Institutional clients demand maintenance research on new issues as a condition for participating in the offering.

Shares of common stock represent ownership of business assets. The value of business assets fluctuates with the overall growth in the national economy as measured by the gross national product (GNP) or the gross domestic product (GDP). The holder of common stock has the last lien on an issuer's assets in times of default. Buyers of equity issues have higher risk profiles compared to buyers of debt; however, a portfolio of equities generally outperforms a portfolio of debt securities over a 10-year period.

Pricing new equity issues is an imprecise art. Buyers of equity issues are concerned about a company's cash flow, growth in earnings, ability to pay dividends, and price appreciation of an issue. Current yield is usually a secondary consideration. Pricing of new equity securities is more complex than pricing debt securities because investors must evaluate the future business environment of the company, its industry, and national economic conditions. Investors buy equity issues based on expectations of future company earnings in an uncertain business environment. The variables to consider in pricing equity issues are:

1. Credit rating of the issuer.
2. The offering price compared to other companies in the group.
3. Current financial condition of the company's income statement and balance sheet, estimated cash flow, book value, off-balance sheet assets, and earnings.
4. Position in the industry.

The Euro-equities market is still in a developmental stage. The primary risk in investing in Euro-equities is the timely clearance and settlement of transactions. Several organizations, such as CEDEL, Euro-clear, NSCC/ISCC, and MCC/MSTC, are developing service facilities to accommodate investors in clearing and settling trades quickly.[2] For example, on certain European and Asian exchanges that don't have centralized clearing facilities, settlement can take weeks or months.

PRIVATIZATION OF STATE-OWNED COMPANIES

Margaret Thatcher's Conservative Party achieved popularity when it privatized British Telecom in 1984. Privatization of British Telecom raised $4.6 billion for the U.K. government, and it helped broaden ownership of U.K. common shares in the global share floatation.

Privatization of companies is the opposite of nationalization—where a government assumes financial and political control of a company. Nationalization is endorsed by socialist, labor, and communist parties who want state regulation of key industries' commercial activities. For example, many privately owned French companies were nationalized during Francois Mitterand's presidency in 1982. The British Labor Party nationalized large numbers of companies that are now being privatized under Margaret Thatcher's government. In certain cases, a government provides seed capital to fund a new company with the intention of privatizing it later. Government-funded companies provide employment and new products for domestic consumption or export.

Privatization is the process of selling shares of state-owned companies to private investors. The motivation to privatize a company usually stems from a change in the political philosophy of a country's majority party. Socialist, labor, and communist political parties favor the nationalization of a country's essential companies, such as banking, utilities, defense, and transportation companies. Leaders of these parties may legislate partial or complete national ownership of essential companies. When the politics in a country favors conservative, probusiness governments, governmental policy changes from nationalization to privatization of state-owned enterprises. The changing political and business cli-

---

[2] NSCC/ISCC, located in New York City, is affiliated with the Depository Trust Corporation (DTC). It is an acronym for the National Securities Clearing Corporation/International Securities Clearing Corporation. MCC/MSTC, located in Chicago, is a wholly owned subsidiary of the Midwest Stock Exchange. It is an acronym for the Midwest Clearing Corporation/Midwest Securities Trust Corporation.

mate created by nationalization versus privatization policies causes enormous uncertainty in capital markets. Investors become uncertain about the future prospects for a company that risks being nationalized. Consequently, they usually avoid investing in such companies.

Privatization began in West Germany when Konrad Adenauer won the general elections in 1957. Chancellor Adenauer and Finance Minister Ludwig Erhardt believed that the West German economy would benefit from private ownership. In 1961, the Federal Republic of Germany sold 20 percent of its shares in Volkswagen, and over 1.5 million people bought shares in the company. In 1965, the German government sold nearly 60 percent of its shares in VEBA, the West German electrical utility company. Nearly 2.5 million people subscribed to VEBA shares when they were offered to the public.

The United Kingdom is the world's leader in privatization. Many of these enterprises were offered at attractive discounts to the market and rose substantially in after-market dealings. For example, in 1981, British Aerospace was sold at £1.50 which rose to £5.66 in 1986. Cable and Wireless was offered at £1.12 and increased to £6.90. In November 1984, the British government sold off its interest in British Telecom for an estimated value of $4.6 billion at an offering price of £1.30 per share. British Telecom had nearly doubled in price by 1986. During the next five years, shares of other privatized British enterprises will be offered to public and institutional investors at attractive prices.

In the next five years, we estimate that 15 governments will announce privatization programs. In such programs hundreds of state-owned companies will be privatized, closed down, or offered in joint venture with other investors. The sale of state-owned companies is an effort to increase the coffers of state treasuries and to return control to the private sector for improved management and operating efficiency. Other countries will be putting their state-owned enterprises up for sale in the international markets. Many will have huge market capitalizations when they become privatized. For example, the Nippon Telegraph and Telephone Co. (NTT) of Japan has an estimated net worth of $21 billion, which is about equal to the market capitalization of General Motors.

When a government privatizes a company, its shares are offered by allotment through investment bankers at attractive prices to prospective investors. The subscription price is often below the current market value as an incentive for making substantial purchases.

TYPES OF FIXED-INTEREST SECURITIES ISSUED

The largest volume of securities underwritten and issued in the international markets are fixed-interest securities that are listed on a stock exchange or traded off the exchange between banks and other financial institutions. These securities may be denominated in specific currencies that allow investment managers to hedge interest rate or foreign exchange risks through the use of financial futures and options contracts. The interbank market can be used to hedge foreign exchange rates risks. The following is a partial list of different categories of fixed-interest securities traded on foreign markets:

Eurobonds. Debt securities denominated in a currency other than the issuing country, issued in bearer form; not registered for sale in the United States.

ECU Bonds. Debt securities whose principal and interest is denominated in European currency units (ECUs).

Dual Currency Bonds. Debt securities with the principal denominated in one currency and the interest denominated in another currency.

Yankee Bonds. Debt securities of U.S. corporations denominated in a currency other than the U.S. dollar.

Fixed-Rate Coupon Bond. Debt securities with a coupon that is fixed at a specified interest rate until called or until maturity.

Floating-Rate Coupon Bond. Debt securities with a variable interest rate that can change at a specified interval based on a standard rate such as LIBOR or 90-day U.S. Treasury bills.

PUBLIC FINANCE

Foreign national and state governments raise money to fund their expenditures through the direct taxation of personal income and corporate profits, taxes on dividends and interest payments, and indirect taxation such as sales tax or value-added tax (VAT). Most government expenditures far exceed the revenues generated through taxation—leaving a substantial budget deficit. Since 1980, the budget deficits of many European, Latin American, and North American countries have tripled from their 1980 base figure. For example, in 1980, France ran a deficit of 286.5 million francs; in 1984, the deficit ballooned to 834.6 million francs. In 1980, Italy ran a deficit of 36.1 billion lira, which rose to 106.7 billion lira in 1985. The French and Italian governments illustrate the magnitude of fiscal irresponsibility from national leaders who don't attempt to balance budgets. Instead, they rely on the credit worthiness of their countries to borrow money, which creates mammoth public debt for future generations. Governments have a distinct advantage over corporate borrowers in issuing interest-bearing securities; unlike corporate borrowers, they can legislate tax incentives for investors.

Budget deficits can be funded through bank loans or by issuing government obligations. Countries that can't borrow in world financial markets rely on commercial bank loans to meet their needs. Credit-worthy nations borrow funds to meet budget maturities ranging from one month to 30 years.

The burgeoning growth of public debt by issuing government securities has a profound impact on the world's aggregate money supply. Growth in the aggregate money supply without corresponding growth in real productivity eventually leads to high wage-price inflation rates, high interest rates, currency devaluations, and major currency value realignments among nations.

The trend in the velocity and growth of public debt among Western nations is alarming. A few governments, such as West Germany, are making serious efforts to reduce deficits by controlling expenditures to achieve a balanced budget.

PROCEDURES FOR CLEARING
AND SETTLING TRANSACTIONS OF PRIMARY
AND SECONDARY OFFERINGS

A major problem with international equities and debt securities markets is the correct clearance and settlement of transactions. Delayed or failed delivery of certificates, lost securities, faulty currency settlements, and incorrect matching of buyers and sellers are common problems for international investors. Several clearing organizations, such as CEDEL, Euro-clear, ISCC/NSCC, and MCC/MSTC, have formed to handle these problems. They were established to coordinate transactional activities between agent banks, exchange clearing facilities, and participants such as insurance companies, securities brokers, and private banks. CEDEL and Euro-clear specialize in clearing Eurobonds and selected equities listed on certain exchanges. ISCC/NSCC and MCC/MSTC specialize in clearing securities listed on the Canadian and London Stock Exchanges. Eventually, many national and supranational clearing and settlement facilities will be linked—to process transactions quickly with minimal error.

Proper transaction settlement requires specific obligations from the buyer and the seller. Specific instructions are given to their respective agent banks about settling a transaction. Settlement of a transaction usually occurs between agent banks in coordination with the clearing facility of an exchange. The settlement terms require satisfying the following conditions and written instructions for an agent bank:

1. Identification by description and code of the security to be transferred from seller to buyer.
2. The amount of money in the designated currency to be paid to the seller. Buyers are responsible for making the necessary currency conversion prior to settlement.
3. The buyer must designate a securities depository bank to hold certificates; the seller must designate a cash depository bank to hold its funds.
4. The parties of a transaction must point to each other.
5. A settlement date must be agreed upon.

In conclusion, investors who participate in international markets must know the risks of clearing transactions. Parties to a transaction must follow specified procedures for providing accurate instructions to an agent bank and a central clearing facility.

The International Financial Markets

Part Two provides an overview of the demographics, government, money and banking systems, background on the economy, and a description of primary financial markets in 15 countries. Countries such as Spain, Belgium, Luxembourg, Israel, and South Africa were omitted, however, due to space limitations. We will write about developed and developing countries in future publications.

During the next decade, investors will observe these changes and developments in the financial markets of free-world nations:

1. Greater financial market deregulation will foster an environment of intense global competition for capital.
2. Modernization of trading facilities will deemphasize the role of the exchange as a place to conduct business. Most transactions between buyers and sellers will be done off the exchange's floor by automated execution and order routing systems. The exchange will be a reporting and data collection center for member firms.
3. Automation of order entry and execution will facilitate 24-hour trading linkages among the exchanges; the order book will move from one exchange to another. Clearing and settlement of transactions will occur through a linkage of national and international clearing and settlement organizations such as CEDEL and Euro-clear.
4. Derivative financial contracts will be introduced such as index options and futures, interest options, and futures on many foreign exchanges.

5. A substantial increase in the listing of internationally traded equities and debt securities.
6. Investors will use innovative trading strategies such as program trading, portfolio insurance, yield enhancement, and bond immunization programs to protect portfolio value and increase yields.
7. Privatization of state-owned companies will encourage a broader distribution of shareholder's capital in the private sector.
8. A global "universal banking system" where commercial and merchant banks play a greater role in underwriting securities and managing investors' financial assets will be a reality.

For an investor to recognize opportunities for buying undervalued securities denominated in undervalued currencies, he or she must know about a country, its dominant economic sectors, and the key companies within those sectors. An investor should know both the macroeconomic factors that cause a country's currency to become undervalued and the factors that cause a company's shares or debt securities to become undervalued regarding its book value, cash flow, earnings, or credit rating. See Table 1. In addition, knowledge of a country's accounting practices is essential for understanding the valuation of a company's assets. Accounting practices differ widely among countries. For example, West German and Swiss companies have ultraconservative accounting practices that greatly undervalue their actual assets. In Japan, many companies value their real estate holdings at purchase price instead of current market value.

Working knowledge of a country's financial markets is also essential for placing orders for shares or debt securities and for clearing and settling transactions with minimal error and expense. The market-making, clearance, and settlement operations of each financial market differ significantly. An investor can't assume that foreign markets operate like markets in the United States. Lack of knowledge in this area causes expensive errors. For example, a delayed Eurobond transaction settlement due to wrong instructions could cost several days of interim financing.

Our survey of 15 countries and their financial markets has given us interesting insights about present and future trends in their

TABLE 1 **Factors That Can Create Undervalued Investment Opportunities**

1. Changes in government or political parties.
2. General level of interest rates and the spread between short- and long-term rates.
3. Cost of energy-related products such as crude oil, gasoline, natural gas, and coal.
4. Cost of raw materials such as lumber, iron ore, and minerals.
5. The country's tax laws regarding interest, dividends, and capital gains.
6. Trade agreements, tariffs, and import restrictions.
7. Development of new technologies and products.
8. Reduction in the credit rating of an issuer.
9. Revision of the financial accounting practices and the interpretation by accounting firms.

demographics, economies, politics, and capital markets. Competitive forces in the global economy affect the supply and demand for capital, technology, management personnel, skilled and unskilled labor, exports, and information services.

Forecasts indicate that certain countries will show a reduced population by the year 2000, while other countries will have a burgeoning population. For example, the population of West Germany is expected to decline by 3.8 percent by the year 2000, while the population of Canada is estimated to increase by 25 percent. Changes in the size and composition of a country's population can affect its national wealth, per capita income, and political, economic, and social systems.

In recent years, many governments have become more conservative in dealing with problems in the economy. There is a growing trend to privatize state-owned enterprises. The governments of Great Britain, France, West Germany, and Japan have embarked on aggressive privatization programs as part of a national policy to transfer ownership of state-owned enterprises to the private sector. Privatization will raise funds for state treasuries, broaden the base of ownership, and improve the operating efficiency of these enterprises.

The United States is one of few countries in the world that has an abundance of natural resources, technology, fertile agricultural lands, a skilled labor force, and democratic institutions that allow the accumulation of private capital to foster the growth of a market-oriented economy. Most countries lack one or more of these elements, which forces them to compensate in other ways. For example, Japan compensates for its lack of natural resources by encouraging the manufacturing and export of durable goods such as cars, electronics, and optical equipment. Hong Kong has developed a substantial re-export market with the United States—Hong Kong businesses import semifinished goods and re-export them in finished form. Both Japan and Hong Kong receive substantial foreign exchange earnings from their export markets.

A decrease in crude oil prices can help oil-importing countries and hurt oil-exporting countries. Most industrialized nations benefit from a decline in oil prices; for example, the economies of Japan, Germany, Italy, Switzerland, and Sweden benefit tremendously from declining energy prices. Their currencies revalued against the U.S. dollar when oil prices dropped from $22 to $10 per barrel in 1986. The economies of Great Britain, the Netherlands, and Norway, however, are affected negatively when oil prices decline. These examples illustrate how the currency values and share values of key companies are affected differently when there is a major change in world oil prices.

Part Two presents historical and contemporary material on the governments, monetary and banking systems, and economies of selected countries and how such factors influence the structure and efficiency of the primary financial markets. Serious investors in international markets must read primary material to keep abreast of everchanging political, economic, and financial situations. Chapter 20 provides readers with a list of primary and secondary reference sources.

There are striking differences in how countries confront the problem of financing private sectors of the economy. Certain governments actively participate as a partner in financing semiprivate enterprises to induce development of specific technologies and markets. Other governments encourage private enterprise by legislating tax incentives.

A dramatic change in one or more of the categories listed in Table 1 can create opportunities to buy undervalued securities. Investors must interpret the effects from such changes. Many times the expected results of a specific change don't occur. For example, the election of a socialist government in France in 1982 was expected to affect the capital markets negatively. After the elections and subsequent nationalization of many French enterprises, share prices of French companies declined sharply, which later created undervalued situations for astute investors. Several years later, the French stock market became very bullish as the CAC Index reached new highs. A similar situation occurred in the Hong Kong market when China didn't renew its lease as a British territory. Panic selling hit the market, which created excellent buying opportunities as shares in Hong Kong companies regained their value.

Tables 2 through 6 provide a capsule view of each primary financial market covered in the book. They help in making comparisons about the characteristics of different markets. The data were compiled during the years 1984 to 1986.

Fédération Internationale des Bourses de Valeurs

The Fédération Internationale des Bourses de Valeurs (FIBV) is an international organization of member stock exchanges based in Paris, France. The FIBV was founded in 1960 to promote closer collaboration among member stock exchanges and stock exchange

---

TABLE 2   Ranking of World Capital Markets

Country	Primary Exchange	Official Currency	Market Capital (U.S.$ billions)
United States	New York	U.S. dollar	$2,231
Japan	Tokyo	Yen	1,314
United Kingdom	London	Pound sterling	402
West Germany	Frankfurt	Deutsche mark	229
Canada	Toronto	Canadian dollar	157
France	Paris	French franc	134
Italy	Milan	Lira	115
Switzerland	Zurich	Swiss franc	102
Australia	Sydney	Australian dollar	72
Netherlands	Amsterdam	Guilder/florin	61
Sweden	Stockholm	Krona	43
Hong Kong	Hong Kong	Hong Kong dollar	41
Singapore	Singapore	Singapore dollar	23
Total market capitalization			$4,989

SOURCE: Morgan Stanley Capital International Perspective.

TABLE 3   The Primary Stock, Options, and Financial Futures Exchanges

---

Country	Primary Stock Exchange	Primary Option Exchange	Primary Futures Exchange
Japan	Tokyo	None	Tokyo S.E.
United Kingdom	London	London S.E.	LIFFE
West Germany	Frankfurt	Frankfurt S.E.	None
Canada	Toronto	Toronto S.E.	Toronto F.E.
France	Paris	Paris S.E.	MATIF
Italy	Milan	None	None
Switzerland[1]	Zurich	None	None
Australia	Sydney	Sydney S.E.	Sydney F.E.
Netherlands	Amsterdam	EOE	EOE
Sweden	Stockholm	Stockholm S.E.	None
Hong Kong	Hong Kong	None	HKFE
Singapore	Singapore	Singapore S.E.	SIMEX

EOE—European Options Exchange
HKFE—Hong Kong Futures Exchange
LIFFE—London International Futures Exchange
MATIF—Marche a Terme des Instruments Financiers
SIMEX—Singapore International Monetary Exchange
[1] The Zurich Stock Exchange plans to introduce options and financial futures markets by 1988.

TABLE 4   Characteristics of Primary Stock Exchanges—Listed Equities

---

Primary Exchange	Members	Companies	Turnover		Margin Trading	Settlement and Clearing	Days
Tokyo	83	1,802	Y	83.1 billion	Yes	JSSC	3
London	4,978	5,026	BP	105.5 million	No	TALISMAN	Var
Frankfurt			DM	45.3 million	Yes	Kassenverein	2
Toronto	79	933	C$	26.7 million	Yes	CDS	5
Paris	40	906	FF	92.3 million	Yes	SICOVAM	Var
Milan	117	199			Yes	Banca d Italia	
Zurich	24	369	SF	308 billion	Yes	SEGA	3
Sydney	42	1,457	A$	7.54 million	No		10
Amsterdam	440	578	Dfl.	80.8 million	No		10
Stockholm	23	170	SEK	80. billion	No	VPC	
Hong Kong	75	950	HK$	256.7 million	Yes		
Singapore	25	308	S$	8.11 million	Yes	SCCS	10

VAR—variable settlement procedures and dates.
JSSC—Japanese Securities and Settlement Corp
TALISMAN—Transfer Accounting Lodgement for Investors, Stock Management
CDS—Canadian Depository for Securities
SEGA—Schweizerische Effeckten-Giro AG
SCCS—Singapore
VPC—Vardepapperscentralen AB.

TABLE 5 Characteristics of Primary Stock Exchanges—Fixed-Interest Securities and Foreign Government Bonds

Primary Exchange	Listed Fixed-Interest Securities		Turnover		Listed Government Bonds		Turnover
Tokyo	736	Y	35.5	billion		Y	24.6 billion
London		BP	3.79	billion	1,217	BP 281.1	million
Frankfurt		DM	76.3	million			
Toronto		C$					
Paris	2,011	FF	409.7	million			
Milan		L.					
Zurich		SF	2.11	billion			
Sydney		A$					
Amsterdam	1,466	Dfl 73,258		million			
Stockholm		SKK					
Hong Kong		No active markets for debt securities.					
Singapore		S$	103	million			

TABLE 6 Characteristics of Primary Stock Exchanges—Trading and Clearing Linkages with Other International Exchanges

Primary Exchange	Other Exchanges	Trading Linkage	Clearing Linkage
Tokyo	None	No	No
London	Midwest S.E.	No	Yes
LIFFE	CBOT	Yes	Yes
Frankfurt	None	No	No
Toronto	Paris	Yes	Yes
Paris	Toronto	Yes	Yes
Milan	None	No	No
Zurich	None	No	No
Sydney S.E.	EOE	Yes	Yes
Sydney F.E.	COMEX	Yes	Yes
EOE	Montreal	Yes	Yes
	Sydney	Yes	Yes
	Vancouver	Yes	Yes
	AMEX	Yes	Yes
Stockholm	None	No	No
Hong Kong	None	No	No
SIMEX	CME	No	Yes

AMEX—American Stock Exchange
CBOT—Chicago Board of Trade
CME—Chicago Mercantile Exchange
COMEX—Commodity Exchange of New York
EOE—European Options Exchange

associations. Presently, the FIBV consists of 27 members and 16 correspondent members representing stock exchanges located in Asia, Europe, and North and South America.

Sir Nicholas Goodison, president of the FIBV in 1986, presided over the organization during a period of total deregulation in the London financial markets and major changes in other financial markets in Europe, Asia, and South America.

Committee of Stock Exchanges in the European Community and the Interbourse Data Information System

The Committee of Stock Exchanges in the European Community is comprised of 12 member stock exchanges of the European Community (EC). It promotes greater cooperation and linkages among European stock exchanges and other world exchanges. Xavier Dupont, syndic of the Paris Stock Brokers Association, was organization chairman in 1986.

The Interbourse Data Information System (IDIS) is a cooperative effort of EC member stock exchanges that shares information on securities prices, settlement procedures, book-entry transfers, and payment of stock market operations.

Important Caveats On Taxation

For most countries, we present a limited discussion of tax treatment for capital gains, cash and stock dividends, and interest payments for nonresident investors. We aren't experts on tax regulations of the countries. We took information from sources we believe are reliable, but we can't guarantee accuracy of the material. Therefore, readers are advised to consult a qualified tax advisor who knows specific tax laws for a country before making an investment. Tax regulations are complex and subject to change. Many countries have a double taxation agreement with the United States that may include significant benefits for U.S. investors.

Bearer and Registered Securities

Securities in bearer form are not registered with an issuer. They are negotiable securities that can be bought or sold on an appropriate exchange. Registered securities are nonnegotiable because the owner's name is registered with an issuer. Securities in bearer form may not be subject to a withholding tax depending on where they are deposited for safekeeping.

American Depository Receipts (ADRs)

As described in Chapter 1, many foreign issuers have their securities listed on the U.S. markets in American Depository Receipts (ADRs). The list of ADRs is long and subject to change. Prospective investors should check with a broker to see if a foreign issuer has its securities listed in ADR form. In many cases, ADRs are easier to trade because they are approved for trading in the United States and a U.S. bank is the custodian for depository receipts. The purchase cost may be less expensive on a non-U.S. exchange than the corresponding ADRs. Prospective investors should compare purchase costs before making a commitment.

Clearing and Settlement of Transactions

One of the most important achievements in recent years is the development of an organization structure for clearing and settling transactions for internationally traded securities. CEDEL and Euro-clear have made substantial advances in allowing a centralized clearance and settlement facility for depositing securities and foreign currencies. Many national clearing facilities are linking up with CEDEL and Euro-clear to allow the convenient transfer of securities and currencies across international borders. These organizations will play an even greater role in the next decade as financial markets become electronically linked for 24-hour trading.

Ranking Investment Opportunities by Country and Sector

Readers are encouraged to develop a ranking system where potential investment opportunities can be analyzed by country and sectors of the economy. The following hierarchy can be adopted to compare and rank the likelihood of achieving performance from an investment regarding specific countries and sectors of the economy:

Time Zones of the World's Primary Financial Markets

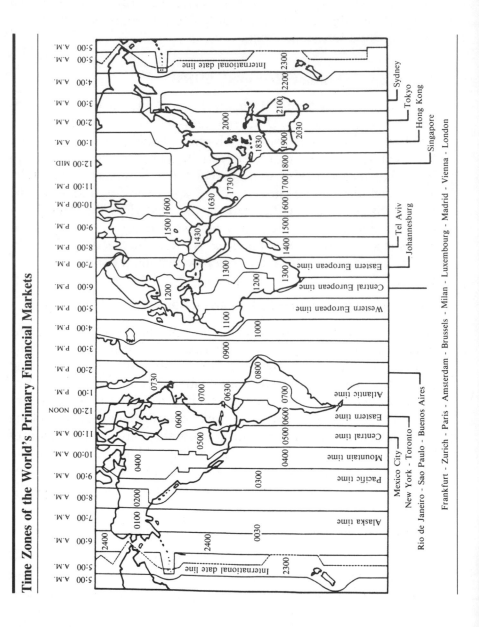

Ranking	Description
1	Most likely to achieve superior results
2	Likely to achieve above average results
3	Likely to achieve average results
4	Likely to achieve below average results
5	Least likely to achieve results

For example, during times of high inflation due to rising world commodity prices, one would rank countries with dominant economy sectors linked to rising commodity prices at 1 or 2, while countries with dominant sectors linked to falling commodity prices would be ranked 4 or 5. One can construct matrices to evaluate investment opportunities by country, sector, or company versus independent variables such as changes in crude oil prices, inflation rate, interest rates, GNP/GDP, population growth, or any other significant variable. This approach produces a quantitative method for comparing multiple investment opportunities.

SUMMARY AND CONCLUSIONS

We present a limited overview of 15 countries and their financial markets in the following chapters. Several books could be written on each country's financial markets. Our purpose is to whet readers' appetites about investing in international markets and provide a general knowledge of how and where to research for undervalued investment opportunities outside the United States.

Japan

The Japanese Archipelago consists of 3,900 islands forming a long mountainous chain in the western Pacific Ocean. Japan covers a total area of 145,809 square miles and has a population of approximately 120 million people. Nearly 42 percent of the population is concentrated in the metropolitan areas of Tokyo, Osaka, and Nagoya. Japan is bordered by the Sea of Japan to the west and north and by the Pacific Ocean to the east and south.

The four main Japanese islands (Hokkaido, Honshu, Kyushu, and Shikoku) have the same latitude range and general climate as the east coast of the United States from Maine to South Carolina. Tokyo, located on Honshu, is the largest city in Japan with a population of 8.2 million people. Tokyo is Japan's capital and financial center. The official language is Japanese, and the official currency is the Japanese yen (Y). (See Figure 8.1.) Buddhism and Shintoism are the primary religions of Japan.

GOVERNMENT

After World War II, Japan's governmental, political, economic, and financial organizations were substantially restructured. The role of the emperor as absolute monarch of Japan was abolished. Postwar leaders established democratic institutions modeled after Western democracies. They wanted to create political and economic systems that provided checks and balances to prevent a recreation of events that led to World War II.

FIGURE 8.1   Exchange Rate for Japanese Yen

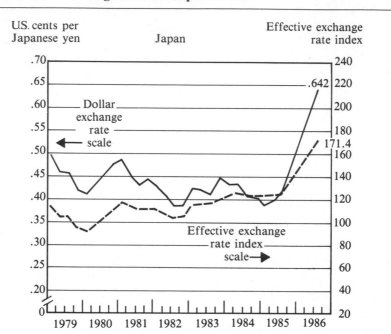

SOURCE: Federal Reserve Bank of St. Louis.

Modern Japan has a parliamentary government. The legislative power is vested in the Diet, which consists of a House of Representatives (511 members) and a House of Councillors (252 members). Members of both houses are elected by direct universal suffrage, except that some members of the House of Councillors are elected by proportional representation.

Executive power is vested in the Cabinet, which is headed by the prime minister. The Cabinet is nominated by the Diet from its members. The prime minister appoints other ministers, a majority of whom must be members of the Diet. Judicial power is vested in the Supreme Court and lower courts as established by law. The major political parties represented in the Diet are the:

1. Liberal Democratic Party—LDP (presently the ruling party).
2. Japan Socialist Party—JSP (the largest opposition party).
3. Komeito Party.

4. Japan Socialist Democratic Party.
5. Japan Communist Party.
6. New Liberal Club Party.

The ruling Liberal Democratic Party (LDP) has remained in power since its formation in 1955.

Members of the House of Representatives are elected to four-year terms unless the House of Representatives is dissolved prior to expiration of their full terms. Members of the House of Councillors are elected for six-year terms.

INTERNATIONAL ORGANIZATIONS

Japan is a member of the United Nations and other international organizations including: the International Monetary Fund, the World Bank, the International Development Association, the Asian Development Bank, the Organization for Economic Cooperation and Development, the Inter-American Development Bank, the African Development Fund, and the International Fund for Agricultural Development.

MONEY AND BANKING

The Bank of Japan was created in 1882 as the central bank of Japan. The Bank is 55 percent owned by the government and 45 percent owned by private investors who have no voting rights. Its functions are similar to other central banks:

1. It issues bank notes.
2. It acts as banker to the government and other banks.
3. It enforces the government's monetary policy.

Most banks rely heavily on the Bank of Japan for refinancing facilities. The most important rate in the Japanese financial system is the Bank of Japan's discount rate for commercial bills, which is known as the bank rate. Adjustment of this rate is one of the four major ways by which the government implements its monetary policy. The other three ways are: (1) adjusting reserve requirements on bank deposits, (2) intervention in the money market, and (3) imposing credit ceilings on banks.

Japan has several of the largest commercial banks in the world with an extensive network of international correspondent banks. The commercial banking system is comprised of foreign exchange banks, foreign banks, city banks, regional banks, and long-term credit banks. These banks perform functions similar to commercial and private banks in the United States.

In addition to private banks, Japan has several important state-owned banks. The Export-Import Bank of Japan is a government-owned institution that finances long-term export credits, raw materials, industrial imports, and Japanese overseas investment. The Japan Development Bank finances long-term developments in the ocean transport, railway, and chemical industries.

THE ECONOMY

Japan's highly advanced and diversified economy developed markedly after the end of World War II. In 1985, Japan had the second largest economy in the free world, accounting for 10 percent of global GNP. Japan is also the world's third largest trading country—ranking next to the United States and the Federal Republic of Germany. Japan's outstanding direct overseas investment totaled $379 billion in 1984, ranking Japan third after the United States and the United Kingdom. The volume of Japan's official development assistance (ODA) to developing nations is the second largest in the world next to the United States.

A combination of ingenuity, hard work, and financial assistance from Western nations helped to rebuild Japan's war-devastated economy. Following the recovery and reconstruction from postwar chaos, Japan returned to stability in the 1950s and experienced rapid growth in the 1960s. Assisted by low labor costs, high levels of savings and capital investment, Japan's gross domestic product (GDP) grew at an annual rate of more than 10 percent until the 1970s.

Japan is poorly endowed with natural resources. Almost all of Japan's raw materials are imported—including most food apart from rice and fish. Japan imports nearly all of its petroleum supplies for energy and manufacturing of chemical products. During the 1970s, Japan's economic growth was disrupted by a sharp rise in crude oil prices. Soaring oil prices during the first oil crisis in 1973–74 caused a major decline in Japan's foreign export earnings and its GDP. The second oil crisis in 1979–80 was less severe than the first, but it had an adverse impact on Japan's economic growth rate. Japan's flexible response to changing world economic conditions enabled its economy to grow steadily during the 1970s. In the 1980s, declining oil prices caused a strong rebound in Japan's economy and currency.

In response to energy needs, Japan is building additional nuclear power plants to nearly double its output of electrical energy during the next decade. In 1984, the country had 28 operating nuclear plants—ranking fourth in the world. In addition, Japanese scientists are developing fusion nuclear capabilities that will replace the more dangerous fission reactors.

The past decade has also seen rapid structural change in Japanese industry and commerce. During high economic growth in the 1960s and early 1970s, expansion was based on development of heavy industries such as steel, machinery, and base chemicals, which consume large amounts of resources. In the last decade, there has been an emphasis on developing value-added industries such as electronics and precision instruments—industries that employ high levels of technology with small amounts of resources.

Industry in Japan is almost entirely privately owned and operated except for the railway system, the telephone and telegraph system, and the tobacco and salt monopolies. In addition, Japan Air Lines (JAL) and an enterprise that constructs electric power generation are government-subsidized; however, the government is considering privatizing certain state-owned enterprises during the next decade.

Japan is a leading manufacturer of motor vehicles, iron and steel products, commercial ships, electronic equipment, general machinery, and precision optical goods. Japanese industry has the most industrial robots in the world. Manufacturers utilize robots for the welding, assembly, handling, and unloading of goods. Robots can improve the efficiency and quality of production for certain assembly-line products. The manufacturing sector accounts for nearly 30 percent of Japan's GDP. The service sector accounts for 20 percent of the GDP; banking, insurance, and real estate account for another 15 percent of the GDP.

Foreign trade is essential to Japan's economy. Large trading companies such as Mitsubishi, Mitsui & Co., and Marubeni Corporation maintain branch offices in the world's leading trade centers to promote the export of Japanese goods and services. The United States is Japan's most important trading partner, accounting for 37 percent of total exports, Japan receives about 20 percent of its total imports from the United States. Members of the European Economic Community (ECC), China, South Korea, Saudi Arabia, and Indonesia also have trade agreements with Japan. Shipping in Japan is not nationalized, but it is supervised by the Ministry of Transportation. Japan has the second largest merchant fleet in the world; the main ports are Yokohama, Nagasaki, and Kobe.

THE SECURITIES MARKETS

Japan is the world's second largest capital market. Japan has eight stock exchanges, several hundred securities firms, and 11 investment trust management companies. Stock exchanges are located in Tokyo, Osaka, Nagoya, Kyoto, Hiroshima, Fukuoka, Niigata, and Sapporo.

Trading on Japan's exchanges was suspended by U.S. military forces in 1945. When trading was resumed in 1949, U.S. occupation forces had revamped its system to the American style. Restructuring of the Japanese stock exchanges was an attempt to reshape Japan's economy. U.S. forces also dissolved family-owned zaibatsu conglomerates, which had dominated the economy for nearly 40 years. Prior to their dissolution, zaibatsu companies had an immense concentration of economic power and wealth in Japan. They were self-financed and therefore never offered shares on a public exchange. After their dissolution, new types of businesses were formed that required substantial equity financing. Stock exchanges played an important role in raising capital to finance the growth of postwar Japan's basic industries.

Under a Japanese securities and exchange law enacted after World War II, stock exchanges are organized on a membership basis. The members organizing an exchange also trade its securities. The exchanges are organized and operated as nonprofit organizations. Because of its market dominance, we will focus on the Tokyo Stock Exchange.

THE TOKYO STOCK EXCHANGE

The Tokyo Stock Exchange (TSE) is Japan's largest exchange—accounting for over 80 percent of total stock exchange business. The Tokyo Stock Exchange is the second largest exchange in the world after the New York exchanges in market value of shares traded. In 1985, 1,476 issuers were listed on the TSE, including 52 foreign companies. At that time, 854 bond issues were listed including issues of foreign companies, foreign governments, and international organizations.

The TSE was founded in 1878 as a public market in response to the need for trading government-granted bonds. During the Meiji Restoration in the 19th century, the new government gave public bonds to the old Samurai class to guarantee their livelihood as Japan's feudal system was dismantled. At the same time, national banks, railways, trading companies, and other large business enterprises emerged. The TSE was formed under regulations modeled after the Stock Exchange of London. For the first 10 years, trading of national bonds dominated the market. In the 1890s, trading in company shares became an important means of financing new business ventures.

TSE membership is divided into three categories: (1) 254 regular members, (2) 12 Saitori members, and (3) seven special members. All memberships are corporate. Regular members buy and sell securities for clients or for their own accounts. The five largest Japanese members are Nomura Securities, Daiwa, Nikko, Yamaichi, and Kokusasi. The Ministry of Finance (MoF) and the stock exchange approve all applications for licensing members. Only securities broker/dealers can become members. Under current Japanese law, commercial and private banks can't become members. Until 1985, Japanese securities dealers were the only TSE members. However, the Ministry of Finance and the TSE permitted the following foreign broker/dealers to obtain memberships: Goldman Sachs, Jardine Fleming, Merrill Lynch, Morgan Stanley, and Vickers da Costa.

Saitori members act as intermediaries in matching bids and offers between regular members. They are appointed by the Ministry of Finance, and they are assigned specific groups of securities to make markets and fix prices in. Saitori members handle transactions in securities listed only in the First Section. Unlike specialists in New York, they can't trade for their own account. All transactions are executed through two methods: the Zaraba method or the Itayose method. In the Zaraba method, transactions are made by an auction process with respect to price and time priorities. In the Itayose method, all orders that reach the floor before the opening are treated as simultaneous orders; each buy order is compared with sell orders until its quantity and price are matched by a sell order. Even though regular members may execute trades away from the Saitori, regular members must report all transactions. Saitori members receive compensation in the form of commissions from regular members. Special members of the TSE are securities firms that specialize in handling transactions on the Tokyo and Osaka Exchanges that can't be made on regional exchanges.

The TSE has five distinct markets: (1) the First Section—for actively traded listed shares and bonds, (2) the Second Section—for less actively traded shares and bonds, (3) the Foreign Section—for trading listed foreign issues, (4) the over-the-counter (OTC) market, used primarily for bond trading, and (5) a financial futures market for trading selected Japanese government bonds.

Each Saitori member is assigned an exchange floor booth where he handles transactions in specific groups of securities listed in the First Section. As mentioned earlier, all transactions involving securities listed in the First Section must be executed through or reported to the Saitori. Regular members can engage in certain off-exchange transactions such as "crossing trades," in which a regular member executes both the buy and sell orders generated between two customers. Or, if the exchange is closed, regular members can make transactions between themselves. The TSE system accommodates large block orders through a Block Transaction System. Large block orders can be handled in three ways: (1) on-floor block purchases, (2) on-floor block sales, and (3) off-floor distributions.

Starting in January 1982, transactions in securities listed in the Second Section have been executed through a Computer-assisted order routing and execution system (CORES). CORES is an automated system that allows for market-making and execution of orders between regular members. The over-the-counter (OTC) market is primarily for bond trading between members. Over 95 percent of all bond trades are made over-the-counter.

GOVERNMENT BOND FUTURES MARKET

Trading in futures contracts was banned in Japan after World War II. U.S. occupation forces prohibited transactions in futures contracts when the Tokyo Stock Exchange reopened in 1949.

With the approval of Ministry of Finance and stock exchange members, the Tokyo Stock Exchange began government bond futures trading in October 1985. With the inauguration of this market, the exchange provides direct access to the new market for existing member firms and for nonmember firms that meet exchange requirements. These nonmember firms are called "special participants"; they include nonmember securities firms and banks that are licensed to deal in Japanese government bonds. See Table 8.1 for contract specifications.

TABLE 8.1 Contract Specifications for Government Bond Futures

Contract	Standardized 6 percent, 10-year, long-term Japanese government bond.
Basic trading unit	Japanese government bonds with a ¥100 million face value.
Contract months	March, June, September, December cycle (Five contract months traded at all times).
Delivery date	20th of each contract month.
Deliverable grade	Japanese government bonds designated by the exchange. Based on 6 percent standard.
Trading hours	9 to 11 A.M. 1 to 3 P.M.
Minimum fluctuation	1/100 yen (¥10 thousand per contract).
Daily price limit	¥1 upward and downward (¥1 million per contract).
Last day of trading	The ninth business day prior to each delivery date. The trading in a new contract month begins on the business day immediately following the last trading day.
Margin requirements for customers	The greater of either 3 percent of the nominal transaction value of ¥6 million.
Margin requirements for members and special participants	2 percent of the nominal transaction value.

SOURCE: Toyko Stock Exchange.

CLEARANCE AND SETTLEMENT OF TRANSACTIONS

Nearly all transactions are settled "regular way" which is on the third business day after execution. Members must settle on that day. Business days include Saturday except for the second Saturday of each month, when the stock exchange is closed. Regular settlements account for 99.9 percent of total trading volume. Other settlement methods include "cash" transactions, which are settled on the same day or the next business day, and "when issued" transactions, in which delivery and payment of new shares are settled after issuance.

Since 1972, the Japan Securities Clearing Corporation (JSCC) has used a book-entry clearing system that transfers ownership of securities by the simple entry on an institution's books rather than actual movement of certificates. The JSCC is a wholly owned subsidiary of the TSE. In 1984, with the enactment of a central depository and clearing of securities law, the Japan Securities Depository Center (JASDEC) was designated as a securities depository organization by the Ministry of Finance. The objective of the JASDEC is establishment of a more complete system for clearance, settlement, and deposit of securities. Japanese securities purchased by nonresidents may be held in custodial banks in Japan.

MARGIN TRADING

Margin trading is a transaction where a securities company lends a customer money or securities needed for the settlement of a regular transaction made on the exchange. Margin trading in Japan was modeled after the U.S. system. However, there are major differences in Japan's system. Margin trading applies only to First Section stocks. A deposit of cash or qualified securities can be used to purchase securities on margin. General margin accounts must be settled within six months of the contract date. The minimum margin rate is presently either 60 percent of the value of the securities or 300,000 yen—whichever is greater; however, minimum margin rates can vary due to changes made by the Minister of Finance.

As of December 1980, the maximum assessment rates for collateral securities were 95 percent for government bonds, 90 percent for government-guaranteed bonds, 85 percent for other bonds, 80 percent for convertible bonds, and 70 percent for shares. Interest rates for margin trades are usually based on the official discount rate. Margin transactions can account for 30 to 40 percent of total volume.

A special margin trading system for designated shares was established in 1978. Margin trading in designated shares occurs under both the general and special margining systems. The new margin trading system calls for making a trade on the following conditions: the volume per transaction is 5,000 shares or more (compared to 1,000 shares or more for the general margining system); the settlement period is three months (compared to six months); the commissions are 60 percent of the present general commission rates; and the interest rate received by the seller is higher than what is received in the general system. Only small numbers of issues qualify for the special margining system. Foreign investors may only deal on margin for short sales or for stock either under conversion or in the registration process.

COMMISSION RATES

Brokerage commissions on equities are fixed depending on the transaction's value, and they range from 0.55 to 2 percent in addition to a fixed charge of 2,500 to 125,000 yen. The commission rates on bonds are also fixed, and they range from 0.25 to 0.8 percent for straight bonds, and 0.55 to 1.15 percent for convertible bonds. Foreign banks and securities houses qualify for a 20 percent rebate on standard commission charges. See Table 8.2 for commission rates.

THE PRIMARY AND SECONDARY MARKETS IN EQUITIES

In the primary market, certain securities dealers are licensed by the Ministry of Finance (MoF) to underwrite new issues. New shares are made available through either a public offering or a rights subscription. New issues are usually listed in the Second Section for a while before they are approved for listing in the First Section.

TABLE 8.2 Commission Rates

(a) Stocks—Subscription Rights Effective from April 1, 1977

(Percentage of Contract Price in Sales or Purchases)

Up to	¥	1 million	1.25%
Over	¥	1 million and up to ¥ 3 million	1.05%
Over	¥	3 million and up to ¥ 5 million	0.95%
Over	¥	5 million and up to ¥ 10 million	0.85%
Over	¥	10 million and up to ¥ 30 million	0.75%
Over	¥	30 million and up to ¥ 50 million	0.65%
Over	¥	50 million and up to ¥100 million	0.60%
Over	¥	100 million	0.55%

(Any fractional sum of less than one yen is discarded)

---

1. The commission rate on contract price less than 200,000 yen is fixed at 2,500 yen.
2. Includes preferred stocks and foreign stocks.

(b) Bonds Effective from July 1, 1976

(Rate per ¥100 of Par Value in Sales or Purchases)

	Total Amount of Par Value			
Kinds of Bonds	*Up to* *¥5 Million*	*Over* *¥5 Million* *up to* *¥10 Million*	*Over* *¥10 Million* *up to* *¥100 Million*	*Over* *¥100 Million*
Government bonds	¥0.40	¥0.35	¥0.30	¥0.25
Government-guaranteed bonds, local government bonds, foreign government bonds, and bonds designated by stock exchanges	.60	.50	.40	.30
Other bonds	.80	.65	.50	.35

(c) Convertible Bonds Effective July 1, 1976

(Percentage of Contract Price in Sales or Purchases)

Total Amount of Par Value	*Up to* *¥1 Million*	*Over* *¥1 Million* *Up to* *¥5 Million*	*Over* *¥5 Million* *Up to* *¥10 Million*	*Over* *¥5 Million* *Up to* *¥30 Million*	*Over* *¥30 Million*
Percentage of contract price	1.2%	1.0%	0.8%	0.7%	0.6%

(Any fractional sum of less than one yen is discarded)

The contract price and total amount of par value are of one lot order that is executed on the same day with respect to the same issue.

The listing criteria for First Section securities are more stringent than for Second Section securities. Securities that either don't qualify for listing in the First Section or are taken from the First Section are assigned to the Second Section. Refer to Table 8.3 for criteria about listing and delisting securities in the First Section.

In the secondary market, First Section securities are traded between regular members using the Saitori. Second Section securities are traded using the CORES system.

Japanese equities are characterized by a low price per share, high price-earning multiples, and low dividends compared to the equities of other countries. Dividends are based on the par value of shares. A round lot ranges from 100 to 1,000 shares depending on share price.

THE PRIMARY AND SECONDARY MARKETS IN DEBT SECURITIES

In the primary market, debt securities are usually classified into government bonds, local government bonds, government-guaranteed bonds, financial debentures, corporate bonds, convertible bonds, and yen-denominated foreign bonds. A samurai bond is a straight bond issued by a foreign government or corporation on the Japanese capital market. Both government and samurai bonds can be issued in registered or bearer form.

Local government and government-guaranteed bonds are called public bonds. The Minister of Finance (MoF) may issue government bonds with a stipulation that the amount doesn't exceed that specified in the budget. Payments of government-guaranteed bonds are guaranteed by the Minister of Finance as to the extent provided for in the resolution of the Diet. Local government bonds are issued with approval of the local assembly and the Minister of Home Affairs in consultation with the Minister of Finance.

When a public or corporate bond is offered publicly for subscription, securities dealers organize a syndicate to underwrite and place an issue. For government and public bonds, the underwriting syndicate consists of city banks, local banks, long-term credit banks, trust banking companies, and mutual and savings banks.

Underwriting syndicates for straight and convertible corporate bonds are composed exclusively of securities companies because

TABLE 8.3 Outline of Criteria for Listing and Delisting (Tokyo Stock Exchange)

	Criteria for Listing	Criteria for Delisting
Capital stock and number of listed shares	(1) Main business in and around Tokyo: ¥500 million or more, and 10 million shares or more. (2) Main business outside of Tokyo: ¥1,000 million or more, and 20 million shares or more.	Less than ¥500 million, or Less than 10 million shares
Distribution of shares	(1) Number of floating shareholders: 2,000 or more. (2) Number of floating shares: a) 25 percent or more of total listed shares (lower limit of 3 million) in the case of total listed shares of less than 20 million. b) 1 million plus 20 percent or more of total listed shares in the case of total listed shares of 20 million–60 million. c) 8.2 million plus 8 percent or more of total listed shares (upper limit of 16 million) in the case of total listed shares of 60 million or more. Note: Floating shareholders have 500 to 50,000 shares and floating shares are held by floating shareholders.	(1) Number of floating shareholders less than 1000. (2) Number of floating shares: a) 10 percent or less of total listed shares (lower limit of 1.5 million) in the case of total listed shares of less than 60 million. b) 3.6 million plus 4 percent or less of total listed shares (upper limit of 8 million) in case total listed shares are 60 million or more.
Net tangible assets	¥1,500 million or more, and ¥100 or more of net tangible assets per share.	

Net profits	(1) Net profits before taxes for the last 3 years: First year ¥200 million or more Second year ¥300 million or more Third year ¥400 million or more (2) Net profits before tax per share. Net profits per share must be ¥15 or more for each of the last three business years and ¥20 or more for the last business year.	(1) No dividends paid for the last 5 years. (2) Excess liabilities at yearend for the last three business years.
Dividends	(1) Must have paid dividends of ¥5 or more per share for the last three years. (2) Prospect maintaining ¥5 or more after listing.	
Trading volume		(1) Monthly average for latest six months of less than 10,000 shares, or (2) No transactions for three months. This doesn't apply when a company falling under (1) or (2) redistributes shares within three months of falling under the criterion of (1) or (2).
Others	No false reports in financial statements. Maintenance of transfer agent. Form of share certificates. Transferability of shares. Five years or more since incorporation.	Suspension of banking account. Reorganization or liquidation. Suspension of business activity. False reports in financial statements. Violation of listing agreement. Restrictions on transfer.

Delisting criteria:

(1) Capital stock and number of listed shares effective since April 1, 1978, as a rule.

(2) Distribution of shares: effective from business term ending at March 31, 1977, except for a company with capital stock that doesn't exceed ¥500 million and that became applicable from the business term ending March 31, 1978.

(3) Trading volume—(1) under trading volume effective from the end of December 1977, except for a company with capital stock that doesn't exceed ¥500 million and that become applicable from the business term ending in December 1978. (2) under trading volume effective from the end of September 1977, except for a company with capital stock that doesn't exceed ¥500 million and that became applicable from the business term ending in September 1978.

SOURCE: Tokyo Stock Exchange.

banks aren't allowed to underwrite corporate issues. The syndicate's composition will vary with each issue, and it may take 10 or more broker/dealers to manage and place an issue.

Many corporate bonds are issued with repurchase agreements (repos). Bonds issued with repurchase agreements (gensaki in Japanese) include a conditional repurchase of bonds by the issuer on a specified date. Gensaki bonds are a substitute for the short-term bond market, which hasn't developed in Japan. Issuers want to raise funds temporarily, while buyers want to invest funds on a short-term basis. Investors who are barred from the call money and bill discount markets participate in the repurchase market, which is considered an efficient place for short-term surplus funds.

In the secondary market, only 3 percent of the bond trading occurs on the TSE, while 97 percent of the total bond volume is handled in the OTC market. Over 600 government, public, and corporate issues are listed on the TSE. Convertible bonds comprise the largest number of listings because they can be converted to company shares listed on the exchange. Yen-denominated foreign bonds also comprise a large percentage of listed bonds.

Issues of corporate bonds and convertible bonds that satisfy the listing requirements of the TSE may be listed subject to the approval of the Minister of Finance. Listing of government and public bonds is exempt by law from approval by the Minister of Finance.

Japanese government bonds have relatively low yields compared to other nations' bonds. Japan has maintained low inflation and low-interest rates during the postwar period. For this reason, many foreign borrowers find it advantageous to issue yen-denominated debt securities to reduce their borrowing costs when interest rates are high in their own countries. A foreign issuer incurs a risk in the currency exchange between the yen and the issuer's national currency that can be hedged in the foreign exchange markets.

Bonds are traded in two sessions, one in the morning and one in the afternoon; select corporate issues are traded in the afternoon session and at-large issues are traded in the morning session.

TAXATION

Withholding tax on interest payments and cash dividends is 20 percent. Withholding for nonresidents isn't charged on bills or

FIGURE 8.2   Nikkei Dow Jones Index

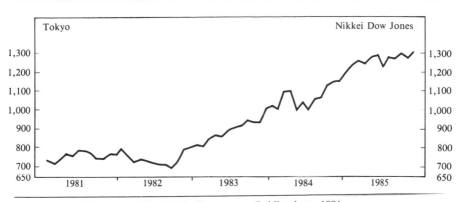

SOURCE: Euromoney Yearbook, Euromoney Publications, 1986.

bonds issued at discount, samurai bonds, or Euro-yen bonds. All withholding may be claimed as a tax credit on U.S. tax returns.

Stock dividends are common in Japan. There are two kinds: stock dividends and free issues. They affect the capital structure of a corporation differently, but they are the same to an investor except for taxes. Stock dividends are the same as ordinary dividends and are taxed, while free issues aren't taxed. It's important for an investor to know the different kinds of shares.

In principle, no capital gains tax exists in Japan; however, there are several exceptions: (1) capital gains derived from continuous stock trading, (2) capital gains from the transfer of large blocks of securities, and (3) capital gains from selling cornering stock.

STOCK EXCHANGE INDEXES

There are two frequently quoted stock indexes:

1. The Tokyo Stock Exchange (TSE) Index.
2. The Nikkei Dow Jones Average.

The TSE Index is a weighted average of the total market value of all shares listed on the First Section of the stock exchange. It includes 28 subindexes. The Nikkei Dow Jones Average is an unweighted average of 225 stocks listed on the Tokyo Stock Exchange. See Figure 8.2.

FIGURE 8.3   Computerized Market Price Transmission System

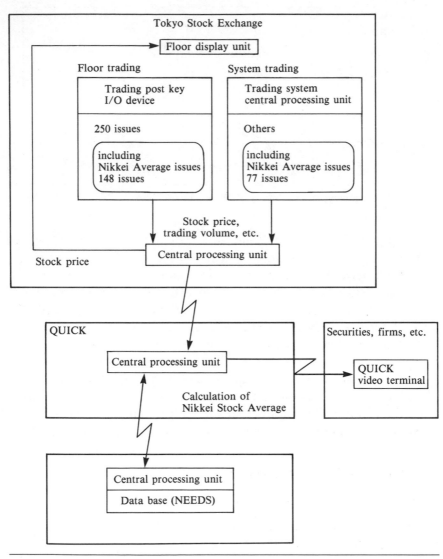

SOURCE: Nihon Keizai Shimbun, Inc.

The Nikkei Stock Average futures contract is traded on the Singapore International Monetary Exchange (SIMEX). As explained in Chapter 19, the SIMEX has trading and clearing linkages with the Chicago Mercantile Exchange (CME). The Nikkei Stock Average futures contract is based on the Nikkei Dow Jones Average. This futures contract can be used to trade the price movement of stocks on the Tokyo Stock Exchange.

Nihon Keizai Shimbun, an information service, was contracted to compute the Nikkei Stock Average minute-to-minute and display this information via QUICK video terminals. See Figure 8.3. Refer to Chapter 19 for more information about this contract.

TRADING LIMITS

Unlike other stock exchanges, the Tokyo Stock Exchange imposes daily trading limits on the price movement of shares. The daily price limit varies with the market price of a specific issue; for example, high-priced issues have a higher daily trading limit than low-priced issues. This practice is similar to the trading limits on U.S. commodity exchanges.

Trading limits prevent sudden, extreme moves in share prices due to an emotional reaction to unexpected market events. Trading limits usually stabilize price moves by providing traders with time to evaluate events that trigger sudden share price movements.

TRADING HOURS

The Tokyo Stock Exchange is open Monday through Friday and certain Saturdays with the following schedule:

Morning session   9 to 11 A.M.
Afternoon session   1 to 3 P.M.
Saturdays*   9 to 11 A.M.

* The exchange is closed on the second Saturday of each month.

MINIMUM ORDERS

The minimal amounts which may be traded are:

Shares   ¥1,000; in some cases ¥100
Straight bonds   ¥1,000,000
Convertible bonds   ¥100,000 or
                     ¥500,000

TABLE 8.4   Selected Information on the 10 Largest Companies
by Market Capitalization as of April 25, 1986

Company	Business	U.S.$ Million	Percent Total
Tokyo Elect. Power	Utility	$ 29,406	2.2%
Toyota Motor	Automobile	25,979	2.0
Sumitomo Bank	Banking	24,739	1.9
Daiichi Kangyo Bank	Banking	21,935	1.7
Fuji Bank	Banking	21,162	1.6
Mitsubischi Bank	Banking	19,950	1.5
Nomura Securities	Brokerage	18,856	1.4
Sanwa Bank	Banking	17,633	1.3
Matsushita El. Ind.	Electrical	17,493	1.3
Industrial Bank	Banking	17,390	1.3
Totals		$214,543	16.2%

Total stock market capitalization: $1,314 billion

SOURCE: Morgan Stanley Capital International Perspective, Geneva, Switzerland.

CHAPTER NINE

The United Kingdom

The United Kingdom of Great Britain and Northern Ireland is composed of two major islands on the European continental shelf. Great Britain consists of England, Wales, and Scotland. Great Britain is surrounded by relatively shallow waters of the Atlantic Ocean, the English Channel, the Irish Sea, and the North Sea. Northern Ireland, in addition to its watery boundaries, shares a 303-mile border with the Republic of Ireland on the south and west. At the narrowest point, there are only 13 miles of water separating Northern Ireland and Scotland.

The United Kingdom of Great Britain and Northern Ireland, henceforth the U.K., has 94,247 square miles of land and 56.5 million people. It has the 14th largest population in the world with an average growth rate of 0.1 percent. The base population is composed of English, Scots, Welsh, and Northern Irish. The Irish represent the largest minority group in Britain. Over the years, many different groups have immigrated to the U.K., including Jews, people from the West Indies, and the South Asian subcontinent.

London, with 6.77 million people, is the capital and financial center of the U.K. With changes in the economy and industrial diversification, there has been a concerted effort to decentralize government, industry, and finance. Other industrial and financial centers include Birmingham, Leeds, Sheffield, Liverpool, Bradford, Manchester, and Bristol, England; Swansea, Wales; Belfast, Northern Ireland; and Edinburgh, Glasgow, and Aberdeen,

---

FIGURE 9.1 Exchange Rate for the British Pound

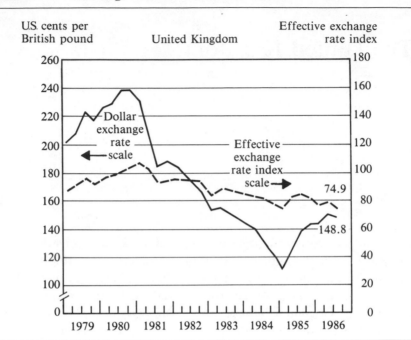

SOURCE: Federal Reserve Bank of St. Louis.

Scotland. Manchester and Liverpool have been industrial and financial centers since the early industrial revolution, while Aberdeen has become important in recent decades due to the discovery of North Sea oil fields.

The official currency of the United Kingdom is the pound sterling (£). (See Figure 9.1.) One pound sterling equals 100 pence. English is spoken in all areas of the country, but 19 percent of the Welsh speak their own language. Bilingual education is encouraged in Welsh schools so that the language won't be lost. Gaelic is spoken in some parts of Scotland and Northern Ireland.

BRIEF HISTORY OF THE BRITISH ISLES

The history of the British Isles is rich and varied. British history can be summarized as one of invasion, settlement, consolidation of power, and growth. Each invader brought new language, laws, and religion to the British Isles, where they meshed with those of previous invaders to create a unique language and culture. The earliest recorded invaders were the Celts. The ancient Romans occupied England from the time of Christ until the 3rd century A.D. The most recent invasion attempt was made by Nazi Germany during World War II. For the purposes of this book, the most significant periods of English history are the periods of exploration and the Industrial Revolution.

During the periods of exploration, the practice began of buying shares in new ventures for risk reduction and profit. This led to the evolution of the London Stock Exchange and the British way of financing new business ventures and expanding existing businesses.

The mechanical revolution and the Industrial Revolution further solidified the British method of financing new ventures. Britain, the first industrialized nation, has remained in the forefront of industrial and technological innovations. The British were the first to industrialize, and they applied mechanization to all aspects of life—from the plowing of fields to the weaving and dying of cloth. The British also realized the need to educate the masses to improve industrial efficiency. The willingness to train workers helped England advance rapidly during the second half of the 19th century.

England's first industrial revolution resulted from the exploitation of iron ore and coal fields. The United Kingdom is undergoing a second industrialization that will keep Britain competitive in today's markets. The government has realized that many industries aren't economically feasible and is encouraging many areas of the country to develop competitive technological industries. For example, the development of the "Silicon Glen" in Scotland rivals the U.S. "Silicon Valley" in northern California for development of semiconductor and microcircuit technologies.

The government has privatized state-owned enterprises such as British Telecom, Trustee Savings Bank, British Gas, and British Airways to reduce the economic dependency of these enterprises on government funds. Privatization has improved efficiency and provided economic incentive for management and employees to increase profitability.

THE GOVERNMENT

The United Kingdom has a constitutional monarchy headed by Queen Elizabeth II. Supreme legislative power is vested in Parliament, which is divided into the House of Lords (hereditary titles) and the House of Commons (elected officials). The two primary political parties are the Conservative Party and the Labour Party. Other political parties include the Social Democrats, the Liberal Party, the Ulster Unionists, and the Scottish Nationalist Party. No minister or department is exclusively responsible for the central administration of domestic policy. The responsibility is shared among governmental departments, and their duties sometimes overlap.

International Relations

The United Kingdom is a member of the North Atlantic Treaty Organization (NATO), Central Treaty Organization (CENTO), European Economic Community (EEC), Organization for the Economic Cooperation and Development (OECD), and the United Nations.

THE ECONOMY

The British economy is broadly diversified into many sectors: industrial, manufacturing, public and private services, retailing, transportation, and utilities. The gross domestic product (GDP) for the U.K. was $349 billion in 1985. Members of the European Community (EC) are the United Kingdom's principal trading partners. Nearly 50 percent of all imports and exports are with EC countries. The United States and West Germany are the largest individual trading partners. About 14.7 percent of total exported goods go to the United States. The U.K. imports about 11.7 percent of its goods from the United States.

England is moving away from traditional industries of coal and iron ore and developing a strong chemicals sector concentrating on pharmaceuticals, dyes, plastics, and artificial fibers. It is also experiencing growth in electrical products and electrical engineering, precision instruments, and vehicle manufacturing.

The economy of Wales was once heavily dependent on coal mining. Wales is now developing an electronics industry. Major American and Japanese high-tech companies have recently located offices and production plants in Wales.

Scotland also is changing its economic base. The new growth industries in Scotland include electrical engineering, semiconductors, computers, medical equipment, and petrochemicals. The development of the North Sea oil fields also has helped stimulate more traditional industries such as coal, steel, shipbuilding, and textiles. Although Scotland looks to the future with high-tech industries, the traditional industries of high-quality textiles, food, and beverages still contribute significantly to Scotland's economy. Whiskey sales contribute a major share of export earnings.

Northern Ireland suffers a number of economic problems for the following reasons:

1. Most industry is located in a small area on the eastern seaboard.
2. It lacks economic diversification.
3. Many people are leaving agricultural areas to work in urban areas.

Since World War II, there has been a steady decline in the traditional sectors of shipbuilding (Belfast has one of the United Kingdom's largest shipyards), linen production, and agriculture. Only recently has Northern Ireland expanded its economic base into other areas; manufacturing of aircraft, textile machinery, engineering products, vehicle components, oil-well equipment, electronic instruments, telecommunications, carpets, and synthetic rubber.

One recent government attempt to stimulate and decentralize the economy has been the privatization of state-owned enterprises. Privatization has the multiple benefits of raising needed funds for the British Treasury, improving the efficiency of a denationalized company, and creating shareholder wealth in the private sector.

MONEY AND BANKING

The Bank of England was established as a private bank by an act of Parliament and given a royal charter as a corporate body in 1694. Under the Bank of England Act of 1946, the bank was nationalized. The bank's affairs are administered by the governor, the deputy governor, and 16 directors, all appointed by the crown. The role of England's Central Bank is multifunctional. It executes monetary policy, acts as a banker to the government, issues banknotes, supervises and provides central banking facilities for the commercial banking system, manages currency exchange rates, arranges government borrowing, and manages the national debt.

The government implements monetary policies through the Bank of England. The bank conducts financial markets operations for the government that influence trends in monetary growth and interest rates. For example, to maintain a decline in the inflation rate, the central bank gradually reduces the rate of growth in the money supply.

The government also affects monetary policy by influencing market conditions through dealings with discount houses. The discount houses hold Treasury, local authority, and commercial bills financed by short-term loans from banks. The Bank of England relieves shortages in discount house accounts by buying bills from them or by lending directly to them.

Since 1981, the bank no longer announces continuous rates at which cash will be supplied to the market. Short-term rates are kept within an unpublished range. Emphasis is now on open-market operations rather than direct lending to discount houses.

The Bank of England intervenes in foreign exchange markets with its Exchange Equalization Account. The Exchange Equalization Account has the official U.K. gold reserves, foreign exchange, special drawing rights (SDRs) on the International Monetary Fund (IMF), and European currency units (ECUs). The bank intervenes in foreign exchange markets when there are undue fluctuations in exchange rates versus the value of the pound sterling.

In October 1986, the United Kingdom deregulated its capital and government debt markets in a move called the "Big Bang." As readers will soon see, Big Bang is synonymous with Big Bank, because many large U.K. and foreign banks acquired U.K. broker/dealers to expand their financial services and investment banking activities globally.

The deregulation permitted expansion of dealers in U.K. government obligations known as gilts. Prior to the Big Bang, there were only two market-making firms in gilt-edged stocks. After the Big Bang, the number increased to 27 authorized dealers and 6 interbroker dealers. The deregulation has enhanced the market-making functions and competition in pricing and distributing gilts.

THE FINANCIAL MARKETS
OF THE UNITED KINGDOM

U.K. financial markets are diversified, and they include the listings of domestic and foreign securities traded on the stock exchange, a listed options market, an unlisted securities market (USM) for smaller capitalization stocks, and a dealer market for trading gilt-edged stocks. Gilt-edged stocks are securities issued by the U.K. government with a life span of many years. The government undertakes the repayment of loans according to set terms and agrees to pay interest at a stipulated rate. During their life, gilt-edged stocks or gilts can be bought and sold on the stock exchange.

Besides the stock exchange, London is home of the London International Financial Futures Exchange (LIFFE). At the LIFFE, financial futures and options contracts are traded on short and long gilts, foreign currencies, and stock indexes. At the London Metals Exchange (LME), contracts on industrial and precious metals are traded for cash or forward delivery among dealers. This chapter will focus on describing activities of the Stock Exchange and the LIFFE.

THE SECURITIES MARKETS

The United Kingdom has five regional stock exchanges plus the Stock Exchange of London located in England, Scotland, and Ireland. In 1973, stock exchanges located in Belfast, Birmingham, Bristol, Dublin, Glasgow, Leeds, Liverpool, Manchester, and Newcastle were joined to form the stock exchange. The London Stock Exchange is the dominant exchange, accounting for 85 percent of total turnover. The London Stock Exchange has the largest listing of securities of any exchange in the world, a listed options market on 52 stocks, an unlisted securities market (USM), and dealer trading in gilts. This section will focus on changes in the London Stock Exchange.

The Big Bang occurred on October 27, 1986, and thereafter British financial markets underwent dramatic changes in structure, operations, and the regulatory environment. The Big Bang resulted from a lengthy dispute between the British government's Office of Fair Trading and Sir Nicholas Goodison and other stock exchange officials. These changes were, in part, caused by concerns that investor protection laws were inadequate and that the stock exchange rule book had restrictive trade practices. In addition, many government officials and stock exchange members felt that the exchange was losing out to competitors in the world market, primarily the New York and Tokyo exchanges. As a result of an Office of Fair Trading investigation into restrictive stock exchange trading practices, the stock exchange agreed to:

1. Abolish fixed commissions; all commissions are now negotiable between customer and broker/dealer.
2. Admit foreign brokerage firms, investment banking firms, commercial banks, and merchant banks to the Stock Exchange Council.
3. Eliminate the distinction between stock brokers and jobbers. Members of the exchange function as market makers who can act either as dealers or brokers in a transaction. They must specify to customers what role they are taking before making a transaction.
4. Admission of corporations and institutions as stock exchange members. Prior to the Big Bang, only individual members were admitted to the stock exchange.
5. Enhanced investor protection through greater market surveillance and computerized transaction recording as well as new rules and regulations to protect investors from unfair trading practices.
6. A new electronic, computerized dealing system called SEAQ (Stock Exchange Automated Quotations). SEAQ is a screen-based dealing system that allows market makers to deal worldwide by computer on a 24-hour basis.
7. Greater access to financial news that can effect market prices and trading patterns.

The legislative instrument governing financial services is the Financial Services Act, which is expected to become law in 1987. This act includes: (1) the regulation of investment businesses, (2) listing of securities, and (3) new powers for controlling shares, debentures, unit trust units, long-term insurance contracts, and options and futures markets. It also will establish an umbrella agency known as the Securities and Investment Board (SIB). The SIB will be similar in scope and function to the U.S. Securities and

Exchange Commission (SEC). Many of the regulatory changes won't be operational until 1987–88. The SIB doesn't cover mainstream commercial banking activities, building societies, or assurance companies.

The stock exchange also became linked with the International Self-Regulatory Organization (ISRO). This organization provides national exchanges with guidelines for establishing improved regulatory and compliance procedures. The SIB will delegate as much regulatory power as feasible to Self-Regulatory Organizations (SROs). The SIB has prepared regulations that are a model for SROs. Important areas of regulation include:

1. An investor compensation plan if the broker/dealer declares bankruptcy.
2. Formal procedures for filing and verifying customer complaints.
3. Compulsory segregation of a customer's cash from the firm's account.
4. Control of unsolicited customer orders.
5. Rules monitoring enforcement of SROs. To give SROs enforcement strength their members won't be able to sue SROs for damages.

As of this writing, the proposed Self-Regulatory Organizations will be:

1. The Association of Futures Brokers and Dealers (AFBD) for members of financial futures and commodities exchanges.
2. The Financial Intermediaries, Managers, and Brokers Regulatory Association (FIMBRA) for smaller securities firms and insurance and unit trust brokers.
3. The Investment Management Regulatory Organization (IMRO) for unit trusts, merchant banks, pension fund managers, and other investment management firms.
4. The Life Assurance and Unit Trust Regulatory Organization (LAVTRO) for life insurance companies, unit trusts, friendly societies, and other firms selling pooled investments.
5. The Securities Association, resulting from a merger of the International Securities Regulatory Organization (ISRO)

and the stock exchange. This agency is for large domestic and foreign broker/dealers dealing in Eurobonds and government and corporate securities.

The restructuring of the financial services sector has caused major changes in how customer accounts are serviced. Nearly 60 stock exchange member broker/dealers have registered to become market makers in specific securities. As market makers, they are obligated to maintain firm, continuous bid-offer quotations on the stock exchange's SEAQ system for actively traded stocks referred to as alpha and beta stocks. They may maintain subject prices on less actively traded securities known as gamma stocks.

THE STOCK EXCHANGE AUTOMATED QUOTATION SYSTEM (SEAQ)

To facilitate trading, the SEAQ system allows market makers to deal on or off the exchange floor. It also integrates the trading activities of regional exchanges. All transactions in officially listed securities must be reported to the stock exchange in a timely fashion. SEAQ will display real-time prices on 3,500 alpha, beta, and gamma stocks; it's designed to respond to entries within one second and can handle 70,000 transactions per hour. SEAQ will support all three of the market sectors:

1. The domestic equities market.
2. The gilt-edged market.
3. Internationally listed equities markets.

On the SEAQ international system, competing market makers input their bid-offer quotes for a range of 500 securities from 17 countries.

Market information from these SEAQ services is delivered via TOPIC, the Stock Exchange's real time viewdata system. TOPIC carries information on current share prices, company announcements, foreign share prices, analytical information, foreign exchange rates, and other useful market information.

SEAQ is segmented in three levels of user access. Level I of the SEAQ service is the Investor Service, which provides information to nonmembers of the Stock Exchange such as private clients and smaller institutions.

FIGURE 9.2 SECQ Information Display

Prices of last trades (buy/sell)

Time now

Last night's closing price

Time of last trade

Market makers offering best buying/selling prices

Quantity of shares Market makers' quoted prices are good for

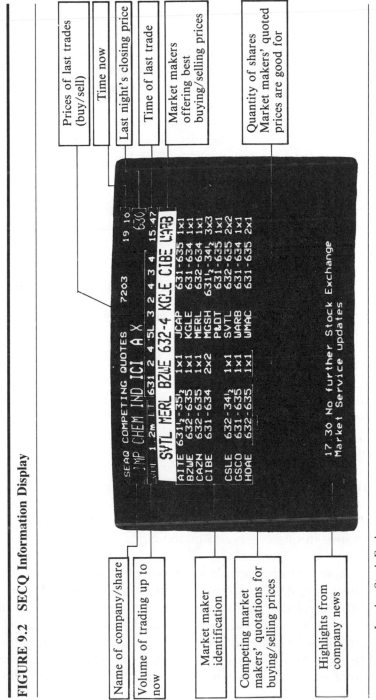

Name of company/share

Volume of trading up to now

Market maker identification

Competing market makers' quotations for buying/selling prices

Highlights from company news

SOURCE: London Stock Exchange.

Level II is the Competing Quotation Service, for members and nonmembers who subscribe to TOPIC. It displays details on all leading equities, competing bid-offer prices from all registered market makers, the latest trade price and volume information for alpha securities, and competing quotes for several thousand securities.

Level III is the Market-Maker Input Service. Market makers use their terminals to enter bid-offer quotations for the SEAQ stocks in which they are registered market makers and to report trades to the exchange. See Figure 9.2.

In addition, SEAQ provides a gilt-edged service to both member and nonmember subscribers. The gilt-edged service shows a display for selected issues where the gilt-edged dealers are making a market.

THE PRIMARY AND SECONDARY EQUITIES MARKETS

In the primary market, newly listed shares can be offered by several methods:

1. Offers of sale
2. Prospectus issue
3. Placings
4. Tender offer
5. Rights issue
6. Capitalization issue

To be listed on the stock exchange, a company must have at least five years of history and 25 percent of its outstanding shares must be owned by outside investors. An issue can become listed on the stock exchange in one of several methods.

1. The most popular method for listing new issues is the offer of sale. The offer of sale occurs with the combined efforts of a stockbroker firm and a merchant bank, although the bank's involvement is not mandatory. The stockbroker firm and the merchant bank arrange and manage the underwriting. They are required to issue a prospectus and an application form. The minimum value of shares offered must be over £500,000, and not more

than 10 percent of the offering can be reserved for preferential applicants such as employees of the issuing company. The merchant bank, company, stockbroker, and market makers agree on an issuing price, at which the shares are offered to investors. Any unpurchased shares are left with the underwriter to hold or sell in the secondary market.

2. A prospectus issue is an issue in which a company offers its own securities to the public for subscription. A full prospectus must be published and distributed to investors.

3. Placings are permitted by the stock exchange where the total funds raised by a company won't exceed £3 million. The securities are bought by the issuing broker who places the majority of shares with clients. Any unplaced shares may then be traded in the secondary market.

4. The tender offer is an aggressive way to float a company's shares on the stock market by auction. The issuing house presents a price for prospective subscribers. The subscribers then apply to buy the number of shares they want at a price that will allow for full subscription of the shares.

5. A rights issue occurs when a company already listed on the stock exchange makes an offering of additional shares to existing shareholders. The British term *underwriter* is used to describe an institution or client who, for a commission, agrees to take up shares at the issue price if applications from the public or existing shareholders are insufficient. A British underwriter is not part of the selling syndicate.

6. A capitalization issue occurs when shares are fully paid out of reserves and are distributed to existing shareholders in proportion to their existing holdings.

In addition, the unlisted securities market (USM) and the over-the-counter (OTC) market can offer new issues. Both markets are subject to legislative requirements. For the USM to offer a new issue, the company must have a three-year operating history and 10 percent of outstanding shares must be owned by outside investors. The USM is bound by its "general understanding" with the stock exchange. The "general understanding" between the USM and the stock exchange is the agreement regulating activity of the two organizations.

In the over-the-counter market, the market maker, who handles all aspects of an issue including trading, defines his own terms for new issues. The secondary market for an OTC stock is generally handled by one dealer; however, more dealers may make a market in it if the issue becomes actively traded. The Department of Trade and Industry has only recently approved the National Association of Securities Dealers and Investment Managers (NASDIM) as a regulatory body for the OTC market.

The secondary market for listed shares is one of the most active in the world, surpassed only by the New York and Tokyo exchanges. As described earlier, trading is automated via the SEAQ system.

THE TRADED OPTIONS MARKET

The Traded Options Market was established in April 1978, and it has become an expanding business for the stock exchange. The stock exchange makes an active market in listed put and call options on selected company shares, the Financial Times 100 Share Index (FT SE-100), and gilt-edged securities. On company shares, one option contract equals 1,000 shares, that is, a round lot of an underlying security. Presently, options are listed on only 52 companies. They are traded as "American-style" options with standardized exercise prices, expiration dates, and margining procedures. Contracts may be offset or exercised prior to their expiration date. Option contracts are cleared, exercised, and assigned through the London Options Clearing House (LOCH), which is wholly owned by the stock exchange.

Options are traded on the FT SE-100 Share Index. This index is capitalization-weighted and represents the composite value of the 100 largest public companies. The base date was set at January 3, 1984, at a value of 1,000. At the base date, the index comprised 69 industrial companies, 5 oil companies, 21 financial companies, 2 mining finance companies, 2 investment trusts, and 1 overseas trader. These leading 100 companies account for 70 percent of the total market value of U.K. equities.

Options on gilt-edged securities have a contract size of £50,000 nominal of a specific government security. When a gilt option is exercised, the holder is entitled to receive (in the case of a call) or sell (in case of a put) £50,000 nominal of a specified gilt. An example of a specified gilt would be Treasury 11¾ percent of 1991.

THE PRIMARY AND SECONDARY DEBT SECURITIES MARKETS

Gilt-edged stocks (gilts) are the debt obligations of the U.K. government. Principal and interest on gilts are guaranteed by the government. Gilts are issued with maturities ranging from three to 15 years or longer. Short gilts mature within 5 years, medium gilts mature between 5 and 15 years, and long gilts mature after 15 years.

Nearly two-thirds of the stock exchange's daily turnover is in gilts. Their market value is as high as £1,500 billion. Gilt-edged securities are issued by, and registered with, the Bank of England as an agent for the government. The issuing of gilts finances long-term government debt and changes money supply availability. Gilts are offered by prospectus in minimum units of £100,000.

The secondary market in gilts operates similarly to the trading of U.S. government securities. The Bank of England has appointed 27 primary dealers and 6 interbroker dealers; interbroker dealers facilitate dealings among market makers by helping them offset portfolio imbalances and provide liquidity in gilts markets. Interbrokers deal only with market makers on the stock exchange. Primary dealers function as market makers in gilts and have direct access to the Bank of England. Debt securities are called loan stock in the United Kingdom. The types of loan stock available are:

Debenture Stock. A fixed-income security issued to a company's creditors that is normally secured by a trust deed giving trustees a legal mortgage over a company's freeholds and leaseholds and a floating charge over the rest of its property.

Unsecured Loan Stock. A fixed-income security not collateralized by specific assets.

Convertible Loan Stock. Gives holders the right to exchange the stock into another class of security (usually ordinary shares) at specified dates and under certain conditions.

Local Authority, County, and Corporation Stock. Fixed-interest securities issued by local governments, county councils, or city corporations. These issues are rarely traded in the secondary market.

TAXATION

The flat tax rate on shares and loan stock is 30 percent; however, the first £5,300 of aggregate gains per year is exempt from withholding taxes. Capital gains on gilts are taxable only if held for less than one year. Nonresidents don't pay a capital gains tax unless the assets are used to conduct trade or business in the United Kingdom through a branch or agency.

Dividends are subject to a 30 percent withholding tax for residents and nonresidents. A nonresident can apply to reclaim those taxes if the nonresident's country has a double taxation treaty with the United Kingdom.

Residents and nonresidents are subject to a 30 percent income tax on interest from domestic loan stock. A nonresident can reclaim this tax if he is a citizen of a country that has a double taxation treaty with the United Kingdom. Certain government bonds pay tax-free interest to nonresidents if they apply for it.

The purchaser of securities pays a transfer stamp duty tax with the exception of gilt-edged securities. Individuals and institutions or residents with the EEC pay a value-added tax (VAT) on commissions.

STOCK EXCHANGE INDEXES

There are four primary stock market indexes in the United Kingdom. The most frequently quoted index is the Financial Times 30 Index, which is a geometric average of 30 ordinary industrial shares. The base value was 100 as of July 1, 1935. See Figure 9.3.

The Financial Times Actuaries Shares Indexes were introduced on April 10, 1962. They are composed of major sector groups of share listings. One index is comprised of 750 companies, and the other has 500 company shares. The Financial Times Government Securities Index was created in 1926 with a base value of 100. It is comprised of a monthly arithmetic mean of selected government securities. The Financial Times 100 Share Index (FT

FIGURE 9.3   Financial Times Index

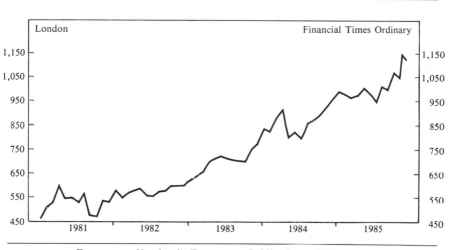

SOURCE: Euromoney Yearbook, Euromoney Publications, 1986

SE-100) was created in 1984. It was designed to trade financial futures and options as is done on U.S. exchanges with the S&P 100 Index. The FT SE-100 index includes the 100 largest publicly traded companies on the stock exchange.

HISTORY OF THE STOCK EXCHANGE

In the beginning, London coffeehouses near the Royal Exchange building were the trading center for loan stock and shares. Many of the early issues traded helped to finance the development and expansion of Great Britain as a mercantile and industrial nation. In 1694, the Bank of England was founded as a private bank with capital of £1.2 million raised by public subscription of its shares.

The first stock exchange building was built in London in 1773; it was moved to the present site in 1801. In 1973, a new stock exchange building was built and installed with modern trading and telecommunication facilities. By 1965, the regional stock exchanges in England, Ireland, and Scotland were united to form the Federated Stock Exchanges of Great Britain and Ireland. The London Stock Exchange is the primary exchange.

GENERAL INFORMATION ON THE LONDON STOCK EXCHANGE

Stock Exchange Members and Regulatory Authorities

Members of the stock exchange are individuals or corporations such as brokerage firms, commercial and private banks, and other institutions. Foreign firms are permitted to have stock exchange membership. All stock exchange members also act as broker/dealers. Broker/dealers may register to become market makers in selected issues listed on the exchange. Stock exchange activities are regulated by the Securities and Investment Board (SIB) and designated Self-Regulatory Organizations. Stock exchange rules are administered by the Stock Exchange Council. The council is composed of the chairman, two deputy chairmen, and 43 members. The responsibilities of the council include:

1. Formulating and implementing the stock exchange's policies, rules, and regulations.
2. Supervising the regulation of trading.
3. Regulating new issues.

Trading Hours

Official trading occurs through the SEAQ system between 9:30 A.M. and 3:30 P.M. Monday to Friday. Trading may occur when the stock exchange is closed, but all transactions must be reported to the exchange in a timely fashion.

Table 9.1 shows the 10 largest companies, ranked by market capitalization, on the London Stock Exchange.

Types of Securities Traded

1. Shares of domestic U.K. companies.
2. Shares of foreign companies.
3. Loan stock of U.K. companies.
4. Gilt-edged securities issued by the U.K. government.
5. Investment trusts.
6. London traded options.

TABLE 9.1   Selected Information on the 10 Largest Companies by Market Capitalization as of April 25, 1986

Company	Business	U.S.$ Million	Percent Total
British Telecom	Communications	$ 21,974	5.4%
British Petroleum	Energy Sources	15,014	3.7
Shell T & T	Energy Sources	12,647	3.1
Glaxo Holdings	Health Care	11,105	2.8
BTR	Multi-industry	9,670	2.4
Imperial Chemical	Chemicals	9,109	2.3
BAT Industries	Beverages/Tobacco	9,023	2.2
Marks & Spencer	Merchandising	8,695	2.2
General Electric	Electrical	7,833	1.9
Barclays	Banking	5,569	1.4
Totals		$110,459	27.4%

Total stock market capitalization: $402 billion

SOURCE: Morgan Stanley Capital International Perspective, Geneva, Switzerland

7. Traditional options.
8. Securities of companies on the Unlisted Securities Market (USM).

Settlement and Clearing

Settlement of shares and loan stocks is "for the account," generally a period of 10 business days. Actual settlement occurs in six business days. Margin trading is not permitted on the stock exchange. Members settle their accounts through the TALISMAN system, which is owned by the stock exchange and linked to company registers. The TALISMAN system is being linked to other non-U.K. clearing and settlement facilities such as the NASDAQ, stock exchanges of the European community through IDIS, and the Midwest Clearing Corporation in Chicago, Illinois.

Government securities and new corporate bond issues are settled the next business day. The Bank of England has a computerized book-entry system for U.K.-registered securities.

On the day of a transaction, a contract note is sent to the investor specifying the transaction details and the account day when payment will be due.

THE LONDON INTERNATIONAL FINANCIAL FUTURES EXCHANGE (LIFFE)

The London International Financial Futures Exchange (LIFFE) began operations as the largest financial futures exchange outside the United States on September 30, 1982. The LIFFE is located in the Royal Exchange Building near the Bank of England and the stock exchange. The structure and operations of the LIFFE were modeled after the Chicago Board of Trade. The LIFFE was established to allow financial institutions to hedge, trade, and establish arbitrage positions to offset risks associated with interest rates, currency exchange, and stock index prices.

Members of the LIFFE are individuals, brokerage firms, banks, and other financial institutions. The International Commodities Clearing House (ICCH), owned by major U.K. clearing

TABLE 9.2 Futures and Options

Contract	FT-SE 100 Future	Option on FT-SE 100 Future
Unit of trading	Valued at £25 per full index point (e.g. value £25,000 at 1,000)	1 FT-SE 100 futures contract
Delivery/expiry months	March, June, September, December.	March, June, September, December.
Delivery day/ exercise day/ expiry day	First business day after the last trading day.	Exercise by 17.00 on any business day. Delivery on the first business day after the exercise day. Expiry at 17.00 on last-trading day.
Last trading day	11.20 The last business day in the delivery month.	16.05 Five business days prior to last business day in delivery month.
Quotation	FT-SE Index ÷ 10 (e.g. 100.00)	Multiples of 0.01
Minimum price movement (tick size and value)	0.05 (£12.50)	0.01 (£2.50)
Initial margin (straddle margin)	£1,000 (£100)	See footnotes.
Trading hours	09.05-16.05	09.07-16.05

banks, matches and clears transactions between parties and provides financial guarantees against the default of a member. There are currently 11 futures contracts and 5 options contracts listed for trading. Even though certain contracts may appear identical to contracts traded on U.S. futures exchanges, they aren't fungible with U.S.-listed contracts.

In June 1985, the LIFFE introduced put and call options trading on the exchange. Unlike futures options in the United States, purchased option contracts are marginable. In other words, an option buyer pays only a portion of the full premium upon purchasing a put or call option on a futures contract. In most respects, futures and options trading on the LIFFE is similar to trading contracts on U.S. exchanges except that there are no formal position limits. All trading occurs within a specified hour by open

---

TABLE 9.2 *(concluded)*

Contract	Sterling Currency Future	Option on Sterling Currency
Unit of trading	£25,000 traded against U.S. dollars.	£25,000 traded against U.S. dollars.
Delivery/expiry months	March, June, September, December.	March, June, September, December with three nearby months.
Delivery day/ exercise day/ expiry day	Third Wednesday of delivery month.	Exercise by 17.00 on any business day. Delivery on the third business day after the exercise day. Expiry at 17.00 on last trading day.
Last trading day	10.31 Two business days prior to delivery.	16.02 Three business days before the third Wednesday of expiry month.
Quotation	US$ per £	U.S. cents per £
Minimum price movement	0.01 cents per £	0.01 cents per £
(tick size and value)	($2.50)	($2.50)
Initial margin	$1,000	
(straddle margin)	($100)	
Trading hours	08.32-16.07	08.34-16.02

Note: 17.00 = 5 P.M.
SOURCE: London International Financial Futures Exchange.

TABLE 9.3

Contract	U.S. Treasury Bond Future	Option on U.S. Treasury Bond Future
Unit of trading	U.S.$ 100,000 par value notional U.S. Treasury bond with 8 percent coupon.	1 U.S. Treasury bond futures contract.
Delivery months	March, June, September, December.	March, June, September, December.
Delivery day/exercise day/expiry day	Any business day in delivery month at seller's choice.	Exercise by 17.00 on any business day; extended to 20.30 on last trading day. Delivery on the first business day after the exercise day. Expiry at 20.30 on the last trading day.
Last trading day	09.00 Chicago time (usually 15.00 London time) seven CBOT working days prior to last business day in delivery month.	16.10 First Friday preceding by at least six CBOT working days the first delivery day of the U.S. Treasury bond futures contract.
Quotation	Per $100 par value.	Multiples of 1/64.
Minimum price movement	$1/32	1/64
(tick size and value)	($31.25)	($15.625)
Initial margin	$3,000	
(straddle margin)	(zero)	
Trading hours	08.15-16.10	08.17-16.10

outcry among members in designated areas of the exchange. Initial and variation margin requirements are set by the exchange. Contracts are standardized as to trading unit, expiration months, quotations, and specific delivery requirements. There are no physical commodities traded on the exchange floor.

Tables 9.2 through 9.5, list contract specifications for futures and options contracts listed on the LIFFE.

TABLE 9.3 *(concluded)*

Contract	Short Gilt	Three-Month Sterling Interest Rate
Unit of trading	£100,000 nominal value notional gilt with 10 percent coupon.	£500,000
Delivery months	March, June, September, December	March, June, September, December
Delivery day	Any business day in delivery month at seller's choice.	First business day after the last trading day.
Last trading day	11.00 Two business days prior to last business day in delivery month.	11.00 Third Wednesday of delivery month.
Quotation	Per £100 nominal	100.00 minus rate of interest.
Minimum price movement	£1/64	0.01
(tick size and value)	(£15.625)	(£12.50)
Initial margin	£1,500	£500
(straddle margin)	(£125)	(£200)
Trading hours	09.05-16.20	08.20-16.02

Note: 1700 = 5 P.M.; 20.30 = 8:30 P.M.
SOURCE: London International Financial Futures Exchange.

TABLE 9.4

Contract	*Long Gilt Future*	*Option on Long Gilt Future*
Unit of trading	£50,000 nominal value notional gilt with 12 percent coupon.	1 long gilt futures contract.
Delivery months	March, June, September, December.	March, June, September, December.
Delivery day/exercise day/expiry day	Any business day in delivery month at seller's choice.	Exercise by 17.00 on any business day. Delivery on the first business day after the exercise day. Expiry at 17.00 on the last trading day.
Last trading day	11.00 Two business days prior to last business day in delivery month.	16.15 Six business days prior to the first delivery day of the long gilt futures contract.
Quotation	Per £100 nominal	Multiples of 1/64
Minimum price movement	£1/32	1/64
(tick size and value)	(£15.625)	(£7.8125)
Initial margin	£1,500	
(straddle margin)	(£125)	
Trading hours	09.00-16.15	09.02-16.15

TABLE 9.4 *(concluded)*

Contract	Dollar-Mark Currency Future	Option on Dollar-Mark Currency
Unit of trading	$50,000 traded against deutsche marks.	$50,000 traded against deutsche marks.
Delivery/expiry months	March, June, September, December.	March, June, September, December with three nearby months. See footnotes.
Delivery day/exercise day/expiry day	Third Wednesday of delivery month.	Exercise by 17.00 on any business day. Delivery on the third business day after the exercise day. Expiry at 17.00 on last trading day.
Last trading day	10.32 Two business days prior in delivery.	16.04 Three business days before third Wednesday of expiry month.
Quotation	DM per U.S. dollar	Pfennigs per U.S. dollar.
Minimum price movement (tick size and value)	DM 0.0001 per U.S. dollar (DM 5.00)	0.01 pfennigs per U.S. dollar (DM 5.00)
Initial margin (straddle margin)	DM 2,500 (DM 250)	
Trading hours	08.34-16.04	08.36-16.04

Note: 17.00 = 5 P.M.
SOURCE: London International Financial Futures Exchange.

TABLE 9.5

Contract	Three-Month Euro-dollar Interest Rate Future	Option on Three-Month Eurodollar Interest Rate Futures Contract
Unit of trading	U.S. $1,000,000	1 Eurodollar futures contract.
Delivery months	March, June, September, December.	March, June, September, December.
Delivery day/exercise day/expiry day	First business day after the last trading day.	Exercise by 17.00 on any business day. Delivery on the first business day after the exercise day. Expiry at 17.00 on last trading day. Automatic exercise of in-the-money options on last trading day.
Last trading day	11.00 Two business days prior to the third Wednesday of delivery month.	11.00 Last trading day of Eurodollar futures contract.
Quotation	100.00 minus rate of interest	Multiples of 0.01 (i.e., 0.01%)
Minimum price movement	0.01	0.01
(tick size and value)	($25.00)	($25.00)
Initial margin	$500.	
(straddle margin)	(zero)	
Trading hours	08.30-16.00	08.32-16.00

TABLE 9.5 *(concluded)*

Contract	Deutsche Mark	Swiss Franc	Japanese Yen
Unit of trading	All currencies are traded against U.S. dollar. DM 125,000	SF125,000	Y12,500,000
Delivery months	March, June, September, December.		
Delivery day	Third Wednesday of delivery month.		
Last trading day	10.32	10.33	10.30
	Two business days prior to delivery.		
Quotation	US$ per DM	US$ per SF	US$ per 100 Yen
Minimum price movement (tick size and value)	0.01 cents per DM ($12.50)	0.01 cents per SF ($12.50)	0.01 cents per 100 Yen ($12.50)
Initial margin (straddle margin)	$1,500 ($100)	$1,500 ($100)	$1,000 ($100)
Trading hours	08.34-16.04	08.36-16.06	08.30-16.00

Note: 17.00 = 5 P.M.
SOURCE: London International Financial Futures Exchange.

CHAPTER TEN

The Federal Republic of Germany

The Federal Republic of Germany lies in the heart of Western Europe bordered by France, Switzerland, Austria, Czechoslovakia, East Germany, Belgium, Denmark, and the Netherlands. Including West Berlin, it comprises an area of 96,000 square miles. West Germany has large reserves of coal and smaller amounts of iron ore, crude oil, and natural gas. In 1985, West Germany had a population of 61.5 million. Several German dialects are spoken throughout Germany. The deutsche mark is the official currency. See Figure 10.1. Roman Catholicism and Protestantism are the primary religions.

The Federal Republic of Germany consists of the *länder* (states) of Baden-Württemberg, Bayern (Bavaria), Bremen, Hamburg, Hessen (Hesse), Niedersachsen (Lower Saxony), Nordrhein-Westfalen (North-Rhine Westphalia), Rheinland-Pfalz, Saarland, Schleswig-Holstein, and West Berlin. Major industries and companies are located throughout West Germany with a heavy concentration in West Berlin and Nordrhein-Westfalen.

GOVERNMENT

After the fall of the Third Reich during World War II, the country was divided into East and West Germany. East Germany became part of the Soviet bloc, and doesn't have any capital markets. West Germany became a federated republic with a constitution codified in the Basic Law of 1949. It consists of 11 federal states including

FIGURE 10.1   Exchange Rate for the Deutsche Mark

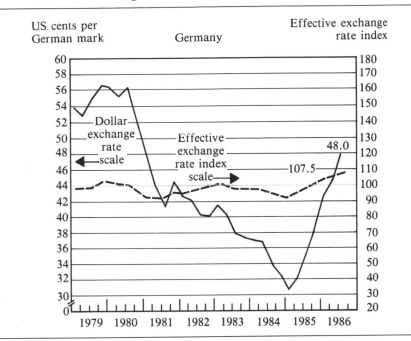

U.S. cents per
German mark   Germany   Effective exchange
                                          rate index

SOURCE: The Federal Reserve Bank of St. Louis.

the city-state of West Berlin. West Berlin is integrated into the legal, economic, financial, monetary, and social systems of West Germany, but maintains a political status of its own. Bonn is the capital of West Germany. The federal states have legislative sovereignty over matters not reserved to the federal government.

The Basic Law provides for a Federal President (Bundespraesi-dent), a Lower House of Parliament (Bundestag), an Upper House of Parliament (Bundesrat), a Chancellor Bundeskanzler), and a Federal Constitutional Court (Bundesverfassungsgericht). Since 1949, West Germany has been governed by six chancellors over 10 electoral periods. Since October 1982, a coalition of the Christian Democratic Union party (CDU) and the Free Democratic party (FDP) has governed.

There are presently five parties in the Bundestag in Bonn. They are the Social Democratic party (SDP), the Christian Democratic Union (CDU), the Christian Social Union (CSU), the Free Democratic party (FDP), and the Greens *(Die Grünen)*. The German Communist Party (DKP) has only a small percentage of the popular vote. The FDP and CDU parties have the largest representation of delegates in the Bundestag.

INTERNATIONAL RELATIONS

West Germany is a founding member of the European Economic Community (EEC), and it belongs to the North Atlantic Treaty Organization, the United Nations, and most of its affiliated agencies. The country is a member of the International Monetary Fund, the World Bank, and the Bank of International Settlements. West Germany is also a party to the General Agreement on Tariffs and Trade (GATT).

INTERNATIONAL AND DOMESTIC ECONOMIES

West Germany has developed into one of the world's leading industrial nations since the end of World War II. In 1985, it ranked third in the free world in economic output after the United States and Japan, and it ranked second in world trade. The West German economy is based on private ownership. The state exerts major influence through ownership in sectors such as transportation, communications, and energy. State-owned enterprises comprise about 10 percent of the net added value. Government is adopting a privatization program to transfer ownership for several of these enterprises from the public sector to the private sector.

Following an average annual 4.5 percent growth rate in the GNP during the 1960s, the economy's average growth declined to 3.1 percent in the 1970s. Increases in oil prices from 1973 to 1974 hurt the growth rate. The second major oil price increase and world recession in 1979–80 caused a moderate decline of 1 percent in real terms in 1981–82. From 1983 to 1985, the real GNP increased sharply to 7.1 percent.

The European Community (EC) is West Germany's largest import/export partner. Nearly 50 percent of West Germany's exports go to the EC. Likewise, Germany imports over 50 percent of its requirements from the EC. The United States and Japan are important trading partners with West Germany.

INDUSTRIAL PRODUCTION

Industrial activity makes the largest contribution to West Germany's GNP. It comprises about 50 percent of total net added value, and it accounts for nearly 45 percent of total employment. The engineering sector, which has a workforce of over 1 million, is the biggest branch of industry in West Germany. Electrical, automobile, and chemical industries constitute other primary sectors of the economy.

The high productivity of the West German economy is attributed to extensive research and development (R&D) programs. Federal and state governments and private industry sponsor research in energy, information, space science, biotechnology, and medical and environmental technologies. Basic and applied research are conducted at universities, academic societies, and industry facilities. Nearly 2.8 percent of the GNP is devoted to nonmilitary R&D. This is a larger percentage than any other country. West Germany is also the third largest user of applied robots in industry after the United States and Japan.

The aftermath of World War II left West German industry in a shambles—factories, plants, and machinery were destroyed during the war. Reconstruction and modernization of West German industry occurred during the 1950s and 1960s. There are 49,000 industrial establishments in West Germany. About two percent of these firms employ over 1,000 employees. Large-scale enterprises are important since they account for 39 percent of all employees. Multinational companies such as Siemens, AEG-Telefunken, Daimler-Benz, Bayer, and BASF employ several hundred thousand people.

Craft trades (builders, car mechanics, and electricians) make important contributions to the West German economy since they employ large numbers of skilled workers and produce value-added products and services for the economy.

The capital goods sector is particularly significant. Its share of total industrial output expanded from 45 percent in 1980 to 49 percent in 1985. The main factors in this expansion were motor vehicle manufacture, electronics, and the production of office and data processing equipment.

The West German economy depends heavily on imported crude oil for conversion to energy, base chemicals, and synthetic products. The economy benefits from low crude oil prices. A large increase in the price of world crude oil hurts economic growth and the balance of payments.

SERVICES

The service sector showed the strongest growth in the economy from 1970 to 1985. Its share of added value increased from 34 percent in 1970 to 42 percent in 1985. The expansion in banking, insurance, transportation, and communications contributed to the strong growth.

AGRICULTURE

The agricultural sector employs few people but supplies nearly 67 percent of West Germany's food requirements. The main crops include cereals, sugar beets, potatoes, corn, and vineyards. Increased capital investment has improved agricultural productivity. Agriculture contributes only 2.2 percent to total added value.

INVESTMENT

Modernization of plants and the increased demand for automatic data processing equipment have played a major role in the growth of capital goods investment. Investment in plants and equipment represented 19.5 percent of GNP in 1985. Slower growth in construction investment, due to a reduction in housing starts, resulted in a decline of investment share of GNP between 1980 and 1985.

EMPLOYMENT AND LABOR CONDITIONS

West Germany's labor force grew by 950,000 in the past 10 years to 27.8 million in 1985, including 2.2 million foreign workers. During the same period, unemployment rose from 1.1 million to 2.3 million. In medium and large corporations, there is mandatory labor representation on Supervisory Boards, a practice known as codetermination. According to recent Bank of Japan statistics, West German workers lose fewer days annually to labor disputes than workers in the United States and Japan.

THE BANKING SYSTEM AND MONETARY POLICIES

West Germany has an extensive system of commercial and private banks. West German banking laws are quite strict with severe penalties for violators. In addition, bank officers are encouraged to maintain substantial assets hidden off the balance sheet (stille reserven) for use in emergencies to preserve bank solvency. West German banks are the major shareholders of West German companies.

There are three major types of banks in West Germany:

1. Commercial banks.
2. Savings banks and their central clearing institutions.
3. Credit cooperatives.

Regulations that previously restricted competition have been lifted gradually since 1946. The West German banking market is open to foreign banks; there were 300 foreign banks operating there in 1985.

West German banking laws permit universal banking where commercial banks can act as broker/dealers, underwriters of securities, investment advisors, and managers. Commercial banks can make on- and off-exchange securities transactions for customers and manage customers' assets. Unlike the United States, banks are primary members of the West German stock exchanges. The three largest commercial banks—Deutsche Bank, Commerzbank, and Dresdner Bank—are prestigious international investment banks active in trading, underwriting, and managing syndications of equity and debt securities. Deutsche Bank Capital Corporation manages the Germany Fund which is listed on the New York Stock Exchange and described in Chapter 2.

The Bundesbank is the central bank. It formulates and carries out monetary policy in West Germany. The Bundesbank regulates the circulation of money and credit in the domestic economy. Although independent of federal government directives in exercising its obligations, the Bundesbank must support general West German economic policies. In every year since 1974, the Bundesbank has announced monetary expansion target ranges for the coming year. These goals have been achieved regularly since 1982.

The Bundesbank may grant credit to the federal government and the states only up to the amount of DM 8.5 billion. Such credit may be used exclusively to bridge short-term cash needs within a given fiscal year, but not to finance budgetary deficits. West Germany has no direct credit controls, nor are there interest rate limitations.

Banking supervision is exercised by the Federal Banking Supervisory Office in cooperation with the Bundesbank. It is complemented by a deposit insurance program voluntarily organized by all three major bank types.

The Bundesbank located in Frankfurt/Main is responsible for stabilizing the mark on international markets. Under terms of the EMS, West Germany must maintain the value of the mark within a margin of ± 2.25 percent on either side of its central exchange rate against other currencies participating in the EMS. Currency adjustment occurs through intervention, adjustment of fiscal and monetary policies or, if necessary, through realignment of the exchange rate. The mark is freely convertible into U.S. dollars. It has traded on a floating exchange rate basis against all currencies except for EMS currencies.

As discussed in Chapters 4, 5, and 7, the European currency unit (ECU) has become an internationally accepted bond currency. The mark is an important component of the ECU. Because the Bundesbank is concerned that the ECU, as a European parallel currency, might bypass the central bank's monetary objectives, it has prohibited use of the ECU in West Germany under the Currency Act.

ACCOUNTING PRACTICES OF WEST GERMAN COMPANIES

Accounting practices for West German companies are ultraconservative. Earnings, profitability, and asset valuation of a company are usually understated to avoid excessive taxation by federal and state governments and to prevent escalation of salaries, wages, and employee benefits. Companies also keep hidden reserves to meet unforeseen future liabilities. A balance sheet for a West German company reflects neither the company's true earning power nor the value of its assets. For these reasons, fundamental analysis of a West German company's balance sheet and income statements as used by brokerage analysts in the United States wouldn't be accurate in analyzing the earnings per share, book value, and cash flow.

A brokerage analyst needs an in-depth knowledge acquired through extensive contacts with a company and its management to accurately evaluate its true net worth, earning power, and growth rate.

THE WEST GERMAN SECURITIES MARKETS

West Germany's capital markets are among Europe's largest, and they are fourth largest in the world with $229 billion in capitalization. Securities trade on the country's eight independent local stock exchanges. The Frankfurt Stock Exchange accounts for over 52 percent of the total volume. The Düsseldorf Stock Exchange accounts for 30 percent of the total volume. Smaller exchanges are located in Berlin, Bremen, Hamburg, Hanover, Munich, and Stuttgart.

While trading in listed securities is not legally confined to these exchanges, they handle the bulk of trading volume in equity transactions. In contrast, domestic and foreign-funded debt are traded off the exchanges, usually between banks and other financial institutions. West German investors have traditionally been yield-oriented investors, and they therefore tend to invest in fixed-interest securities. Trading in equities on the Frankfurt Stock Exchange accounts for only 29 percent of the total volume, whereas dealings in fixed interest securities account for 71 percent.

West German stock exchanges offer three different market segments for securities trading:

1. **The official market.** Trading in shares that have been admitted to the official listing (the Official List) by the Admissions Committee of the exchange based on disclosure in a listing prospectus. *Kursmakler* are order book officials appointed to handle transactions and set standard prices for their designated securities.

2. **The regulated, unlisted market.** Trading in shares not admitted to official listing. Companies admitted to this market are exempt from publishing a full-listing prospectus. Admission is granted by a special committee that is also responsible for supervising price establishment. Trading occurs between banks and *freie Makler. Freie Makler* are independent dealers who handle transactions in the regulated, unlisted market between members. They may trade for their own account.

3. **The unofficial, unregulated market.** Trading in over-the-counter securities by telephone or at the stock exchange between banks or through *freie Makler* firms during unofficial hours.

For official listing, West German stock exchanges require public disclosure of all information needed for an evaluation of the listed securities. This information includes the history and nature of the business, real property and other assets, investments, and participations involving more than 25 percent of the investment entity's voting equity.

The *Kursmaklerkammer* is a public body that represents and supervises the *Kursmakler. Kursmakler* are officials appointed in agreement with the stock exchange board of governors and the *Kursmaklerkammer* executive board by the appropriate state minister. They are entrusted with certain issues and responsible for controlling settlement prices and editing the official list. A *Kursmakler* acts as an order book official for selected shares, but can't trade for his or her own account except in specific circumstances. A *Kursmakler* acts solely as an intermediary between the persons admitted to deal at the stock exchange and to fix official prices. As commercial brokers, *Kursmakler* receive commissions for handling transactions.

Clients can place either limit or market orders for shares through instructions to their bank, or they can stipulate that the bank is to sell "at best" or buy "at bottom"; the official price fixed at the exchange on the day of an order's execution. The *Kursmakler* collects all price and order data and then estimates the best price (standard price) that will fill most orders in his or her book. The book is closed each day from noon to 12:15 P.M. to determine the standard price for each security. For actively traded shares, variable prices are quoted throughout the trading session. In executing orders for clients, banks may utilize services of the *Kursmaker* or *freie Makler. Freie Makler* act as market makers who can deal with the *Kursmakler,* banks, and other authorized dealers to execute transactions.

VIEW DATA SYSTEM

The Düsseldorf and Frankfurt Stock Exchanges cooperate with the Chamber of *Kursmakler* and the BDZ Stock Exchange Data Center to distribute current prices and market data on standard and variable prices for all West German shares and selected foreign shares. Information includes turnover, the 10 most active shares, options market data, and graphs of stock indexes.

AUTOMATED CLEARING AND SETTLEMENT

Delivery and settlement of West German securities occurs through a system of automated clearing and collective deposits. Customer transactions are done as credit and debit journal entries between member banks. Physical securities aren't exchanged, but they are represented as electronic journal entries. West German exchanges don't permit margin transactions. All transactions must be settled by the second business day.

TAXATION OF WEST GERMAN SECURITIES

Shares, Common Stocks

All dividends distributed to foreign investors (nonresidents) are subject to the flat withholding tax of 25 percent of the gross dividend. Foreign investors receive a tax credit if the distributed profits of the corporation don't originate in West Germany.

Fixed-Interest Securities

Foreign investors pay no withholding taxes. The 25 percent withholding tax for bonds has been abolished. To avoid double taxation, most international conventions reduce the 25 percent flat rate withholding tax to 15 percent. The first 25 percent of funds withheld are paid to the governments, and 10 percent are refunded on request. The remaining 15 percent of funds are credited against or deducted from foreign personal income tax according to respective national laws. The German office to write for a refund is:

Bündesamt für Finanzen
Koblenzer Str. 63–65
D-5300 Bonn-Bad Godesberg
Federal Republic of Germany

PRIMARY AND SECONDARY MARKETS IN EQUITIES

West Germany's capital markets offer broad representation of most of the privately owned industrial and financial sectors. The stocks of over 450 West German companies trade either listed or unlisted on one or more West German stock exchanges. Primary offerings of listed equity securities have increased from DM 3.97 billion in 1980 to DM 9.34 billion in 1985. The underwriting of new issues represents a growing proportion of all capital increases. They occur primarily from the exercise of subscription rights.

Two types of limited liability corporations issue equity shares that are freely transferable and may be publicly traded:

1. Aktiengesellschaften (AG), stock corporations.
2. Kommanditgesellschaften auf Aktien (KGaA), limited partnerships.

Capital stock carries a par value of not less than DM 50 per share. Shares are normally fully paid and nonassessable.

Even though banks are the primary underwriters of new issues, an independent organization called Portfolio Management (PM), located in Munich and headed by Bernd Ertl, has become active in underwriting new issues since 1981. PM is not a stock exchange member, and it underwrites West German companies in syndication with other investment banking firms.

In the secondary market, listed securities are traded in an auction style with an open outcry of buyers and sellers. A number of listed securities change hands in the interbank dealer markets on and off the exchanges. Share prices are determined by open outcry. Prices are quoted continuously throughout the trading day for active securities. A round-lot transaction is 50 shares. Odd lots are priced at an official "single quotation" once a day by the appointed broker's matching all market orders. Less actively listed and regulated, unlisted securities are quoted only once a day. Settlement occurs on the second business day following a transaction.

TRADING IN OPTIONS

Put and call options on West German shares have been traded European style since 1970. Active primary and secondary markets for options occur on the Frankfurt Exchange. Options on 43 West

German and 13 foreign companies are approved for trading. Options are traded based on 50 shares of an underlying security. Option transactions may be concluded only at specified terms that expire on the 15th of the expiration month. Option terms run to the 15th calendar day of the expiration months of January, April, July, and October.

The option's exercise price is set close to the security's share price. An option buyer has a choice of exercising an option, transferring an option to another party, or allowing it to expire. An option buyer can transfer an option to another buyer up to three days before the expiration date. An option seller (option writer) can't transfer the obligations from the option to another writer.

If an option buyer exercises an option, the price at which the securities must be delivered or accepted is the exercise price, which had already been agreed on for the customer's account. Exercise prices are fixed according to the following scale:

DM 2.50 or a multiple thereof up to and including DM 30.
DM 35.00 or a higher multiple of 5 up to and including DM 100.
DM 110.00 or a higher multiple of 10.

When transferring an option, the seller and the buyer agree on the premium the seller shall receive.

PRIMARY AND SECONDARY MARKETS FOR FIXED-INTEREST SECURITIES

Like equity issues, fixed-interest securities are generally underwritten and distributed through banking syndicates. The aggregate value of fixed-interest securities greatly exceeds equity issues. However, the gap between the two has narrowed since 1980. Fixed-interest securities include government, public, mortgage, corporate, and foreign-issued issues. The representative maturities for new debt issues have averaged 10 years.

Foreign participation in West Germany's fixed interest markets has grown substantially since August 1984, when the government removed the withholding tax on income from domestic debt issues. In May 1985, the government authorized foreign-owned banks to lead manage DM issues, and it permitted the issuing of DM-denominated floating rate notes, zero coupons, and dual-currency bonds. Interest rate options are traded European style on a limited number of fixed-interest obligations.

THE FOREIGN CURRENCY EXCHANGES

Frankfurt, Düsseldorf, Hamburg, Munich, and Berlin are centers of spot currency exchange dealings. The Frankfurt Foreign Currency Exchange is affiliated with the stock exchange. Unlike stock exchange trading, foreign currency exchanges operate with a conference telephone. The official exchange rates are fixed in Frankfurt. Closing bid and asked rates are computed for each currency. The Bundesbank only intervenes in Frankfurt. Since the introduction of the European Monetary System (EMS) in March 1979, the obligation to intervene has become more important. In buying and selling foreign currencies in Frankfurt, the Bundesbank keeps the official exchange rates within EMS limits.

Apart from the U.S. dollar, the Canadian dollar, and the Japanese yen, 14 European currencies are officially listed in Frankfurt. The Belgian franc, French franc, Italian lira, Dutch guilder, Danish krone, and Irish pound are covered by the EMS agreements. The official exchange rates are the basis for the bank's foreign exchange business with nonbank clients.

The Foreign Currency Exchange accounts for a small percentage of Frankfurt's total volume in foreign currency transactions. However, the fixing and publication of official exchange rates is important for West German businesses making payment transactions denominated in foreign currencies.

THE BUNDESBANK'S ROLE IN AFFECTING INTEREST RATE AND FOREIGN CURRENCY VALUE CHANGES THROUGH DIRECT INTERVENTION ON THE STOCK EXCHANGE

The Bundesbank can cause immediate interest rate changes of West German government obligations through direct intervention on the floor of the Frankfurt Stock Exchange. On the Frankfurt Stock Exchange, government bonds are traded in a room next to the main trading floor. Unlike other world financial markets, the Bundesbank has a representative in the bond trading room. If the Bundesbank wants to raise interest rates, the representative sells government obligations to depress prices and raise interest rates. Recall that bond prices and interest rates are inversely related. If the bank wants to lower interest rates, its representative buys government obligations to raise bond prices and lower rates.

Upstairs from the main trading floor, foreign currencies are officially fixed against the deutsche mark each day between 1 and 2 P.M. The Bundesbank has a representative who is authorized to buy and sell deutsche marks against other currencies to affect foreign exchange rates. A *Kursmakler* presides over the official fixing of major currencies. Representatives of commercial and private banks participate in the fixing of currencies. Foreign exchange rates can be highly variable in the interbank market, and rates change dramatically from hour to hour. Official foreign currency rates allow West German banks to transact international business for customers at a fixed rate each day instead of the highly variable interbank market rates.

THE FRANKFURT STOCK EXCHANGE (FRANKFURTER WERTPAPIERBÖRSE)

Unlike many countries, West Germany doesn't have a large central stock exchange. The Frankfurt Stock Exchange is the largest exchange in West Germany; it accounts for 52 percent of the total turnover of all exchanges.

Frankfurt/Main has been a prominent financial center in Europe since the Middle Ages when international trade fairs were held there. Frankfurt was an active center in the foreign currency and gold dealings hundreds of years before the exchange's opening in 1402. Early stock exchange dealings were mainly bills of exchange. Regular trading in bonds and promissory notes began in the late 18th century. Modern Frankfurt is an international banking center where the Bundesbank and 358 domestic and foreign credit institutions are represented.

The first exchange list of the Frankfurt Stock Exchange was printed in 1727. The first dividend-yielding shares traded in Frankfurt were from the Austrian National Bank, and were issued in 1820. The stock exchange moved into its permanent home in 1879. The stock exchange building suffered extensive damage during both World Wars I and II. The exchange building was nearly destroyed in an air raid in 1944. It was completely rebuilt in 1957 with new offices, telephones, and electronic display equipment. A second trading floor for fixed-interest securities was opened in 1966. The foreign currency exchange was enlarged in 1971.

The Frankfurter Allgemeine Zeitung Index (F.A.Z. Index)

The F.A.Z. Index is a broad representation of shares traded on the Frankfurt Exchange. Table 10.1 lists the 10 largest companies by market capitalization included in the F.A.Z. Index. The index is capitalization-weighted. See Figure 10.2.

GENERAL INFORMATION ON THE FRANKFURT STOCK EXCHANGE

Stock Exchange Authorities. The Board of Governors, the Admission Board, the Board of Arbitration, the Disciplinary Board, and the Kursmaklerkammer all function as stock market authorities.

Banks as Agents. Customer orders can only be placed through banks represented on the stock exchange. Banks can execute their

---

TABLE 10.1 Selected Information on the 10 Largest Companies by Market Capitalization as of April 25, 1986

Company	Business	U.S.$ Million	Percent Total
Daimler-Benz	Automobiles	$122,823	10.0
Allianz	Insurance	15,087	6.6
Siemens	Electrical	14,617	6.4
Deutsche Bank	Banking	12,607	5.5
Münchener Rück	Insurance	8,898	3.9
Bayer	Chemicals	8,251	3.6
BASF	Chemicals	7,388	3.2
Hoechst	Chemicals	7,115	3.1
Volkswagen	Automobiles	6,925	3.0
VEBA	Utilities	6,092	2.6
Totals		$109,740	47.9%

Total stock market capitalization: 229 billion

SOURCE: Morgan Stanley Capital International Perspective, Geneva, Switzerland.

FIGURE 10.2 F.A.Z. Index

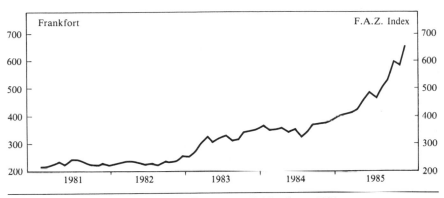

SOURCE: Euromoney Yearbook, Euromoney Publications, 1986

orders through a *Kursmakler* or *freie Makler* who are admitted to the exchange.

Stock Market Hours. Official trading hours are from 11:30 A.M. to 1:30 P.M. The exchange conducts business Monday through Friday. *Kursmaklers* close their books from noon to 12:15 P.M. to calculate standard prices.

Price Quotations. *Kursmaklers* fix the standard price for shares once a day based on the supply and demand of orders at specified prices. In actively traded issues, consecutive trading is permitted for lots of 50 shares or more with continuous price quotations. Prices are displayed during the trading day on electronic boards. Final market statistics are published in the official list edited by the Kursmaklerkammer Frankfurt am Main. They are available each trading day at 4:30 P.M.

Listing of Shares. Shares are listed in these categories:

1. Industrial shares (Industrie)
2. Bank shares (Banken)
3. Transport shares (Verkehr)
4. Insurance shares (Versicherungen)

Fixed-Interest Securities.   The following list contains fixed-interest securities:

1. Bonds of federal and state governments
2. Municipal bonds
3. Bonds of special institutions
4. Industrial bonds
5. Convertible bonds
6. Debentures and bonds of mortgage banks and public credit institutions

This classification corresponds with groups on the official list. In addition, there are officially listed shares and fixed-interest securities for foreign issuers.

Stock Exchange Contracts.   All dealings executed on the exchange are cash transactions with settlement occurring on the second business day after the trade date.

Transaction Costs.   Security transactions involve taxes and fees that amount from 1¼ to 1½ percent of the final share amount. Fees on fixed-interest securities range from ¾ to 1 percent.

ANNOUNCEMENT OF OFFICIAL SHARE PRICES

Prices for the Frankfurt Stock Exchange are published in the official list edited by the *Kursmaklerkammer* Frankfurt/Main and are available each day after 4:30 P.M. In addition, the *Kursblatt Der Frankfurter Wertpapierbörse* lists the prices and turnover for shares, options, and fixed-interest securities. The abbreviations listed below appear in reference to the official dealing prices on the official list. They explain the market situation in which prices are set:

b = paid (bezahlt), if all orders were executed.
G = money (geld), if there were only orders to buy.
bB = paper (brief), if there were only orders to sell.
bG' = paid and money, if not all limited buying orders could be executed at established prices.

B′ = paid and paper, if not all limited orders to sell could be executed at the established price.

T = estimated price (taxe).

* = small amounts without turnover.

− = no official price established.

CHAPTER ELEVEN

The Dominion of Canada

The Dominion of Canada is the second largest country in the world next to the Soviet Union. In 1867, the British Parliament passed the British North America (BNA) Act, which federally united three separate colonies (Canada, Nova Scotia, and New Brunswick) into "one Dominion under the name of Canada." Since that time, the act was renamed the Constitution Act of 1867. In 1982, the British Parliament passed the Canada Act, which repatriated the Constitution to Ottawa. With the passing of this act, it was not necessary for important constitutional amendments to be made in the British Parliament. The Constitution Act of 1982 includes the Charter of Rights and Freedoms and other procedures for amending the Constitution. Canada is a member of the British Commonwealth of Nations. Its economic ties to the U.K. have all but disappeared.

Canada is bordered by the Arctic Ocean to the north, the Atlantic Ocean to the east, the United States to the south, and Alaska to the west. Canada has an area of 3.85 million square miles with a population of 25.4 million people, which makes it one of the least populated countries per square mile in the world. Canada has 10 provinces, and the Yukon and Northwest Territories. The country is richly endowed with mineral deposits, oil and gas reserves, farmland, forests, and fishing and wildlife areas. English and French are the official languages. The Canadian dollar (C$) is the official currency. One Canadian dollar equals 100 cents. See Figure 11.1.

FIGURE 11.1   Exchange Rate for the Canadian Dollar

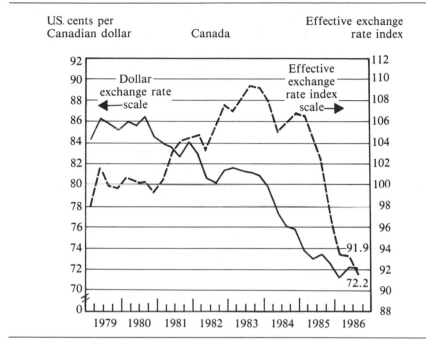

SOURCE: Federal Reserve Bank of St. Louis.

GOVERNMENT

The Dominion of Canada is a constitutional monarchy; the British monarch is the nominal head of state. Canada's Constitution and government are modeled after the United Kingdom. The Queen of England is represented in her absence by the Canadian governor-general appointed by recommendation of the Canadian prime minister. The Canadian government has a federal structure with 10 provincial governments and two northern territories. Ottawa, Ontario, is the capital of Canada and the location of Canada's Parliament, which is styled after the bicameral British system.

Parliament consists of the queen, the Senate, and the House of Commons. The Senate has 104 seats, and the House of Commons has 282 seats. The primary political parties are: (1) the Liberal Party, (2) the Progressive Conservative Party, (3) the New Democratic Party (NDP), (4) the Social Credit Party, and (5) the "separatist" Parti Quebecois. The Liberal and Progressive Conservative parties are the leading political parties in Canada. The NDP represents a coalition party of liberals and conservatives. The Parti Quebecois appeals to the nationalistic sentiments of French Canadians in Quebec. Quebec is populated with French-speaking Canadians who have periodically proposed political and economic separation of their province from English-speaking Canada. The separatist movement in Canada has caused social and political unrest.

The provinces wield considerably more political power than individual U.S. states. Provincial government is modeled after the federal government except that there is no upper house attached to elected legislatures. Municipal government operates under the wing of the provinces.

INTERNATIONAL RELATIONS

Canada is a member of the British Commonwealth of Nations, the United Nations, the North Atlantic Treaty Organization (NATO), the Caribbean Common Market (CARICOM), and the Organization for Economic Cooperation and Development (OECD).

THE ECONOMY

In 1985, Canada's gross national product (GNP) was C$ 453.7 billion. The economies of Canada and the United States are highly interdependent, which sometimes creates major economic and political problems for Canadians. The United States is Canada's most important trading partner; it accounts for 75 percent of total exports and 72 percent of total imports. Other trading partners include Japan, the United Kingdom, West Germany, the Soviet Union, China, and France. Canada's principal exports are motor vehicles and parts, forest products, nonferrous metals, energy products, minerals, and foodstuffs. Motor vehicles and parts contribute 26 percent of the total export earnings.

Canada has vast natural resources, which makes it a leading supplier of minerals, nonferrous metals, oil and gas, forest products, and fish. Canada is one of the world's major producers of nickel, copper, gold, zinc, silver, lead, natural gas, iron ore, potash, and uranium. Canada is the second largest producer of gold in the free world next to South Africa.

Other natural resources include forests that make Canada the world's leading exporter of newsprint, pulp, and paper products. Cultivated farmland helps Canada to be one of the world's largest exporters of wheat.

The large number of rivers and natural waterways allow Canada to produce an abundant supply of hydroelectric power. Hydroelectric power has permitted Canadian industry to grow rapidly.

In recent decades, Canada has diversified and become a strong service and manufacturing country that supplies the United States and other countries with semifinished and finished goods. The important sectors of the economy include public services, manufacturing, transportation, communications, finance and insurance, and wholesale and retail trade.

In the banking and financial sectors, the interdependent economies of Canada and the United States can create serious problems for Canada by causing unwarranted changes in the Canadian inflation rate, commercial lending, and foreign exchange rates. For example, if the U.S. Federal Reserve Board raises the discount rate or if yields on U.S. government obligations rise, lending rates and yields on Canadian government obligations must rise also to prevent an outflow of capital from Canadian financial institutions to the United States. An outflow of capital from Canada causes a devaluation in the Canadian dollar with a subsequent rise in inflation, even though the fundamental economic conditions in Canada may not warrant such a situation. The alternative is for the Canadian government to impose foreign exchange controls to decrease the outflow of Canadian funds. However, foreign exchange controls cause other undesirable effects. This situation worsens as the United States runs larger and larger deficits in its federal budget and foreign trade accounts, creating a major economic concern for the Canadian government without a solution in sight.

MONEY AND BANKING

The Bank of Canada is the central bank and is directly responsible for monetary policy. The bank was modeled after the Bank of England. The bank performs the functions of most central banks; it exercises control over interest rates, the management of cash reserves, credit supply, money supply, and foreign currency exchange. The bank oversees the commercial banking system and acts as the government's fiscal agent. Although independent in theory, the Bank of Canada has been a servant to the federal Department of Finance since 1961.

Commercial banking in Canada is conducted predominantly by the 11 privately owned banks chartered by Parliament. Chartered banks are the largest deposit-taking institutions in Canada and a major source of commercial financing. The Bank Act of 1980 raised competition between foreign-owned and domestic banks by allowing subsidiaries of foreign banks to act as full-service banks in competition with Canadian banks.

Under current law, banking institutions can't become members of Canadian stock exchanges, and they can't underwrite corporate issues. However, recent changes in Canada are relaxing these restrictions.

THE SECURITIES MARKETS

There are five Canadian stock exchanges, and they are located in Toronto, Montreal, Vancouver, Calgary, and Winnipeg. They are not linked in operation, and they compete for listings. The Canadian capital markets are the fifth largest in the world with a total market capitalization of $157 billion. The Toronto Stock Exchange (TSE) is the largest Canadian exchange accounting for 78 percent of total market turnover. This chapter will focus on Toronto financial markets. The right of dealing on the Toronto Stock Exchange (TSE) is granted to an applicant broker upon purchasing a seat from an existing member and upon approval by both the board of governors and by the members. TSE members may be individuals, partnerships, or corporations. Members are allowed to own more than one seat. Banks and other financial institutions aren't eligible to own a seat. In 1985, the TSE had 79 members.

A National Contingency Fund was established in 1969, cosponsored by the Canadian Stock Exchanges and the Investment Dealers Association. At the fund's discretion, individual clients can be compensated for losses through the financial failure of securities firms associated with any sponsoring organizations.

THE OVER-THE-COUNTER (OTC) MARKET

The over-the-counter (OTC) market is a free market where all trading in all types of bonds occurs. Bonds and other debt securities aren't listed on the stock exchanges. Many equities not listed on Canadian or U.S. exchanges are also traded in the OTC market in a similar manner to bond trading.

Canada has two bond rating services: the Canadian Bond Rating Service and the Dominion Bond Rating Service. They specialize in evaluating the quality and assigning ratings to Canadian government, municipal, and corporate bond issues. Before investing in these securities, an investor should consult these services for more information.

The usual denomination of Canadian bonds is C$ 1,000. Bonds are issued with maturities of 1 to 15 years or longer. Interest is usually paid semiannually. Both registered and bearer bonds are available. Corporate bonds can be issued as mortgage, collateral trust, convertible, sinking fund, or straight bonds. Canadian bonds can differ significantly from U.S issues. Investors should read the indenture to determine the benefits and risks of each issue.

OTC market prices are determined by negotiation between buyers and sellers through a telephone and TELEX network. Transactions occur between broker/dealers, investment councillors, and major financial institutions.

The rules and details of the OTC market are controlled by the Investment Dealers Association (IDA). Rules cover all major aspects of trading and delivery practices including trading units.

THE TORONTO STOCK EXCHANGE

The Toronto Stock Exchange (TSE) was founded in 1852 by a group of Toronto businessmen. The TSE founding was a response to the need for financing the rapid growth of Canadian railways, mining, and other key industries in the mid-19th century.

The TSE is a nonprofit organization owned and operated by members. The TSE is the largest stock exchange in Canada and the fifth largest exchange in North America. The TSE maintains active markets for trading shares, bonds, options, and financial futures contracts. In addition, the TSE is one of the most sophisticated exchanges in the world for computer-assisted trading. In 1985, 939 companies were listed for trading. Some companies list more than one type of stock, and, as a result, 1,402 issues were traded. Interlisted issues are listed on both the TSE and on a U.S. exchange. In 1985, 121 Canadian issues were listed in Toronto and on a U.S. exchange. See Table 11.1 (page 218) for a listing of the 10 largest Canadian companies.

The TSE is a participating member of the International Federation of Stock Exchanges (FIBV). The FIBV represents principal stock exchanges around the world. J. Pearce Bunting, president of the TSE, has served two terms as FIBV president.

Under exchange rules, all transactions in listed shares by member firms and their affiliated companies must be made on the floor of the exchange with certain exceptions.

ORDER HANDLING, TRADING, AND INFORMATION SYSTEMS

Large orders are handled by designated market makers or registered traders who represent member firms and deal at specified trading posts on the exchange floor. Specific issues are assigned to each trading post. Designated market makers and registered traders match bid and offer prices by an open outcry auction process at the trading posts. When a buyer and seller agree on a price, it is reported to the exchange and displayed on a tape and on other electronic information systems.

Smaller orders on both active and less actively traded securities are traded by computer. The Market Order System of Trading (MOST) and the Limit Order Trading System (LOTS) encompass all stocks traded on the Toronto market. The MOST system routes small market orders directly from brokerage firms to where stocks are traded. Trades are instantaneous, and confirmation of the trade is immediately transmitted back to the source of the order. The MOST system is enhanced by a commitment from designated market makers and registered traders to guarantee market orders of up to 599 shares at one price for all stocks traded through the system. For a limited number of stocks, they will guarantee a fill on 1,099 shares.

The LOTS trading system fills limit orders that come to the floor until market prices move to the specified price so that the order can be filled. LOTS ensures that floor traders have more time to trade larger and more complex orders.

The TSE has reached an agreement with both the American Stock Exchange (AMEX) and the Midwest Stock Exchange (MWSE) to establish a two-way trading link. The TSE, AMEX, and the MWSE are primary markets for a number of North American issues.

EXAMPLE 11.1 Board Lot for an Official Quotation

On shares at C$ 100 and over:	10
On shares at C$ 1.00 and under C$ 100:	100
On shares at C$ 0.10 and under C$ 1.00:	500
On shares under C$ 0.10:	1,000

A board lot for an official price quotation can range from 10 shares for stocks at C$ 100 or more, to 1,000 shares for stock under C$ 0.10. A special board lot of 100 shares exists for shares of IBM. See Example 11.1.

COMPUTER-ASSISTED TRADING SYSTEM (CATS)

In 1977, the TSE installed a proprietary Computer-Assisted Trading System (CATS) for executing certain transactions through computer terminals. With this system, certain orders are executed from the offices of member firms by computer instead of on the exchange floor. CATS is used for all less actively traded common and preferred shares on the TSE. In 1985, 793 stocks were traded exclusively through the CATS, which accounted for 20 percent of all TSE trading and the value of shares traded. The value of shares traded in the system reached nearly $4 billion.

Recently, the TSE sold its CATS system, which can be modified to particular exchange conditions, to other exchanges. The Tokyo, London, and Paris exchanges have installed similar computerized systems to execute transactions in less actively traded issues. The CATS system allows for international trading linkages with other exchanges and financial institutions. Other Asian and European exchanges are installing computer-assisted systems to trade securities off the exchange floor.

TYPES OF TRANSACTIONS

There are two types of transactions permitted on the exchange: cash transactions and margin transactions. Settlement is completed with a seller's delivery of securities and a buyer's cash payment. For cash transactions, settlement must be made within five business days following the trade date. Transactions are settled

TABLE 11.1   Selected Information on the 10 Largest Companies
by Market Capitalization as of April 25, 1986

Company	Business	U.S.$ Million	Percent Total
Bell Canada	Communications	$ 7,202	4.6
Seagram	Beverages	5,489	3.5
Imperial Oil	Energy sources	5,026	3.2
Canadian Pacific	Multi-industry	3,861	2.5
Northern Telecom	Communications	3,580	2.3
Thomson Newspapers	Publishing	3,166	2.0
Alcan Aluminum	Nonferrous metals	3,132	2.0
Imasco	Beverages/tobacco	3,021	1.9
Toronto Dominion Bank	Banking	2,583	1.6
Moore Corporation	Business services	2,430	1.5
Totals		$39,490	25.1%

Total stock market capitalization: U.S.$ 157 billion

SOURCE: Morgan Stanley Capital International Perspective, Geneva, Switzerland.

through the Securities Settlement System (SSS), a wholly owned subsidiary of the Canadian Depository for Securities (CDS.)

Margin transactions are settled with the client depositing marginable securities or cash to cover the required transaction percentage upon settlement. There is no limit on contractual time agreements when margin trading occurs within Canada. Short selling is provided for, but 150 percent of the margin is required in this particular contract. Members must report all short sales to the exchange at least twice a month. Foreign investors aren't restricted from margin trading.

Most securities firms finance margin lending through bank loans. Securities dealers that need to borrow stock to cover their needs can do so through the Canadian Depository for Securities (CDS) or from another dealer.

OPTIONS TRADING

In 1976, the TSE introduced an exchange-traded option market that has grown dramatically. The mechanics of options trading and margining are similar to the Chicago Board of Options Exchange (CBOE). Options contracts are traded American style with standardized exercise prices and expiration dates. An option contract has 100 shares of an underlying security. An active secondary market exists for buyers and sellers. Options contracts may be closed out either by offsetting the sale or purchase or through exercising the option.

Puts and calls are available on all underlying securities listed for option trading. In 1985, options on 35 companies were available for trading. Options are also listed on Canadian government long-term bonds and on a broad-based market index option (TIX) based on the TSE 300 Composite Index.

Trans Canada Options, Inc. (TCO), was created in 1977 as the guarantor and clearing facility for all equity, bond, and index option contracts traded on the Toronto, Montreal, and Vancouver stock exchanges. TCO is owned by all three exchanges and funded by its clearing members.

In 1984, the TSE announced that individuals or partnerships could trade for their own account in the options market. In 1985, the first independent traders, called competitive options traders (COTs), started trading in all of the exchange's options products. COTs encourage competition in the options market and ensure that all orders are executed at the best price available.

TRADING HOURS

The TSE is open Monday through Friday with official trading from 10 A.M. to 4 P.M. Both securities and option contracts are traded continuously during these hours.

THE PRIMARY AND SECONDARY MARKET IN EQUITIES

In the primary market, Canadian securities laws require that listed companies disclose their financial position by prospectus, by audited shareholder reports, and by communicating to shareholders any new company developments. Securities are registered on behalf of the issuer to keep accurate ownership records. Each security is assigned a CUSIP number for identifying eligible Canadian securities. A CUSIP number is a nine-digit number permanently assigned to each issue that identifies a single issue.

Canadian issuers that apply for a dual listing on the TSE and a U.S. exchange must also comply with U.S. securities laws and exchange listing requirements. New Canadian-based issues must undergo a quiet period of 90 days following issuance before they can be sold in the United States.

The TSE requires the following minimum listing requirements for newly listed issues:

1. The company must have at least 200 public shareholders; each one must hold a board lot or more.
2. The market value of publicly traded shares must be at least $350,000.
3. The financial requirements for each company vary with the listing category, such as industrial, mines, and oil and gas. Some companies have multiple category listings.
4. Sponsorship by an exchange member can be a significant factor in determining a company's suitability for listing.

In the past few years, the TSE improved access to capital markets for smaller industrial and resource companies by designing a new procedure called the Exchange-Offering Prospectus (EOP). The EOP enables resource and industrial companies to issue a question-and-answer disclosure document instead of issuing a prospectus. Under the new policy, listed companies and companies conditionally approved for listing may raise capital by using an EOP to issue additional shares or undertake an initial public offering.

In the secondary market, common and preferred shares, convertible preferred shares, rights, and warrants are traded either through designated market makers (DMMs), registered traders, or the CATS system depending on order size and the issue's activity. Designated market makers maintain fair and orderly markets in their allocated stocks of responsibility. Floor DMMs set opening prices for their stocks, maintain posted bid and offer quotations, and show accurate and constantly updated market sizes on both the bid and the offer throughout the trading session. DMMs are permitted and, in some cases, required to trade for their own accounts. When the DMMs trade for their own account, it usually is to stabilize prices if a large imbalance of buy or sell orders occurs in a security. DMMs fulfill an important bridging function between buyers and sellers and contribute to the liquidity and market-making function of the exchange.

FIGURE 11.2   Toronto 300 Composite Index

Index

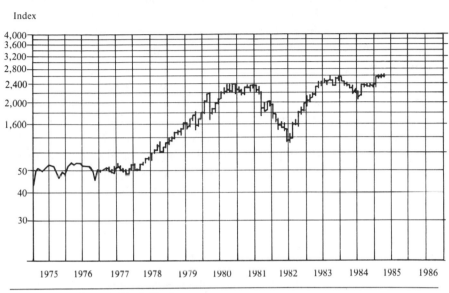

SOURCE: Toronto Stock Exchange.

PRIMARY STOCK INDEXES

The primary stock market index for the Toronto Stock Exchange is the TSE 300 Composite Index. The TSE 300 Index was created in 1977. It is comprised of 300 stocks divided into 14 groups and 41 subgroups. Each of the stocks, industry groups, and subgroups are weighted to reflect their trading activity influence. All 1,400 TSE-listed issues must meet minimum standards to be included in the index; a company must be a Canadian corporation to be eligible. Its shares must be quoted for a period of time with a quoted market value of at least C$ 3 million, and the stock must trade at least 25,000 shares a year for a total value of C$ 1 million. See Figure 11.2. Both index option and financial futures contracts are traded on the TSE 300 Composite Index.

Another index derived from TSE-listed stocks is the TSE High Technology Index, which consists of 27 stocks of companies in the technology sector such as computer manufacturing, semiconductor electronics, and communications.

TAXATION

Half of capital gains less losses of residents are taxable as ordinary income. Unless precluded by a tax treaty, nonresidents are subject to income tax on half of the gains from disposal of only certain assets, such as Canadian real estate and shares in private Canadian companies.

Cash dividends from Canadian companies are subject to a 15 percent withholding. A stock dividend is deemed to have no value for tax purposes. Withholding on interest from Canadian government and corporate bonds is generally 15 percent; however, there are many exceptions depending on the type of issuer, issue date, and currency denomination of the issue. Investors should consult a tax adviser to determine the correct tax treatment of specific issues.

THE TORONTO FUTURES EXCHANGE

Futures trading began on the Toronto Stock Exchange in 1980 when interest rate futures contracts were introduced. In January 1984, the Toronto Futures Exchange (TFE) was officially established as a futures exchange in Ontario. Exchange membership includes individuals, banks, trust companies, securities dealers, commodity dealers, and financial institutions from Europe, the United Kingdom, Asia, Australia, the United States, and Canada. In 1984, 182 members held 260 seats. The TFE shares a trading facility with its sponsor—the Toronto Stock Exchange. Trading of financial futures and options contracts occurs in trading pits located on the Toronto Stock Exchange floor even though it is a separate organization.

Trading and margining financial futures contracts are handled similarly to U.S. futures exchanges. Buyers and sellers of contracts deposit initial margin funds with brokers. Positions are marked to market daily. Clients in losing positions must deposit variation margin funds or their positions are closed out by their broker. Presently, the Canadian futures markets don't have the liquidity that U.S. futures exchanges have; but they are new and growing in volume as traders become more aware of them.

All transactions made on the TFE floor are cleared through Intermarket Services, Inc. (IMS), a wholly owned subsidiary of the

TABLE 11.2

Silver Option Contract (SVR)	
Contract size	100 ounces of .999 fineness silver bullion
Trading hours	9:05 A.M. to 4 P.M. (Eastern)
Price multiple	In multiples of one cent (for all premium levels)
Position limits	20,000 puts and calls on the same side of the market
Reporting levels	500 or more aggregate long or short positions of any single class
Exercise limits	20,000 contracts over a five consecutive business day period
Last trading day	The third Friday of each expiry month
Expiration day	The Saturday following the third Friday of each expiry month
Exercise notice tender day	Any business day
Delivery day	The fifth business day following receipt of the exercise notice
Settlement	A silver certificate issued by an approved depository

Long-Term Canada II Bond Futures (GCB)			
Contract size	$100,000 face value 9% theoretic coupon rate		
Trading hours	9 A.M. to 3:15 P.M. (Eastern). Trading ends at 11 A.M. on the last day of trading in a delivery month		
Minimum price fluctuation	1/32 of a point or $31.25 per contract		
Daily price limit	2 points or $2,000 per contract		
Expanded price limit	3 points or $3,000 per contract		
Minimum client margin	Speculative		$2,000
	Hedge		$1,000
	Spread		$ 625
Position limits	1,200 contracts in total (spec)		
	6,000 contracts in total (hedge)		
Reporting levels	400 contracts in total (spec)		
	600 contracts in total (hedge)		
Last trading day	The sixth last business day of the delivery month		
Delivery notice tender day	Any business day from five business days prior to the first business day of the delivery month up to and including the sixth last business day of the delivery month		
Delivery day	The fifth business day following tender of a delivery notice		
Deliverable issues	Eligible bonds must not mature or be callable for at least 15 years from the date of delivery with a face value of $100,000. The exchange will determine from time to time which issues are deliverable		

SOURCE: Toronto Futures Exchange

TFE. The IMS substitutes as the buyer to every seller and the seller to every buyer, and it guarantees daily settlement of gains and losses. Financial futures contracts are traded on 91-day government of Canada Treasury bills, 18-year government of Canada Treasury bonds, 15-year government of Canada Treasury bonds, the TSE-300 Composite Index, the Oil and Gas Index, and U.S. dollar futures. In addition, an option contract is traded on 100 ounces of silver bullion. For more details, see the contract specifications for Toronto Futures Exchange contracts in Tables 11.2 through 11.5.

TABLE 11.3   TSE 300 Composite Index Futures

Underlying index	TSE 300 Composite Index
Contract size	Valued at 10 times the TSE 300 Index futures price
Trading hours	9:30 A.M. to 4:15 P.M. (Eastern). Trading ends at 4 P.M. on the last day of trading in a contract month
Minimum price fluctuation	One index point or $10 per contract
Daily price limit	150 index points or $1,500 per contract
Expanded price limit	225 index points or $2,250 per contract
Minimum client margin	Speculative $1,500
	Hedge $1,000
	Spread $ 200
Position limits	2,000 contracts in total (spec and hedge)
Reporting levels	300 contracts in total (spec and hedge)
Last trading day	The third Friday of the contract month
Settlement	On the last day of trading in a contract month all open positions will be marked to market and terminated by cash settlement. Spot value of the TSE 300 Composite Index will be used as the cash settlement price rounded to the the nearest whole number
Settlement day	The first business day following the last day of trading

SOURCE: Toronto Futures Exchange.

TABLE 11.4

91-Day Canada Treasury Bill Futures

Contract size	$1,000,000 face value
Trading hours	9 A.M. to 3:15 P.M. (Eastern). Trading ends at 11 A.M. on the last day of trading in a delivery month
Minimum price fluctuation	.01 or $24 per contract
Daily price limit	.60 or $1,440 per contract
Expanded price limit	.90 or $2,160 per contract
Minimum client margin	Speculative $1,500
	Hedge $1,000
	Spread $ 625
Position limits	300 contracts in total (spec)
	3,000 contracts in total, 750 per month (hedge)
Reporting levels	100 contracts in total (spec)
	300 contracts in total (hedge)
Last trading day	Day of the Bank of Canada auction preceding the last Friday of the delivery month
Delivery notice tender day	Any of the last three Bank of Canada auction days immediately preceding the last Friday of the delivery month
Delivery day	Any of the last three Fridays of the delivery month
Deliverable issues	Seller may substitute bills with maturities ranging from 89 to 93 days with a discounted value of $1 million at maturity

U.S. Dollar Futures (USD)

Contract size	$100,000 U.S.
Trading hours	8:30 A.M. to 4 P.M. (Eastern). Trading ends at 11 A.M. on the last day of trading in a contract month
Minimum price fluctuation	.01 or $10 per contract
Daily price limit	2.50 or $2,500 per contract
Expanded price limit	3.75 or $3,750 per contract
Minimum client margin	Speculative $1,500
	Hedge $1,500
	Spread $ 150
Position limits	6,000 contracts in total (spec and hedge)
Reporting levels	600 contracts in total (spec and hedge)
Last trading day	Two business days prior to the third Wednesday of the delivery month
Delivery notice tender day	Two business days prior to the third Wednesday of the delivery month
Delivery day	Third Wednesday in the delivery month
Settlement	Settlement is made in Canadian funds

SOURCE: Toronto Futures Exchange.

TABLE 11.5

Oil and Gas Stock Index Futures and Spot Index Contracts

Ticker symbol	TOX
Underlying index	TSE Oil and Gas Index
Contract size	$10 × Index Futures price
Contract months	The current month plus the following two months
Trading hours	10 A.M. TO 4:15 P.M. (Eastern)
Price quotation	Quoted in index points rounded to the nearest whole number
Minimum price fluctuation	One index point or $10 per contract
Daily price limit	250 index points or $2,500 per contract
Expanded price limit	375 index points or $3,750 per contract

Spot Index Contracts

TSE 300 Composite Index (TSE)	*TSE Oil and Gas Index (TOI)*
Valued at $10 × the TSE 300 Composite index	Valued at $10 × the TSE Oil and Gas Index
9:20 A.M. TO 4 P.M. (Eastern)	9:20 A.M. to 4 P.M. (Eastern).
Quoted in index points rounded to the nearest whole number	Quoted in index points rounded to the nearest whole number
Minimum fluctuation of one index point or $10 per contract	Minimum fluctuation of one index point or $10 per contract
Position limit of 2000 contracts (spec and hedge)	Position limit of 2000 contracts (spec and hedge)
Reporting level of 300 contracts (spec and hedge)	Reporting level of 300 contracts (spec and hedge)
At the end of each day, all open positions are marked to market and automatically terminated by cash settlement. There are no overnight positions carried	At the end of each day, all open positions are marked to market and automatically terminated by cash settlement. There are no overnight positions carried

SOURCE: Toronto Futures Exchange.

CHAPTER TWELVE

The Republic of France

The Republic of France consists of metropolitan France and its overseas departments and territories. France is situated in Western Europe and bordered by Spain, Italy, Switzerland, Belgium, Luxembourg, and West Germany. France has an area of 214,110 square miles with a population of 54.7 million according to the 1984 ccnsus. Paris, the largest city in France with 2.3 million people, is the capital and financial center. The French franc (FF) is the official currency; one French franc = 100 centimes. See Figure 12.1.

GOVERNMENT

The Constitution establishing offices and institutions of the Fifth Republic was adopted in 1958. The principal offices and institutions are: (1) the president, elected for a seven-year period; (2) the government, consisting of a prime minister, appointed by the president, and other members (ministers, delegate ministers, and secretaries); (3) the Council of Ministers, composed of the president and other ministers; and (4) Parliament, divided into a National Assembly and a Senate. Members of the National Assembly are elected for a five-year period. There are 491 deputies in the National Assembly. Members of the Senate are elected for nine years by an electorate of locally elected officials. The Senate has 317 senators.

The Constitution defines the president's role as an arbitrator whose duty is to assure the continuity and the orderly functioning

FIGURE 12.1 Exchange Rate for French Franc

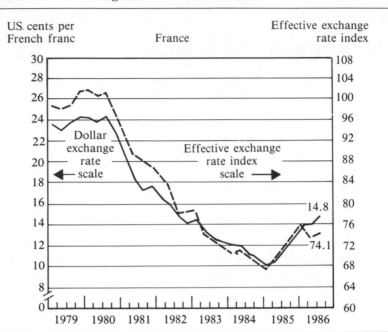

SOURCE: Federal Reserve Bank of St. Louis.

of government. The Constitution charges the government with determining and directing national policy, and charges the prime minister with directing government operations. The Constitution limits Parliament's role by enumerating the matters on which it can legislate. The National Assembly can require the government to resign if it fails to be supported in a vote of confidence or if a motion of censure is adopted.

Political parties consist of: Rally for the Republic (RPR), the Union for French Democracy (UDF), the Union Center, the Republican party, the Democratic Left, the Socialist Party, and the Communist Party.

INTERNATIONAL ORGANIZATIONS

France is a member of the United Nations, the European Economic Community (EEC) and the Common Market, the European Coal and Steel Community, the European Atomic Energy Committee, the World Bank, the International Monetary Fund (IMF), the Organization for Economic Cooperation and Development (OECD), and the General Agreement on Tariffs and Trade (GATT).

THE ECONOMY OF FRANCE

France is the fifth largest industrial and economic power in the world and the fourth largest exporter of goods and services. France benefits from a highly diversified economy with significant contributions from the industrial, service, and agricultural sectors. It claims the fourth largest gross domestic product (GDP) among OECD countries. Foreign trade is important to France; imports and exports account for 24 percent of the GDP. France's total export of goods and services accounts for nearly 5 percent of world trade. The European Community (EC) is France's largest trading partner; it accounts for nearly 50 percent of total exports and imports. West Germany, Italy, and the United States are also active in trading with France.

INDUSTRIAL SECTOR

Industry is the most important sector of France's economy. About 7.1 million people (34 percent of the labor force) are employed in industry. Including construction and public works, the industrial sector accounted for 37 percent of the value added of all sectors. Major industries include electronics, telecommunications, aerospace engineering, transportation, fashion and perfume, and motion pictures. French industry is a leading manufacturer and exporter of automobiles, textiles, tires, and aircraft parts. France is also the fourth leading nation in use of applied robots for welding, assembly, and material handling in the world.

France is an important producer of iron ore; it produces an estimated 15 million metric tons per year. It exports nearly 31 percent of all goods produced. The French steel industry is the seventh largest in the world. France has substantial reserves of bauxite, antimony, magnesium, and radioactive minerals. France was once a leading producer of coal, but coal production has declined sharply to an estimated 20 million metric tons.

France lacks sufficient internal petroleum resources to meet its national energy requirements. It imports large quantities of crude oil. The French government has embarked on a national energy policy that calls for energy conservation, developing nuclear power, and diversifying energy sources. France has developed alternative energy resources in hydroelectric, geothermal, and nuclear power to reduce its dependence on imported oil. In 1981, nuclear power produced more electricity in France than the combined outputs of fossil fuel and hydroelectric installations.

AGRICULTURAL SECTOR

France has the highest agricultural production in Europe; it accounts for 26 percent of the European Common Market's (ECC) total agricultural output. France is a major producer of sugar beets, meat, feed grains, milk, and cheese for the ECC. Nearly 85 percent (116 million acres) of France's total area is arable or wooded land. Farmland accounts for 43.6 million acres; pasture accounts for 31.1 million acres; vineyards account for 2.7 million acres, and forests account for 36 million acres. Approximately 6.7 million acres of arable land aren't cultivated. France is a leading producer of fine wines and champagne.

Agriculture, forestry, and fishing represent 4 percent of France's value added in all sectors. This sector employs 1.7 million people, or 7.8 percent of the total labor force; Common Market policies markedly affect the agricultural sector. These policies can directly affect the production of key crops and their prices by establishing import/export quotas among Common Market countries for French agricultural products. Reduced export quotas or low prices can have a negative impact on France's foreign exchange earnings.

COMMUNICATIONS AND TRANSPORTATION SECTORS

The communications and transportation sectors of the French economy employ many skilled workers. They are essential to both France's private and public sectors. Telecommunications, including telephone, TELEX, and telegraph service, are a state monopoly operated by the Ministere des P.T.T. Capital expenditures for the P.T.T. were budgeted at FF 31.1 billion in 1984. The French government has made a major technological and financial commitment to develop space satellites and telecommunications. France is a leading developer of optical fiber technology and the fifth largest exporter of telephone equipment. Through formation of the Minitel videotext system, France has become a pioneer in interactive communications. Videotext allows interactive communication for commercial and personal uses between computers linked by telephone. The transportation industry uses Minitel to share information on freight costs, tariffs, shipping schedules, and regulations.

The transportation industry plays a key role in the economy. France is the fourth largest exporter of automobiles and trucks. The automotive industry, led by Renault and the Peugeot-Talbot-Citroen group, exports 50 percent of its products to foreign markets. French engineering firms have designed and supplied equipment to build subways in Montreal, Mexico City, and certain South American cities.

The national air, road, inland waterway, and railway networks comprise a major component of the French economy. Inland waterways are especially important in movement of bulk commodities, fuels, minerals, and building materials.

STATE-OWNED ENTERPRISES

During 1981–82, the socialist government of Francois Mitterrand nationalized large numbers of companies, banks, and other institutions. Nationalization of French companies brought the number of state-owned or controlled companies to 4,300. The breakdown of nationalized companies in each sector is: *(a)* chemicals—54 percent, *(b)* electronics—60 percent, *(c)* synthetic fibers—75 percent, *(d)* armaments—75 percent, and *(e)* iron and steel—80 percent. These industries employ 11 percent of the total workforce, which accounts for 17 percent of the GDP and 35 percent of the national investment.

Several well-known public enterprises include Air France, Air Inter, Electricite de France (EDF), Gaz de France (GDF), Bank of France, and Renault. Nationalization of private industries created havoc in capital markets for a time due to radical changes in management personnel, legal status, business practices, and uncertainties about compensation for shareholders. State-owned enterprises are classified as:

1. Public establishments that are industrial or commercial.
2. Nationalized corporations.

3. State corporations.
4. Mixed-economy corporations.

Under the conservative government formed in 1986, most state-owned enterprises will be privatized from 1986 until 1991. Many state enterprises have operated at substantial losses; in 1985, the state budget provided for capital contributions of FF 15.21 billion to state-owned enterprises. The privatization policies of the new government will create a large supply of new equity and debt securities for syndication and distribution to investors in world capital markets.

The opposite approaches to government involvement in business by socialist and conservative parties causes high economic uncertainty in France's financial markets. Growth and development of French business enterprises requires efficiency in management and labor, government stability, and long-range planning by business and government leaders. Uncertainty about the government's position on nationalization of businesses discourages foreign investment and capital formation. Most investors will take economic risks but not political risks with their capital. State control of businesses can occur: (a) in an economic emergency, (b) to provide seed capital for joint government and business ventures, or (c) for national security reasons.

Success in France's economic future lies in the ability of businesses to be efficient, adaptable, and responsive to competitive forces, and to attract foreign investment. Socialist politicians and their nationalization policies hurt economic interests because managers of state-owned enterprises are more responsive to politicians than the competitive forces of the marketplace.

BANKING SYSTEM AND MONETARY POLICY

France's banking system is composed of the Banque de France, savings institutions, mutual and cooperative banks, trade and finance banks, and a postal checking account service that uses the post office as a central clearing system. The postal checking account system competes with bank checking account services. There are 310 banks in France and 420 financial institutions that transact types of business similar to banks. The 483 savings banks are officially recognized as nonprofit public institutions.

In addition, there are several thousand financial institutions, many having received state support, with a special legal status founded on mutual society principles. They include: Crédit Agricole Mutuel, Crédit Mutuel, Crédit Populaire, and Crédit Cooperatif.

The Banque de France was organized in 1800 and nationalized in 1945. It is the central bank and the bank of issue for the French franc (FF). France owns all capital stock. In 1985, the bank had total assets of FF 702 billion. The Banque de France is comprised of a governor, two deputy governors, and a board of 10 members. Its principal banking functions are:

1. Participation in formulating monetary and credit policies.
2. Making advances to the Treasury under special agreements.
3. Conducting open-market operations in short-term government securities.
4. Administering France's foreign exchange reserves; trading in gold and foreign currencies.
5. Acting as Treasury depository.
6. Discounting commercial paper.
7. Issuing bank notes.

The basic monetary and credit policies are administered by the Bank and National Credit Council within policies established by the government. France's recent monetary policy has been structured to control the inflation rate by limiting growth in broader monetary aggregates (M2R). In addition, the bank has imposed mandatory reserve requirements based on increases in the amount of credit extended by banks.

THE FRENCH SECURITIES MARKET

France has seven stock exchanges: the Paris Bourse and six regional *bourses*—Bordeaux, Lille, Lyons, Nancy, Nantes, and Marseilles. The Paris Bourse is the largest exchange, and it accounts for over 95 percent of turnover for all French exchanges. Equities, corporate bonds, and government bonds are traded on the exchanges. Shares can be in registered or bearer form. Commercial and merchant banks are agents and custodians for clients in placing orders with the Agents de Change on the exchanges. Orders generated by banks and their customers account for 80 percent of all transactions made on stock exchanges. Dual listing of a

FIGURE 12.2   SICOVAM

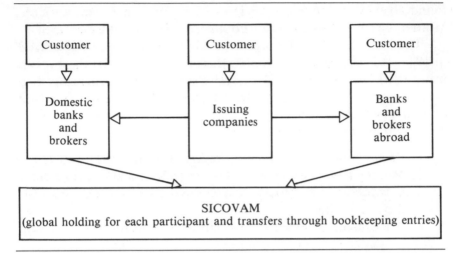

security is prohibited on French exchanges. Approximately 181 foreign companies are listed. France's capital markets are the sixth largest in the world with $134 billion in total market capitalization.

In recent years, greater participation by French and foreign investors has prompted the *bourses* to update trading facilities. French *bourses* are being modernized and deregulated to prepare for global trading. The exchanges are implementing new trading pits for continuous trading, computer-assisted trading and quotation procedures (CATS), facilities for block trading, and the creation of counterparty companies.

In 1949, French exchanges installed SICOVAM—an acronym for the Société Interprofessionelle pour la Compensation des Valeurs Mobilières. SICOVAM is a system of automated clearing and settlement for securities through bookkeeping entries. SICOVAM is a central depository trust for securities; it holds 85 percent of all shares and 60 percent of all bonds registered in France. SICOVAM insures against the loss of securities, and it will eventually eliminate the need for issuing shareholder certificates. Customers receive confirmations of their buy/sell transactions from SICOVAM. See Figure 12.2.

Financial futures contracts on bonds were introduced in February 1986, with the creation of Marché á Terme des Instruments

Financiers (MATIF). The opening of the MATIF financial futures market enables institutional investors to hedge interest rate exposure and bond prices.

Each of the stock exchanges is comprised of three markets:

1. *Cote officielle*—the official market.
2. *Second marché*—the second market.
3. *Marché hors-cote*—the unlisted market.

Companies applying for listing on the *cote officielle* must satisfy the following requirements:

1. Must have been profitable for the last three years.
2. At least 25 percent of a company's stock must be issued for trading.
3. The stock issuance must be a minimum of 320,000 shares for the Paris Bourse, and 80,000 shares for regional exchanges.

There are over 642 companies listed on the official market.

The *second marché* was established in 1983 to expand the listing of medium-sized companies that can't meet the stringent requirements of official listing. The second market has experienced significant growth in new listings of equities and debt issues—from 52 listings in 1983 to over 130 listings in 1986. Companies listed on the *second marché* must issue at least 10 percent of their common stock. There are no earnings qualifications for listing.

The *marché hors-cote* is the over-the-counter market established for companies that can't be accepted for listing by any of the seven exchanges. Rules for introduction and trading of shares are less stringent than for the official and second markets. The *agents de change* (stockbrokers) have an exclusive monopoly in dealing shares on this market. The Professional Association of Brokers supervises this market as to prices and supply and demand for securities traded.

Listing on the *cote officielle* and the *second marché* requires the approval of the Commission des Operations de Bourse (COB). A company's quarterly and annual reports must be filed with the COB.

Listed equity and debt securities are traded on the stock exchanges through *Agents de Change* who are intermediaries between buyers and sellers. *Agents de Change* are appointed by the Minister of Economy after they pass qualifying examinations.

They are independent of the banks and financial institutions that must transact orders through them. They have an exclusive legal monopoly for trading securities in France. They act as brokers for a security except in special situations. *Agents de Change* advise clients, manage clients' portfolios and share joint liability and responsibility if a client or broker defaults on a transaction. The collective liability is guaranteed by a fund (Fonds Commun), which is administered by the Compagnie des Agents de Change (brokers' association) through the executive body of the Chambre Syndicale des Agents de Change.

Securities on the *cote officielle* are traded on:

1. *Marché a reglement mensuel* (RM)—the forward market where trading is done in lots; payment and delivery is made on the last business day of the month.

2. *Marché au comptant*—the cash market in which any quantity may be negotiated for immediate settlement and delivery. Securities traded on the *second marche* and *marche hors cote* are settled as cash transactions.

QUOTATIONS

On French exchanges, only one price is quoted for a security at any moment. The quoted price is binding on both buyers and sellers. Shares are quoted in francs and centimes. Convertible bonds, indexed bonds, and bonds denominated in foreign currencies are quoted in francs and centimes with accrued interest included in the price. All other bonds and debentures are quoted as a percentage of their par value excluding accrued interest. The Daily Official List publishes the amount of accrued interest as a percentage of nominal value.

Customers may enter orders with the Agents de Change as:

Au mieux.   Market orders to buy or sell.
Cours limité.   Limit orders at a specified price to buy or sell.
Premier ou dernier cours.   Orders to be filled at the opening or closing prices.
Sans forcer ou soignant.   Orders to be filled at the discretion of the *agent de change;* this order is used in illiquid markets when large orders need to be filled over time.

Ordre stop. A stop order either to buy when the price rises above a fixed limit or to sell when the price falls below a fixed limit; a stop order becomes a market order to be filled at the next price quoted when the price has been reached.

Depending upon the type of settlement—cash or forward—one of two price quotations can be made:

Par casiers. Quotation for the cash market.
À la criée. Quotation for the forward market.

In addition, customers can enter orders for a specified time:

Jour seulement. Order is valid for the day only.
Revocation. Order is valid until filled or cancelled. On the cash market, revocation orders are valid until the last day of the month. On the forward market, they remain valid until the next settlement day.

THE CAC INDEX

The most important stock index in France is the Compagnie des Agents de Change (CAC). The CAC is published every day and consists of a general index, a special index for nine large economic

---

TABLE 12.1   Selected Information on the 10 Largest Companies by Market Capitalization as of April 25, 1986

Company	Business	U.S.$ Million	Percent Total
Aquitanine (Elf)	Energy sources	$25,324	4.0
Air Liquide	Chemicals	3,834	2.9
Compaigne du Midi		3,200	2.4
Avions Dassault	Aerospace	2,701	2.0
Generale des Eaux		2,548	1.9
Michelin	Industrial parts	2,523	1.9
Thomson-CSF	Electrical	2,318	1.7
Peugeot	Automobiles	2,190	1.6
Compaigne Bancaire	Financial services	2,123	1.6
Moet-Hennessy	Beverages	2,092	1.6
Totals		$28,853	21.6%

Total stock market capitalization U.S.$ 138 billion

SOURCE: Morgan Stanley Capital International Perspective, Geneva, Switzerland.

FIGURE 12.3   CAC General Index

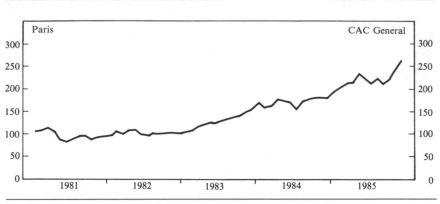

SOURCE: Euromoney Yearbook, Euromoney Publications, 1986.

sectors, and an index of industrial securities collecting six of the nine indexes. The CAC is a capitalization-weighted index composed of 250 issues. Table 12.1 lists the 10 largest capitalized companies traded on the Paris Bourse and included in the CAC Index. Base: December 31, 1981 = 100. See Figure 12.3.

THE PRIMARY AND SECONDARY MARKETS IN EQUITIES

In the primary market, new equity issues can be underwritten by banks and certain financial institutions. The Banque de France regulates the underwriting and issuance of new issues. In France it is mandatory that a company's capital increases be approved by a two-thirds majority vote at a special shareholders meeting where at least 50 percent of the company's shareholders are represented. French law requires that shareholders be offered preemptive rights regarding capital increases. As a result, new issues generally take the form of rights issues for existing shareholders on a pro rata basis, usually at a price that is at a discount to the market price at time of the issue. The shareholders of most French companies are registered with the issuer.

In the secondary market, equity securities are traded on the Paris Bourse in the morning and on all French exchanges in the afternoon. Prices are established by *Agents de Change* according to the number of shares bid for and offered. Opening cash market prices can't differ by more than ± 5 percent from the previous day's close; opening forward market prices can't differ by more than ± 8 percent from the previous day's closing prices. Orders may be written at the best market price *(au mieux)*, at a price limit *(cours limité)*, or the opening or closing prices *(premier/dernier cours)*. All prices quoted must be endorsed by the Chambre Syndicale.

An unlisted market for stock options exists, but they are usually bought and sold in private transactions with no secondary market. The Paris Bourse plans to introduce listed options trading within several years.

THE PRIMARY AND SECONDARY MARKETS IN FIXED-INTEREST SECURITIES

The French government, municipalities, government agencies, and state-owned enterprises issue over 80 percent of all fixed-interest securities. Banks and certain financial institutions are authorized to underwrite and place government and corporate debt issues. The Direction du Tresor determines an annual timetable for scheduling large bond offerings. Smaller bond issues (under FF 1 billion) are offered on an unscheduled basis *(petit marché)*. New issues are generally split between fixed-rate and floating-rate issues. Institutions purchase over 80 percent of the fixed-interest issues.

In the secondary markets, listed government and corporate debt securities are traded by *agents de change* and banks. Maturities may range from under one year to over five years.

TAXATION OF SECURITIES

There is a 15 percent withholding tax levied on dividends. Nonresidents are not taxed on capital gains. Interest from government bonds is paid without withholding taxes, but interest on other types of fixed-interest securities may be subject to a 10 percent withholding tax.

GENERAL INFORMATION ON THE PARIS BOURSE

Dealings in securities, gold, and currencies have occurred in Paris during the past nine centuries interrupted by periods of war and revolution. In 1141, King Louis VII consolidated trading activities in houses built on a bridge that crossed the Seine. However, the modern *bourse* didn't exist until Napoleon II authorized construction of the building in 1808; it opened for trading in 1827.

Stock Exchange Authorities

There are 101 *Agents de Change* belonging to 61 different firms. The Chambre Syndicale is composed of 8 *Agents de Change* who are elected annually.

Stock Market Hours

The Bourse is open Monday–Friday in two sessions:

1. A morning session from 9:30 to 11 A.M., which is limited to the 30 most active stocks.
2. A normal session from 11:30 A.M. to 1:30 P.M. for public and private bonds and from 12:30 to 2:30 P.M. for all French shares and foreign securities.

Types of Securities

Equities.   There are four types of equities:

1. Ordinary shares–voting common stock.
2. Preferred shares–shares with dividend preference rights without voting privileges.
3. Investment certificates–voting right certificates.
4. French Certificates–shares of foreign companies listed in Paris.

Fixed-Interest.   There are seven types of fixed-interest securities:

1. Government bonds–bonds backed by the full faith and credit of the French government.
2. Straight bonds–bonds without clauses granting conversion or warrant privileges.
3. Convertible bonds–bonds that may be converted by the holder to ordinary shares.
4. Floating-rate bonds–bonds with an interest rate that is subject to change in relationship to money market rates.

5. Warrant bonds–bonds with warrants attached that can be converted to ordinary shares on a subscription basis.
6. Participating certificates–securities issued by a nationalizated French company.
7. Public or Semi-public Authority bonds–bonds issued by public and semipublic authorities.

Transaction Charges

A brokerage commission is the rate of commission fixed by an official sliding scale, and it decreases as transaction size increases. It varies from 0.65 percent to 0.215 percent for shares, and 0.45 percent to 0.045 percent for bonds. Commissions for large transactions are negotiable. Fiscal charges are stamp duty stands at 0.30 percent of transactions up to FF 1 million and 0.15 percent thereafter. The value-added tax (VAT) comes to 18.6 percent of commission fees.

CHAPTER THIRTEEN

The Republic of Italy

The Republic of Italy borders the countries of France, Switzerland, Austria, and Yugoslavia. Italy is a peninsula surrounded by the Mediterranean and Adriatic Seas with a land mass covering 116,318 square miles. The country has modest agricultural resources and a few mineral resources; the most valuable resource is natural gas. Northern Italy is highly industrialized compared to the poorer regions of southern Italy. The government provides incentives for establishing more industry in southern Italy. Rome, located in central Italy, is the capital. Milan, in northern Italy, is the financial center. In 1985, Italy's population was 57.2 million. The Italian lira is the official currency. See Figure 13.1.

GOVERNMENT

After World War II and the overthrow of the fascist government of Benito Mussolini, the Republic of Italy was proclaimed in 1946 and a president was elected that same year. The present Constitution, enacted in 1948, provides for the powers of a democratic state divided among the Parliament, the executive branch, and the judiciary. The head of state is the president, who is elected by Parliament in a joint session with regional representatives; the president holds office for a seven-year term. Parliament consists of the Senate (315 elected members) and the Chamber of Deputies (630 elected members). Parliamentary elections must be held every five years, although they have been held more frequently. Historically,

FIGURE 13.1   Exchange Rate for the Italian Lira

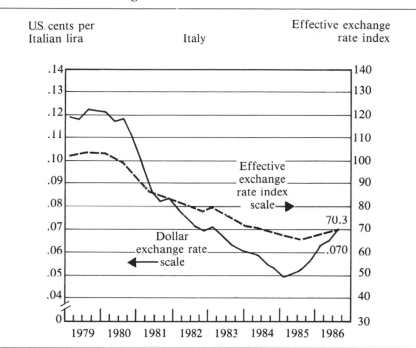

SOURCE: Federal Reserve Bank of St. Louis.

the Christian Democratic Party has been the largest political party in Italy although, except for the period for 1948 to 1953, no party has had a majority. The main opposition parties are the Communist Party and the Italian Social Movement. After the 1983 elections, the government was a five-party coalition of Christian Democrats, Socialists, Republicans, Social Democrats, and Liberals.

INTERNATIONAL RELATIONS

Italy is a founding member of the European Economic Community (EEC), a member of the North Atlantic Treaty Organization (NATO), and a member of the United Nations and many of its agencies. Italy is also a member of the International Monetary Fund (IMF), the International Bank for Reconstruction and Development (the World Bank), the Asian Development Bank, and the Interamerican Development Bank.

DOMESTIC ECONOMY

The Italian economy has developed rapidly since World War II. Large-scale, technologically advanced industries have developed beside traditional agricultural and industrial enterprises. For example, Olivetti has been transformed from a typewriter company to a supplier of modernized office equipment for Europe and North America. Fiat is a major manufacturer of automobiles and commercial vehicles.

Even though Italy is a private-enterprise economy, much industrial growth has come from the establishment of large public-sector companies. The government participates in significant areas of the economy including: banking, communications, shipping, and transportation through the Istituto per la Ricostruzione Industriale (IRI), Ente Partecipazioni e Finanziamento Industria Manifatturiera (EFIM), Ente Nazionale Energia Elettrica (ENEL), and Ente Nazionale Idrocarburi (ENI).

Between 1960 and 1974, Italy's gross domestic product (GDP) grew an average of 5.1 percent per annum in real terms. In 1975, industrial output fell 3.5 percent in response to the world recession caused by dramatic oil price rises from 1973 to 1974. Between 1976 and 1980, the economy grew an average of 4.0 percent per annum, compared with an average growth rate over the same period of 1.0 percent per annum for industrial countries as a whole. From 1981 to 1983, the Italian economy recorded negative real growth at an average rate of −0.4 percent per annum; this compares with a positive growth rate of 1.2 percent per annum for industrial countries. This trend was reversed in 1984 when Italy's GDP grew by 2.6 percent in real terms. Italy's balance of payments is very sensitive to changes in oil prices.

The most important sectors of GDP, in terms of total value added, are industry and marketable services, which account for over 40 percent of the GDP. Public-sector services have maintained a 10 percent share of the GDP. Machinery and precision instruments account for over 20 percent of total principal exports. Principal imports are crude oil, coal, agricultural, forestry, and food products.

Foreign trade is a major component in overall growth. Export performance was strong from 1980 through 1985 with an average increase of 18.6 percent per annum. Italy runs annual trade deficits with imports exceeding exports ranging from L. 3 to 11 billion per year. Italy exports over 45 percent of its total goods to the European Community (EC). West Germany, France, OPEC, and the United States account for significant export destinations. Italy imports nearly 43 percent of its total goods from the EC followed by West Germany, OPEC, and France.

INDUSTRIAL PRODUCTION

Italy has compensated for a lack of natural resources by specializing in the transformation of raw materials into finished durable and consumer goods for both domestic consumption and export. Italian companies have begun to robotize industries to reduce labor costs and improve production quality. Italy is modernizing its industries to catch up with West Germany, the United Kingdom, and France. Although state-owned enterprises play an important role in the economy, small- and medium-size private businesses have led Italy's economic growth in recent years.

Among the most important nationalized sectors are the railways (Ferrovia dello Stato), electricity (ENEL), and hydrocarbons (ENI). Italy's principal industrial production sectors are automobiles, machinery, chemicals, food processing, jewelry, leather goods, and textiles.

AGRICULTURAL SECTOR

With the rise in living standards following World War II, demand for agricultural products has expanded and diversified. Italy no longer produces a self-sufficient supply of foodstuffs. Total output and growth in the agricultural sector has declined steadily since 1960. For wheat, the principal cereal crop, Italy produces 80 percent of its needs. Fruit and vegetables are grown in considerable variety and abundance. They make an important contribution to export earnings. Italy is also one of the largest wine producers in the world. Small farms remain an important feature of the agricultural sector's economic organization. Plans to improve and mechanize the agricultural sector have been hampered due to small farms' inability to adapt to mechanization. Small farms lack the necessary capital to purchase heavy machinery and employ skilled labor.

SERVICE SECTOR

The marketable service sector has grown rapidly during the post-war period; it represents 41 percent of the GDP. Tourism has developed throughout the country; it contributed over $7 billion to the inflow of foreign exchange since 1983. However, in recent years, threats of terrorism directed against tourists have reduced earnings in the tourism industry.

EMPLOYMENT AND LABOR CONDITIONS

The largest proportion of the workforce is employed in the services sector. Over 25 percent of all workers are employed in the industrial sector; construction accounts for one quarter of this sector. Agriculture occupies 10 percent of the workforce; 60 percent of all agricultural workers are self-employed. Unemployment figures, adjusted for the wage supplement fund, have risen since 1980.

INVESTMENT AND CONSUMER EXPENDITURE

As a percentage of GDP, gross investment has stayed between 16.5 percent and 17.6 percent. Of total investment, the construction sector makes the largest contribution, accounting for almost 50 percent of total expenditures. The next largest contributions are made by the investment capital and transport equipment sectors.

MONETARY AND BANKING SYSTEM

The Italian banking system is regulated by three regulatory bodies: the Interministerial Committee for Credit and Saving (CICR), the Ministry of the Treasury, and the Bank of Italy. The Bank of Italy exercises monetary policy by controlling the monetary base through operations in primary and secondary government securities markets and through the discount window and advances to banks.

The importance of equity markets has traditionally been limited in Italy. Credit institutions have played a predominant role in total domestic financing. Commercial and savings banks accept demand

and short-term deposits from the public, and they supply short-term credit to the corporate sector and households. Nine banks represent 40 percent of the banking system. They are incorporated under public law or controlled by the IRI.

EXCHANGE-RATE POLICY
AND EXCHANGE CONTROLS

Italy's foreign exchange-rate policy is governed by membership in the European Monetary System (EMS). Under this agreement, the Bank of Italy must intervene to keep the lira within a margin of ±6 percent of the central parity price established in European Currency Units (ECUs). For other countries, the EMS specifies a margin of ± 2¼ percent. In July 1985, the lira central rate was devalued by ±6 percent against the ECU, and the central rates of other EMS currencies were revalued by approximately 2 percent.

Italian law guarantees repatriation of foreign capital and unlimited remittance of earnings from investments made to establish or expand productive enterprises. For nonproductive investments, including investments in securities, the law guarantees remittance of earnings up to 8 percent per annum on the lira amount of foreign capital invested, and it guarantees repatriation of the full amount originally invested after two years from the investment date.

THE ITALIAN SECURITIES MARKETS

Equity and debt securities are traded on 10 Italian stock exchanges or in transactions off the stock exchanges by large financial institutions. In order of importance, the exchanges are: Milan, Rome, Turin, Genoa, Naples, Florence, Bologna, Venice, Trieste, and Palermo. The largest trading volume occurs on the Milan Stock Exchange, which is located in Northern Italy. The major investors are banks, insurance companies, and mutual funds.

Mutual funds allow the public to participate in markets through buying units in Italian mutual fund companies. Legislation in 1983 permitted the establishment of domestic mutual funds for the first time. Domestic mutual funds have made a significant contribution to increased market capitalization (over 13.4 billion lira in 1985). The Instituto Mobiliare Italiano and Ruinione Adriatica de Sicurta were the first Italian companies to create mutual funds. By 1990, over 30 mutual funds will be available, which will create a sizable pool of investment capital. Securities prices are quoted and traded in the Italian lira (L.).

Although trading in listed securities occurs primarily on an exchange, trading activity also occurs off the exchanges. There is limited trading in securities that aren't listed on an exchange. Securities issued by the Italian government, other than short-term issues, are listed, although trading usually occurs off the stock exchanges. Only brokers may be members of an Italian Stock Exchange, and only Italian nationals can be brokers.

The Commissione Nazionale per le Societa e la Borsa (CON-SOB) was created in 1974 to regulate trading on all securities markets. It has authority to suspend trading on any security under certain conditions. CONSOB issues and administers listing standards and trading regulations for Italian stock exchanges, and it approves the listing of securities on exchanges. Italian securities regulations are less stringent than U.S. securities laws; for example, there are no prohibitions against using insider information for securities trading. All companies with listed securities are required to report semiannually to CONSOB. Accounting and financial reporting requirements aren't equivalent to U.S. requirements. Certain material disclosures aren't allowed, and information is available less frequently. The principal requirements for listed securities are:

1. Minimum capital of 500 million lira.
2. Net assets of 1.5 billion lira.
3. Profit in the last two years.
4. A dividend payment in the previous year.
5. Shares that are freely transferable with full voting rights.
6. Minimum of 20 percent public ownership.

CLEARING, SETTLEMENT, AND DELIVERY OF SECURITIES

Clearinghouse service is performed locally by the Banca d'Italia (Central Bank of Italy) on behalf of its participants. Clearinghouse participants are banks, stockbrokers, and primary financial and trustee companies. Clearing operations include the purchase and/ or sale of securities, collection of checks, payment of promissory notes and drafts, and payments for third parties. *Interstanza* is a service performed by Banca d'Italia for the monthly clearing of debit and credit balances relevant to forward dealings of listed shares and convertible bonds.

The Banca d'Italia and Monte Titoli S.p.a. function as centralized depositories for securities. Banca d'Italia began in 1980 as a central depository. Membership to its central depository system is reserved for banks and stockbrokers. Monte Titoli is a joint stock company created in 1978 as a central depository. Banks, stockbrokers, and other financial institutions are participants in the Monte Titoli central depository system. Securities eligible for deposit include registered shares, savings shares, and fungible bearer shares. Due to currency regulations, securities of nonresident beneficial owners aren't eligible for deposit.

Italian securities markets have tremendous back office problems in clearing and settling transactions. Settlement and delivery of securities transactions can take months. Stock exchange officials are aware of the problem, and they are developing a fully computerized settlement and delivery system between banks and stock exchanges to facilitate the clearing and settlement of securities transactions within a period of several days.

The problem is particularly acute for foreign investors who need securities in a negotiable form. Most U.S. institutions use a DVP/RVP system to receive and deliver certificates. Italian exchanges and banks may be several years away from implementing a fully automated, electronic journal entry system acceptable to non-Italian institutional investors. Presently, bearer certificates can only be delivered out of Italy if they are properly stamped. Under Italian law, most shares are issued in registered form except for saving shares. Saving shares are exempt from registration and may be issued in bearer form. Saving shares are a form of nonvoting preferred shares issued by Italian companies. They pay a higher dividend than a company's common shares. In addition, Italian companies have certain tax incentives for issuing saving shares versus common stock or convertible bonds. Saving shares are a popular investment among Italian residents because they are issued in bearer form.

THE MILAN STOCK EXCHANGE
(BORSA VALORI DI MILANO)

The Milan Stock Exchange (MSE) was founded in 1808 by a decree from Viceroy Eugene Napoleon. The MSE is an unincorporated entity formed and governed by Italian law. Both equity and debt securities are traded on the exchange. The Milan Stock Exchange accounts for 90 percent of total equity volume and over 80 percent of total volume of fixed-interest securities. No foreign shares are listed on the MSE.

Five Italian stock exchanges, including Milan, have two trading boards, a main board plus a second board for companies with securities that don't meet main board requirements. The main board holds daily auctions for securities, whereas the second board meets once a week, usually on Wednesday afternoons.

CONSOB issued new listing requirements for the main board in 1984. For a new listing on the main board, a company must meet minimum net worth requirements of 10 billion lira for industrial companies, and 50 billion lira for insurance companies and banks. A company must: publicly distribute a minimum of 25 percent of the securities from the class to be listed, have no restrictions on transferability of the class of securities to be listed, have one year of audited financial statements and, have been profitable for the

---

TABLE 13.1 Selected Information on the 10 Largest Companies by Market Capitalization as of April 25, 1986

Company	Business	U.S.$ Million	Percent Total
Fiat S.p.a.	Automobiles	$15,642	13.6
Assicurazioni	Insurance	11,539	10.0
STET	Telecommunications	6,889	6.0
Olivetti	Office equipment	5,527	4.8
RAS	Insurance	4,364	3.8
SIP	Communications	3,811	3.3
Montedison	Chemicals	3,226	2.8
Alleanza Assicurazioni	Insurance	3,097	2.7
La Fondiaria	Insurance	3,023	2.6
Mediobanca	Banking	2,700	2.3
Totals		$59,818	51.9%

Total stock market capitalization U.S.$ 115 billion

SOURCE: Morgan Stanley Capital International Perspective, Geneva, Switzerland.

FIGURE 13.2   Milan Stock Exchange Historical General Share Index (M.I.B.) (base February 1, 1975 = 1,000)

SOURCE: Milan Stock Exchange.

past three years. CONSOB has the authority to waive or vary such requirements. Listing requirements on the second board are less stringent; they generally require a net worth of 1 billion lira and permit some restrictions on transferability.

MILAN STOCK EXCHANGE INDEX

The Milan Exchange General Historical Index (M.I.B.) is the primary stock index that investors and economists watch to gauge changes in market psychology. See Figure 13.2. Equity prices are displayed on electronic boards on the trading floor; bond prices are posted on blackboards. The stock exchange Electronic Data Processing (EDP) center relays prices and other essential stock market information in real time over a video and printer price network. TELEKURS is connected into the EDP center to relay the same information to international markets.

PRIMARY AND SECONDARY MARKETS FOR EQUITIES

Legislation requires registering of new issues with CONSOB except for offerings to existing shareholders. New issues of equity securities are distributed on a best-efforts or firm-commitment basis, or they are auctioned by banks and other financial institutions. Italian law gives shareholders option and preemptive rights. All increases in equity capital must be approved by company shareholders. Increases in excess of 10 billion lira must be approved by the Ministry of the Treasury in consultation with the Bank of Italy. A company may limit or eliminate option and preemptive rights regarding an issue of additional shares if the issue is approved by the number of shares representing a majority of the company's capital.

Trading in secondary markets is done on and off stock exchanges. Transactions on the exchanges are made by brokers who act as agents. A substantial volume of transactions occurs off the exchanges. Transactions executed off the exchanges are performed through banks with an in-house crossing of buy and sell orders placed by customers. An investor can either place an order directly with a broker or go through a bank or other financial intermediary. Commissions for transactions, on and off the exchange, are made at negotiated rates.

PRIMARY AND SECONDARY MARKETS
FOR FIXED-INTEREST SECURITIES

Fixed-interest securities *(obbligazioni)* issued by the Italian government and its public entities dominate the debt securities markets. They may be issued directly by the government or in underwritings through financial institutions. Interest on *obbligazioni* issued by the Italian government and most public entities is exempt from Italian taxes.

Corporate debt securities may be issued as straight bonds, convertible bonds *(convertibili)*, or bonds with warrants *(obbligazioni con warrant)*. Interest on corporate issues is taxable. A corporation must obtain stockholder approval to raise capital through debt securities. Although there is no limit on bank financing, a corporation generally can't issue unsecured bonds in excess of current paid-in capital. As a consequence, no significant market has developed for corporate bonds.

The Italian government fixed-interest market is composed of three types of securities:

1. *Buoni Ordinari del Tesoro* (BOT)—These are three, six, and 12-year Treasury bills issued at a discount to parity. The yield is the spread between the purchase price and the payment at maturity.

2. *Certificati di Credito del Tesoro* (CCT)—These are floating-rate treasury notes issued for five, seven, or 10 years. The yield is equal to a 12-month BOT plus a spread.

3. *Buoni del Tesoro Poliennali* (BTP)—These are fixed-rate treasury notes with coupons not exceeding three years.

In addition, the Italian government guarantees securities issued by certain public entities such as the ENEE, ENI, CREDIOP, and Ferrovie dello Stato. All Italian government securities are listed except for BOTs. Most trading for government securities occurs off the exchanges.

WITHHOLDING TAXES

Withholding tax on common and preferred stock dividends is 15 percent. Withholding tax on corporate bonds is 20 percent. Government bonds and securities issued by state agencies are exempt from withholding tax. The Italian withholding tax system favors issuing government and state agency debt securities over capital stock and corporate debt, which is detrimental to capital formation in the economy. Funds are directed into financing the economy's public sector at the expense of developing the private sector.

GENERAL INFORMATION ON THE MILAN STOCK EXCHANGE AS OF SEPTEMBER 1983

Exchange Staff, Stockbrokers, and Representatives

There are 155 exchange staff, 117 stockbrokers, and 263 stockbroker representatives.

Stock Market Hours

The exchange is open from Monday through Friday. Official trading hours are from 10 A.M. to 1:45 P.M. The market for unlisted securities, Mercato Ristretto, has a weekly meeting usually on Wednesdays. The official exchange rate for the lira against all leading international currencies is fixed at a floor ring.

Mercato Dei Premi

There is limited trading in put and call options on a few large listed companies such as Fiat, Generali, and Montedison. Options are traded European-style, and they may be exercised or allowed to expire; no secondary market exists for options.

Number of Listings

The following list shows the total number of listings:

1. Shares of common: 199 (14 suspended)
2. Companies quoted: 143 Italian (13 suspended)
3. Fixed-interest issues: 1,048 public issues
                          72 government issues
                          58 ordinary loan issues
                          52 convertible issues
                          29 international institutions

Stock Exchange Contracts

Cash or account (three-days or one-month) transactions are foreseen respectively for bond and share securities.

Transaction Costs

Commission rates are based on a percentage of market value, 0.7 percent for shares; and nominal value, 0.3 percent for bonds, and 0.15 percent for government stocks.

Margin Requirements

The following compulsory cash deposits are made with the stock-broker: 50 percent of the value of equities purchased, 50 percent of the value of equities sold, or delivery of relative certificates within three business days.

Stamp Duty

A stamp duty is charged for every 100,000 lira in amounts of 30 lira for government stocks and bonds. Shares are charged 56.25 lira.

Switzerland

The Confederation of Switzerland is a mountainous country located in central Europe with an area of 16,102 square miles. Switzerland is comprised of 27 cantons (states). It is bordered by France, West Germany, Italy, Austria, and Liechtenstein. Switzerland has a population of 6.49 million. Bern is the capital, but Zurich is Switzerland's largest city and the financial center. Even though the country has few natural resources, it's one of the wealthiest nations in world due to the productivity and ingenuity of its people. Switzerland is a world banking and financial center that has maintained a policy of neutrality through both World War I and World War II.

German is the dominant language of Switzerland, but French and Italian are spoken widely. The official currency is the Swiss franc (Sfr). One Swiss franc equals 100 centimes. See Figure 14.1.

GOVERNMENT

Switzerland is officially known as the Swiss Confederation (Confederatio Helvetica), which was founded in 1848. The Swiss government is a parliamentary democracy with certain powers delegated to the officials in communal, cantonal, and federal parliaments. The political process is implemented through a system of initiatives and referendums that give the Swiss people a direct voice in national and cantonal affairs.

FIGURE 14.1   Exchange Rate for the Swiss Franc

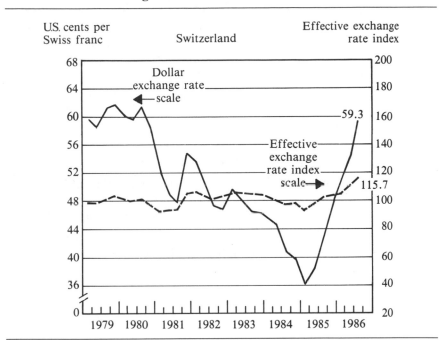

SOURCE: Federal Reserve Bank of St. Louis.

The federal constitution defines the relationship between the federal government and the cantons. The federation guarantees Switzerland's independence and assumes responsibility for foreign policy, defense, pensions, communications, railways, and currency.

The cantons are composed of numerous communes of differing size. The cantons have considerable political power within Switzerland along with the federal government in Bern.

Parliament has two chambers: the National Council and the Council of States. The Federal Council is the executive authority with seven members taken from Parliament. The important political parties are: the Radical Democrats, the Christian Democrats, the Social Democrats, and the Central Democratic Union. The Communist Party was outlawed in 1940 and has been replaced by the Workers' Party.

INTERNATIONAL RELATIONS

Due to Switzerland's policy of strict international neutrality, it is not a member of any political treaty organizations. Switzerland does have an observer in the United Nations General Assembly. Switzerland is a member of two economic treaty organizations: the European Free Trade Association (EFTA) and the Organization for Economic Cooperation and Development (OECD). Switzerland has been a member of the EFTA since its inception in 1960.

Switzerland has a free trade agreement with the European Economic Community (EEC). In any free trade agreement, the Swiss insist on certain preconditions such as the continuation of its foreign-worker policy and protectionist agricultural policies, retention of Swiss autonomy in any armed conflict with other nations, autonomy in internal politics, and autonomy in relations with third-world countries. These preconditions allow for Swiss cooperation in other areas, such as environmental, research, and development policies.

THE ECONOMY

Switzerland has one of the world's highest levels of per capita income at $14,950. The country's prosperity is due to earnings from service sectors such as banking and related financial services, insurance, and tourism. Because of the importance of maintaining a stable economic and political environment to foster growth in the banking and financial sectors, Switzerland's economic policies are strongly influenced by the government's intense desire to control monetary growth and producer and consumer price inflation.

Through its banking system, Switzerland is both a major importer and exporter of capital funds. Nonresidents from around the world make substantial deposits in Swiss banks. These funds are lent to corporations and governments in Switzerland and in foreign countries either through direct loans or through capital-market transactions. Switzerland was one of the few European countries with a functional banking system after World War II. It is now receiving intense competition from England and West Germany. The ability of Swiss banks and capital markets to attract foreign capital depends on Switzerland's political neutrality, a stable currency, and low inflation rates.

The country has a high level of expertise in the design and production of industrial chemicals, pharmaceuticals, processed foods, machinery, appliances, precision instruments, watches, and jewelry. Switzerland isn't endowed with natural resources except for abundant rivers that generate hydroelectric power and forests that supply paper, pulp, and lumber products.

Switzerland's gross domestic product, which has grown steadily since 1983, depends highly on exports. With approximately 35 percent of the GDP given to exports, the Swiss economy is sensitive to external factors. High labor costs help reduce its price competitiveness in world markets. The Swiss depend on skilled labor supplemented by foreign workers from Italy, France, and West Germany. High labor costs are partially offset by a low inflation rate and a high degree of adaptability.

The basic sectors of the Swiss economy are: banking, insurance, and related financial services; agriculture; forestry; energy; manufacturing; construction; tourism; transportation; communications; and foreign trade. Switzerland doesn't publish GDP figures by origin, which makes it impossible to determine the relative contributions of each sector.

The manufacturing sector is highly specialized; it makes a large contribution to the Swiss GDP. Manufacturing includes the production of machinery, chemicals, metals, textiles, clothing, and watches. Most of these goods are made to export.

Foreign trade accounts for over 35 percent of Switzerland's GDP. Switzerland's principal trading partners are the European Community (EC), West Germany, the United States, France, the United Kingdom, and Italy. The EC accounts for 50 percent of all exports, followed by West Germany with 20 percent of all exports.

Switzerland imports a large volume of machinery, chemicals, agricultural products, textiles, clothing, and energy products. Many imported goods are transformed into products to export. The European Community (EC) accounts for 69 percent of all imports, and West Germany has 30 percent of all imports. France, Italy, the United Kingdom, and the United States also supply goods to the Swiss economy.

As for the agricultural sector, Switzerland has a strict protectionist policy toward Swiss farmers and livestock producers. The objective is to remain self-sufficient in the supply of basic foods. Because Switzerland is a landlocked country, agricultural policy maintaining self-sufficiency carries a high national priority that won't be modified by trade agreements with the European Community or other trading partners.

In the energy sector, hydroelectric power is one of Switzerland's primary natural resources. It is almost completely exploited, which makes the Swiss economy dependent on imported oil and petroleum products to meet its energy needs. The dependency on foreign-supplied energy makes the Swiss economy vulnerable to fluctuations in world oil prices and, therefore, consumer price inflation. In 1985, over 66 percent of all Swiss energy production came from foreign suppliers. Low oil prices are highly beneficial to the Swiss economy.

In a move to become energy independent, Switzerland embarked on a long-term program to build nuclear reactors for future electricity needs. The fate of the nuclear energy program is uncertain due to the Chernobyl disaster that occurred in 1986 in the Soviet Union. Five Swiss nuclear power stations now produce 40 percent of all domestic electricity. Switzerland planned to build several more nuclear plants by the year 2,000.

Since 1966, tourism has been a significant factor in foreign exchange earnings. Income from tourism peaked in 1981; it is affected by the relative strengths of various world currencies.

MONEY AND BANKING

The Swiss National Bank (SNB) is the central bank of Switzerland, and it has a profound influence on the Swiss economy. Not only does the SNB control the country's money supply and credit flow, it governs the trading of Swiss equities and debt securities through regulation of subordinate banks.

The SNB controls the money supply and credit flow through open market operations, the use of minimum reserves, and the flotation of bond issues. A primary responsibility of the central bank is controlling the rate of producer and consumer price inflation. Because Switzerland has few natural resources for supplying industries with raw materials, no internal petroleum sources of energy, and a dependency on foreign labor, the Swiss economy is extremely sensitive to inflation. For this reason, the SNB targets small growth in the annual money supply—usually 2 percent or less.

Even though half of the SNB board of governors are appointed by the federal government, the SNB is largely independent in determining monetary policy. Of the 71 banks under SNB jurisdiction five are national banks, 28 are cantonal banks, and eight are local and savings banks. Switzerland also has approximately 100 foreign banks and several hundred finance companies.

A complete discussion of Swiss banking includes the bank secrecy laws. While there are numbered accounts at Swiss banks, the client's identity is known only to a few bank officials. Bank officers regard the revealing of information about clients or their accounts as both a breach of confidentiality and an invasion of privacy. Under Swiss law, bank employees can be prosecuted if they reveal information about customer accounts without proper authorization.

The Swiss regard the right to conduct one's business affairs in private as sacrosanct. The Swiss attitude toward privacy and individual rights has evolved from the time when Switzerland's neighboring countries were ruled by regimes that abused individual freedoms and privacy. People fled to Switzerland from these countries to regain their freedom and rights to privacy. The most recent example occurred during the Third Reich in Germany from 1933 to 1945.

The United States and Switzerland disagree over the Swiss interpretation of privacy rights. Swiss law states that information about clients and their bank accounts can be revealed only if a criminal act has been committed. Swiss law must be violated as well as the law of the country requesting the information. For instance, tax evasion and insider trading are criminal acts in the United States. As of this writing, neither of these acts violates Swiss criminal codes; therefore, a Swiss bank wouldn't reveal information to aid the U.S. government in prosecuting an individual with a Swiss bank account. There is, however, legislation being prepared that would make insider trading a criminal offense in Switzerland.

THE SECURITIES MARKETS

Switzerland has seven stock exchanges in Zurich, Basel, Geneva, Lausanne, Berne, Saint Gall, and Neuchâtel. The Zurich Stock Exchange is the largest exchange; it accounts for over 60 percent of total turnover. The exchanges of Basel and Geneva are more innovative than Zurich because they intend to introduce innovative financial products such as financial futures and options earlier than the Zurich exchange. The Zurich, Geneva, and Basel exchanges account for 90 percent of total turnover. In 1986, Swiss capital markets were the eighth largest in the world with a total market capitalization of $102 billion.

As part of the Commission Tripartite Bourse's policy to integrate the trading, clearing, and settlement systems of the Zurich, Basel, and Geneva exchanges, plans have been made for electronic linkage of the exchanges by 1988. A feature of the proposed system is a computer-assisted trading system, Computerunterstutze Handelssystem (CHS). The CHS system will allow screen trading for less actively traded securities between members. The Commission Tripartite Bourse is working toward a common clearing system, the integration of prices in a common CHS, and new options and financial futures market for Switzerland.

Only licensed banks can be stock exchange members. Foreign banks may conduct trading only on the over-the-counter (OTC) market. Although purchasing a seat on the Zurich exchange isn't mandatory, the membership cost is Sfr 300,000; the minimum capital requirement is Sfr 500,000 with no liquidity requirements. Switzerland operates under a universal banking system; universal banking permits banks of public rights, and commercial, regional, and private banks to conduct all banking and related financial services under one roof. Under the universal banking system, a bank can: trade securities for its own account, act as a securities broker, clear and settle securities transactions, conduct custodial business, provide investment advice, conduct trust business, and underwrite new equity and debt issues.

Any member bank can perform any function without special registrations. The Swiss have a dual-capacity trading system. Because there are no laws or regulations that require trading to occur on the exchange floor, banks may put customer orders through their own books; thus "crossing orders" off the exchange floor. The stock exchange is a facility for conveniently handling transactions and pricing securities.

There are 24 members on the Zurich Stock Exchange and 197 representatives. The five largest members are the Union Bank of Switzerland, Swiss Bank Corporation, Credit Suisse, Swiss Volksbank, and Bank Leu. They account for over 50 percent of total trading volume on the exchange. Trading on the exchange is dominated by Swiss and foreign bonds. There are approximately 370 equities, 1,397 Swiss bond, and 716 foreign bond issues quoted on the official list.

All transactions must be reported to the Stock Exchange Commission. Telekurs, AG, a company jointly owned by a number of large banks is responsible for transmission of prices and other data on securities. Each security dealer must report all securities transactions to the stock exchange register. At the day's end, the stock exchange issues an official quotation sheet that lists all transactions made on the exchange.

Each exchange is under the governmental control of the canton where it is located. Rules vary from canton to canton. The Zurich Stock Exchange is governed by the Stock Exchange Commissionship (Borsenkommissariat) and the Stock Exchange Commission (Borsenkommission). All exchanges are members of the Association of Swiss Stock Exchanges. Under the universal banking system, Switzerland has no investor protection laws because they are covered by banking regulations.

The total value of bonds traded is triple the number of shares. The average share price for Swiss companies is much higher than shares traded on the New York Stock Exchange. The average price of Swiss shares ranges from $400 to $500. Share prices of well-known Swiss companies are as high as several thousand dollars.

THE PRIMARY AND SECONDARY EQUITIES MARKET

In the primary market, there are three types of shares issued by Swiss companies: (1) bearer, (2) registered, and (3) participation certificates. Participation certificates have the same ownership rights as shares of stock, but they don't have shareholder voting rights. Banks underwrite and place all new issues through their syndicates. A new listing must meet the following criteria as outlined in the Official Listing Regulations of the Zurich Stock Exchange:

1. An issuer must prepare and widely distribute a prospectus with current financial information.
2. An issuer must prepare an annual report.

3. An issuer must distribute all official communications to shareholders in a timely fashion.
4. A security must have achieved a wide market with the investing public before it can be listed on the Zurich Stock Exchange.

After the prospectus is published, the subscription period occurs; shares can then be ordered from the bank. At the end of the subscription period, the shares are allocated to the bank's clients. Then, the shares are paid for and the securities are printed.

The Swiss Capital Market Commission, an agency of the Swiss National Bank, controls the amount of money raised each year through primary markets. New issues are underwritten by banks and placed by their syndicates. As in the European markets, current shareholders have preemptive rights requiring the company to offer them rights or newly issued shares first. The shareholders' preemptive rights can be waived by a decision of the company's general meeting.

In the secondary market, trading in equities occurs on or off the exchange floor. All trades must be reported to the exchange, and settlement is made at official prices. The Zurich Stock Exchange has three rings *(la corbeille),* each designated for a particular type of trading. Ring 1 is reserved for the trading of Swiss bonds; trading of shares occurs at ring 2, and foreign bonds are traded at ring 3. See Figure 14.2. Trading at the rings occurs through a combination of open outcry *("a la crièe")* and roll-call methods. Stocks are grouped according to industry, and they are alphabetical within each group. The stock exchange clerk announces each stock, and then trading commences. No stock may be traded at the ring until the clerk has announced it. Once trading has started, traders may return to a previous stock if its industry group is still being announced. When the clerk has completed the roll call for a particular industry group, all trading for those stocks must cease. Roll call on official listed shares occurs twice a day during official trading hours.

Trading of unlisted shares can occur by two methods. For medium and smaller-sized companies that don't fulfill official listing requirements for the Zurich exchange, trading occurs before official trading hours at the exchange prior to official trading. Ring

FIGURE 14.2 Layout of the Zurich Stock Exchange Floor

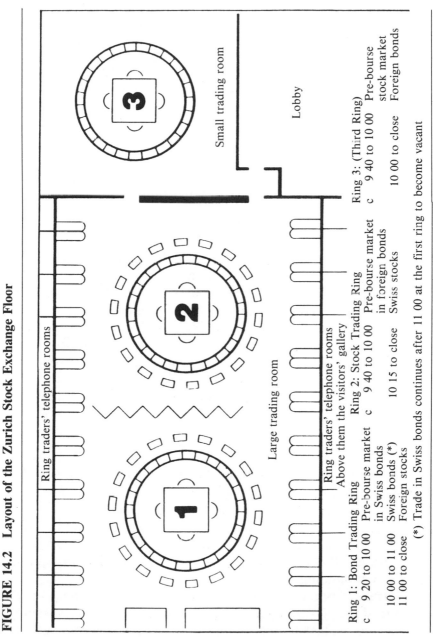

Ring traders' telephone rooms

Large trading room

Ring traders' telephone rooms
Above them the visitors' gallery

Small trading room

Lobby

Ring 1: Bond Trading Ring
c 9 20 to 10 00 Pre-bourse market
in Swiss bonds

10 00 to 11 00 Swiss bonds (*)
11 00 to close Foreign stocks

Ring 2: Stock Trading Ring
c 9 40 to 10 00 Pre-bourse market
in foreign bonds

10 15 to close Swiss stocks

Ring 3: (Third Ring)
c 9 40 to 10 00 Pre-bourse
stock market

10 00 to close Foreign bonds

(*) Trade in Swiss bonds continues after 11 00 at the first ring to become vacant

SOURCE: Zurich Stock Exchange.

3 is used for prebourse trading *(Vorborsen)* in shares. Stocks are generally allowed to trade prebourse only after they have been traded over-the-counter (OTC) on a regular basis.

A small OTC market is maintained by the 24-member ring banks of the Zurich exchange. OTC transactions are executed on the exchange floor and represent less than 5 percent of total equity volume. OTC trading is for stocks neither listed nor traded prebourse. This usually includes shares of local companies with a small public flotation and the shares of companies that operate mountain railways.

THE PRIMARY AND SECONDARY MARKETS IN DEBT SECURITIES

In the primary market, the Swiss National Bank controls the issuance of bonds. They are underwritten as public issues by a banking syndicate. In most cases, the minimum bond denomination is Sfr 5,000, but it may be denominated as Sfr 1,000. Foreign borrowers issue debt securities denominated in Swiss francs.

In the secondary market, as with shares, bond trading occurs on or off the exchange floor. On the exchange, trading occurs at Zurich Stock Exchange rings using the open outcry and roll-call method. Prebourse trading in bonds, with certificates that haven't been printed or delivered, occurs before the official bond market.

TAXATION

Nonresidents aren't liable for federal or cantonal tax on dividends or capital gains. Current income from Swiss government bonds is subject to a Swiss withholding tax of 35 percent unless otherwise reduced by a double-taxation agreement. Capital gains aren't subject to Swiss withholding tax. Profits from traded options and financial futures that qualify as capital gains for nonresidents aren't subject to withholding taxes.

Government bonds and equities are subject to a stamp duty only if one of the parties is a professional securities dealer. A stamp duty is levied against traded options and financial futures only if the documents qualify for a stamp duty.

FIGURE 14.3   U.B.S. Index

Switzerland - SBC General - Price index
From 1/ 1/80 to 25/ 5/87 weekly

High 688.2 6/ 1/87   Low 264.8 17/ 8/82 Last 617.7

SOURCE: Datastream.

STOCK EXCHANGE INDEXES

There are three indexes quoted on the Zurich Stock Exchange. The Swiss Bank Corporation (SBC Index) is composed of 90 companies weighted by market value. An aggregate index and group indexes are computed daily. The base value, as of 1958, is 100. See Figure 14.3. The Credit Suisse Index (SKA Index) has 25 companies weighted by market value. The base value, as of 1959, is 100. The Swiss National Bank Index (SNB Index) is an aggregate of 117 shares quoted on the Zurich, Basel, and Geneva exchanges. The base value, as of 1966, is 100.

As of this writing, there is no trading of stock indexes on the Zurich exchange. The Zurich, Basel, and Geneva exchanges plan to introduce index trading in 1987 or 1988. Table 14.1 lists the 10 largest capitalized companies traded on the Swiss Exchanges.

TABLE 14.1 Selected Information on the 10 Largest Companies by Market Capitalization as of April 25, 1986

Company	Business	U.S.$ Million	Total
Nestle	Food	10,965	10.7
Schweiz Bankgesell	Banking	10,402	10.2
Schweiz Bankverein	Banking	9,425	9.2
Ciba-Geigy	Pharmaceuticals	6,421	6.3
Schweiz Kreditanstalt	Banking	5,940	5.8
Hoffmann-La Roche	Pharmaceuticals	4,985	4.9
Sandoz	Pharmaceuticals	4,122	4.0
Schweiz Ruckversicherung	Insurance	3,078	3.0
Zurich Ruckversicherung	Insurance	2,855	2.8
Winterthur	Insurance	2,556	2.5
Totals		U.S.$ 60,749	59.4%

Total stock market capitalization U.S.$ 102 billion

SOURCE: Morgan Stanley Capital International Perspective, Geneva, Switzerland.

THE ZURICH STOCK EXCHANGE

The history of the Zurich Stock Exchange has been marked by a resistance to government intervention and the need for more space. Since the earliest days of trading, the Swiss have resisted compulsory stock exchange trading; they feel it violates individual freedom.

Even though the official founding date of the Zurich Stock Exchange is 1877, a form of trading was conducted by the *sensale* (brokers or business intermediaries) since the mid-17th century. In 1663, the *Sensale's Order* was published by the Zurich mercantile directorate. The *Sensale's Order* was a set of regulations that established the duties and business conduct of brokers.

In 1883, the first Cantonal Stock Exchange Act in Zurich was established. When this act was introduced, brokers felt it was a violation of their individual rights, and they went on strike for several months. They eventually relented, and the Stock Exchange Act remained law. The act stated that the canton would:

1. Supervise the methods for conducting business.
2. Require brokers to have a government trade permit.

3. Require brokers to deposit a sum of money as a guarantee.
4. Appoint a stock exchange commissioner as a cantonal official at the exchange.

In 1896, a new cantonal law allowed banks and brokers access to the stock exchange for the first time. The most recent law regulating the Zurich Stock Exchange went into effect in 1912; it still governs the exchange today. The Law on Professional Trade covers several major points:

1. The canton, instead of the exchange, assumed responsibility for regular publication of daily quotations sheets.
2. The canton would provide the location and building for the stock exchange.
3. The creation of a committee of stock market experts to advise the canton.
4. The law called for forming a stock exchange association to play an advisory role in the issuance of on- and off-the-floor trading licenses.

As with other European countries, the growth of the Zurich Stock Exchange was facilitated by capital needs for constructing regional and national railways. Zurich became a principal financial center, and its importance in banking grew during World War II, when Europeans transferred their assets to Switzerland to avoid Nazi confiscation.

GENERAL INFORMATION ON THE ZURICH STOCK EXCHANGE

Stock Exchange Authorities

Membership is restricted to the ring banks. Each of the ring banks has a ringside place where traders execute transactions. All bank members must be Zurich Stock Exchange Association members. The stock exchange association forms a general assembly and elects a board of governors to oversee stock exchange operations. The stock exchange is regulated by the Zurich Stock Exchange Association and the canton of Zurich. Securities trade is subject to Zurich securities laws. Members are required to file annual reports with the Zurich cantonal government.

Unlike other exchanges, Swiss exchanges don't have specialists or registered market makers. Transactions are conducted directly between ring members. Transactions aren't restricted to the exchange floor.

Trading Hours

Official trading occurs Monday to Friday from 10 A.M. to 1 P.M. Trading in foreign bonds begins at 10:15 A.M.; trading in foreign stocks begins at 10:30 A.M. Prebourse trading may occur from 9:20 or 9:40 A.M. to 10 A.M. Trading can continue after 1 P.M. if the market is unusually active. The exchange may cease trading before 1 P.M. if the market is inactive.

Types of Securities Traded

The following types of securities are traded on the exchange:

Bearer Shares. Most Swiss shares come in bearer form with a coupon attached. Par value of Swiss shares can range from Sfr 100 to Sfr 500.
Registered Shares. These shares are registered with the issuer in the shareholder's name. For the most part, registered shares are only owned by Swiss citizens or Swiss-controlled companies. Par value is usually Sfr 100.
Participation Certificates. Participation certificates have the same ownership rights as shares of stock except that shareholders have no voting rights.
Convertible Bonds. These bonds can be converted into shares of the issuing company.
Federal Bonds. These bonds are issued and backed by the full faith and credit of the Swiss government.
Public Authority Bonds. The bonds are issued and backed by the full faith of a Swiss canton or municipality.
Warrant Issues. These bond issues have warrants attached that include the right to purchase shares or participation certificates of the issuing company at stipulated prices within a specific period.
Foreign Bonds. These bonds are issued by foreign governments or corporations denominated in Swiss francs. The issues are divided into debentures of Sfr 5,000 and Sfr 100,000 each. They are exempt from the 35 percent withholding tax.

Clearing and Settlement

Securities in cash deals must be delivered and paid for within one to five business days. The settlement "delivery against payment" within the SEGA depository occurs within three business days after a transaction. Schweizerische Effekten-Giro AG (SEGA) is the Swiss company for the clearing and deposit of securities. SEGA uses a book-entry system of transferring ownership of shares. There is no physical transfer of securities. Both banks and SEGA function as depositories for shares. Only fungible shares (bearer securities) can be cleared through the SEGA system.

Margin Trading

Margin trading is permitted, but credit arrangements are made between a customer and the bank. Margin requirements can vary between banks. Stock borrowing is not allowed by the exchange.

Commissions and Fees

The brokerage convention of the Association of Swiss Stock Exchanges establishes the commission rates. Commission schedules are a combination of fixed and negotiable rates depending on the type of security and the size of the transaction. They are as follows:

Bonds. Rates range from 0.6 percent to 0.16 percent of market value. Commissions are negotiable for deals exceeding Sfr 2 million and for deals with foreign currency, bonds exceeding Sfr 1 million. Investment fund certificates are subject to a flat rate of 0.3 percent.

Shares. For trades less than Sfr 50,000, the commission is 0.8 percent for Swiss shares and 1.0 percent for foreign shares of market value. Trades between Sfr 50,000 and 2 million have a minimum charge of 0.2 percent of market value. For trades exceeding Sfr 2 million, rates are negotiable. Table 14.2 lists the trading lots compared to the market value of stocks.

TABLE 14.2   Trading Lots

Market Value of Stock (Sfr.)		Trading Lot (Shares)
More than	To	
	5.	1000 shares
5.	10.	500 shares
10.	50.	100 shares
50.	200.	50 shares
200.	500.	25 shares
500.	2000.	10 shares
2000.	5000.	5 shares
5000.	10000.	2 shares
10000.		1 share

SOURCE: Zurich Stock Exchange.

Quotations Sheet

The quotations sheet *(Kursblatt der Zurcher Effektenborse)* is published daily after the market closes. This chronicle of events is maintained electronically by Telekurs AG. The quotations sheet contains all securities listed on the Zurich exchange, and it categorizes them into Swiss shares, foreign shares, Swiss bonds, and foreign bonds. The quotations sheet includes data on all prices paid during the trading session and the last closing bid and asked prices of the trading day. It also contains information on the closing time of each trading session, official exchange rates, stock exchange statistics, a list of market leaders, settlement dates for the month, official discount and collateral lending rates, and important exchange news such as new listings, delistings, and redemptions.

TRADED OPTIONS MARKET

As of this writing, Switzerland doesn't have a traded options market. Swiss banking and cantonal laws complicate introducing a traded options market. Zurich, Geneva, and Basel are contemplating introducing a traded options market by 1988. Option contracts will be traded by computer instead of market makers on the exchange floor. In addition, they anticipate introducing share index and bond index trading.

Although Switzerland doesn't have a traded options market, the Zurich exchange has fixed-forward transactions and premium trading, which have some similarities with option contracts. Fixed-forward transactions are called "ultimo trading." Ultimo trading involves a set security with a fixed price and specified settlement month.

Premium trading is a contingency or optional transaction in that the buyer can withdraw from taking delivery by paying a premium, usually ranging from 3-10 percent of the security's price, agreed on at the conclusion of a transaction. The buyer can either take delivery of the stock by paying the agreed on price on option day or decline delivery and pay the premium. Option day is the fifth from last trading day of the month.

Only fully paid shares can be traded on a forward basis. Bank shares, insurance company shares, and investment trusts can't be traded on a premium or forward basis.

FINANCIAL FUTURES MARKETS

As of this writing, Switzerland has no domestic financial futures markets, but banks can place trades for clients on foreign futures exchanges. The stock exchanges anticipate creating a futures exchange by 1989. Like traded options markets, Swiss banking and cantonal laws complicate the introduction of a financial futures market. Option and futures contracts may be construed as gaming contracts with obligations that aren't fully sanctioned under Swiss law. Amendments to current laws are needed before a viable financial futures and options exchange can develop in Switzerland.

CHAPTER FIFTEEN

The Commonwealth of Australia

The Commonwealth of Australia is the world's largest continent inhabited by one nation. As an island continent, it is surrounded by the Pacific, Indian, and Antarctic Oceans. Australia is comprised of six states, the Northern Territory, and several other territories. Australia has a total area of 2.967 million square miles—about the size of the United States excluding Alaska and Hawaii. Despite its large geographic area, Australia is populated with only 15.75 million people who are concentrated mostly in the capital cities of

FIGURE 15.1   Exchange Rate for the Australian Dollar

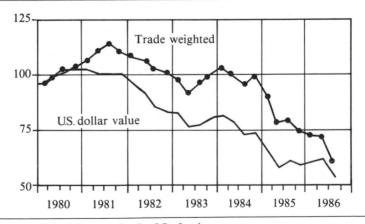

SOURCE: Federal Reserve Bank of St. Louis.

states along the eastern and southern coastal regions. Most of the population is of British heritage. Aborigines, the original inhabitants of Australia, number 170,000 and live in the central region of the country. The vast central region is arid and largely unsuitable for agriculture.

Australia was colonized by Great Britain in 1788 because America—having gained independence in 1776—could no longer be used for British convict settlements. Sydney became a new penal colony for convicts from the British Isles.

Canberra is the capital of Australia. Sydney is Australia's largest city and principal financial center. The Australian dollar (A$) is the official currency; one A$ equals 100 cents. (See Figure 15.1).

FORM OF GOVERNMENT

The Commonwealth of Australia was formed in 1901 as a federated commonwealth comprised of six states, the Northern Territory, and several other territories. The federal government, based in Canberra, New South Wales, is responsible for national interests. Federal legislative powers are vested in the Federal Parliament, which consists of the Queen of England, the Senate, and the House of Representatives. The queen is represented in Australia by the governor-general and six state governors. The Senate is comprised of 76 members. The House of Representatives has 148 members. The executive power of the commonwealth under the constitution is vested in the governor-general. A Federal Executive Council, composed of the prime minister and other federal ministers of state, advises the governor-general. Each of Australia's six states—New South Wales, Victoria, Queensland, South Australia, Western Australia, and Tasmania—has a state parliament. The Northern Territory is a self-governing territory.

Australia has four main political parties:

1. The Australian Labor party, which is the current party in power. This party holds 44 percent of all Senate seats and 55 percent of all seats in the House of Representatives.
2. The Liberal Party, which holds nearly one-third of all seats in the Senate and the House of Representatives.
3. The National Party of Australia.
4. The Australian Democrats.

The party or coalition of parties with a majority in the House of Representatives becomes the ruling government and provides the ministry, including the Prime Minister. All members of the ministry are members of parliament. The cabinet is the major policymaking government agency. The prime minister presides over the cabinet, which comprises nearly half of the full ministry.

INTERNATIONAL RELATIONS

Australia is a member of the British Commonwealth of Nations, the Association of South-East Asian Nations (ASEAN), and the United Nations. Australia provides large amounts of aid to nearby developing countries. The largest recipients of Australian aid are New Guinea, Indonesia, the Philippines, and Thailand. Australia provides limited aid to Laos, Malaysia, and China.

THE ECONOMY

In the last 50 years, significant structural changes have occurred in the Australian economy. Before 1940, Australia depended on production of agricultural and mineral resources. Since World War II, Australia's economic development has been transformed from a resource-based economy to an industrial and service economy. The sudden isolation and demands of World War II caused the development of a wider industrial and manufacturing base. Coupled with economic diversification after 1945, a sustained immigration program provided labor for the rapid development of natural resources and an expanded domestic market.

The last two decades have seen structural adjustment in the Australian economy with changes in the relative importance of different sectors of the economy. These changes have generally corresponded with changes in most other developed countries. Marked growth has occurred in the service sector; its contribution to the gross domestic product (GDP) rose from 59 percent in the 1960s to 73 percent in 1985. The agricultural sector's contribution declined from 13 percent to 5 percent of the GDP in the same period.

Primary production contributed between 20 and 30 percent of Australia's production until the early 1950s. However, primary production accounts for only 10 percent of production in the 1980s, while manufacturing accounts for 18 percent of the gross domestic product (GDP). Australia remains a major producer of agricultural commodities such as wool, mutton, beef, veal, wheat, and sugar. It's also a leading supplier of industrial and energy-related commodities such as coal, alumina, refined lead, mineral sands, iron ore, nickel, and bauxite. More than 50 percent of all agricultural and industrial-based commodities are exported.

Despite the constraints of a small domestic market, Australia's manufacturing industry has benefited from political stability, generous natural resources, steady population growth, and substantial capital investment from within Australia and overseas.

Australia is part of the Pacific Basin group of countries that include New Zealand and many Southeast Asian nations, (Malaysia, Singapore, Hong Kong, and Indonesia). They have active trade arrangements whereby Australia supplies food, mineral resources, manufactured goods, and advanced technologies to neighboring countries. In exchange, Australian consumers and manufacturers receive the benefits of lower labor costs. Because of its active trade arrangements with the developed countries of Southeast Asia, Australia has an expanding economy diversified into service, industrial and manufacturing, mining and oil, energy, and agricultural sectors. In 1985, the GDP was A\$ 209,775 million; it has grown at a rate of 3 to 5 percent annually.

Australia has a broad industrial base that produces manufactured goods with advanced technology. The range of manufacturing includes: garments, food, electronics, household appliances, base metals, precision instruments, oil refining, and plastics.

Australia's manufacturing industry grew rapidly in the postwar period up to the 1960s but it declined in relative terms in the 1970s. Manufacturing contributes about 18 percent of the GDP and accounts for 17 percent of all employment.

Australia is a net exporter of energy. It has massive deposits of coal and uranium and large reserves of fossil fuels and natural gas. Federal and state governments control the exploration and development of coal, uranium, oil and gas, and mineral reserves.

Agriculture, including fishing and forestry, contributed 5.8 percent to the GDP and 42 percent of all exports. Australia is the world's largest producer of wool; wheat is the principal agricultural crop, and Australia is a major producer of cattle, sheep, and poultry.

Transportation is a major component of economic activity because of Australia's size and its scattered natural resources. Shipping fleets and airlines are owned by the government; road transportation is a private industry.

Australia ranked 19th in value of world trade in 1985. Its major trading partners are Japan, the United States, the European Community, ASEAN, New Zealand, and the United Kingdom. Japan is Australia's major export market. It accounts for 21 percent of Australia's rural exports, and 41 percent of all mineral, fuel, and metal exports. Japan also accounts for 75 percent of all iron ore exports and 65 percent of all coal exports. The United States and Japan are Australia's major suppliers of imported goods; each accounts for 22 percent of all imports. Because of the United Kingdom's entry into the European Economic Community (EEC), Australia's exports to the United Kingdom have declined from 9.7 percent to 5 percent.

Australia's major exports are coal and coke, cereals, sugar, wool, nonferrous metals, iron, and meats. Its primary imports are processed industrial goods, capital goods, transportation equipment, and fuels and lubricants.

MONEY AND BANKING

The Australian banking system is modeled on the British system. It is comprised of the Reserve Bank of Australia (the central bank), 14 trading and commercial banks, 11 savings banks, 3 specialist banks, 16 foreign banks, and various nonbank financial institutions. All nationally operated trading and savings banks are subject to reserve bank control; its control over bank liquidity is based on law. The lending ability of trading banks is influenced by a required percentage of deposits (statutory reserve deposits) that are kept with the reserve bank.

Reserve bank responsibilities include managing the note issue, regulating the Australian banking and monetary system, performing banking services for the government, and supervising Australia's international currency operations. There is no bank rate in Australia, but control over bank interest rates is vested in the reserve bank, which has a confidential lender of last resort rate. The reserve bank regulates financial system liquidity through various open-market operations.

FOREIGN EXCHANGE

As a result of deregulation in 1983, the Australian dollar floats freely against, and can be converted into, other currencies. All transactions involving the inflow of funds to Australia are free from foreign exchange control restrictions and formalities, except for interest-bearing investments from foreign governments, their agencies, and international organizations that undertake borrowing or other forms of capital raising in Australia. The range of outgoing foreign exchange transactions is subject to procedural requirements that meet the government's taxation screening policies.

THE SECURITIES MARKETS

Australia has six stock exchanges located in Sydney, Melbourne, Adelaide, Brisbane, Perth, and Hobart. They form the Australian Associated Stock Exchanges (AASE). All stock exchanges are members of the AASE, and they are regulated by the Securities Industry Act. Sydney has Australia's largest stock exchange and Melbourne the second largest. The Sydney and Melbourne exchanges account for 90 percent of total exchange turnover. In 1986, Australian markets ranked ninth in the world with total market capitalization of U.S. $ 72 billion.

The Sydney and Melbourne stock exchanges are linked by computer and a Reuters Economic Videomasters system. Major companies from all sectors are dually listed on the Sydney and Melbourne Exchanges. In recent years, there was speculation about a merger of the Sydney and Melbourne exchanges, but the idea waned as Australia's capital markets became deregulated in April 1984.

The Sydney and Melbourne exchanges operate a market information network called JECNET. JECNET collects and processes trading information about security dealings transacted on all capital city exchanges and gives this information to subscribers through computer terminals.

The stock exchanges are organized as private companies with no specific governmental regulation laws. The Australian Associated Stock Exchanges (AASE) secures uniformity regarding official listing requirements, commission rates, and ethics. Stock exchanges are registered with the National Companies and Security

Commission (NCSC). The right to deal on stock exchanges is granted to members who are Australian stockbroker firms. In 1986, there were 42 member firms on the Sydney exchange and 27 members on the Melbourne exchange. Member firms are organized either as partnerships or corporations. Banks and insurance companies enter the stockbrokerage business by owning no more than 50 percent of existing brokering firms' shares. Foreign ownership in Australian brokerage firms is limited to 50 percent, but this limit may be revised in subsequent years.

Stockbrokers act mainly as agents for their clients, but they can trade for their own accounts. All stock exchanges orders must be handled by members. Besides regular stockbrokers, there are brokers who specialize in handling odd-lot orders; they are called odd-lot specialists. These brokers accumulate odd-lot orders at a discount and then consolidate them into round lots for buying or selling at a premium.

There is significant offshore trading, with major business occurring on the stock exchanges in London and New York. Outside the formal markets, nearly 80 percent of all trading in debt securities is done off the stock exchange floor between members and banks.

The Australian financial markets became deregulated on April 2, 1984, after many years of negotiation with the Trade Practices Commission. The results of deregulation included: (1) brokerage commissions became fully negotiable, (2) corporate membership was permitted, and (3) the extent of ownership in stockbrokerage firms by banks, insurance companies, and foreign financial institutions was allowed to increase.

PRIMARY AND SECONDARY MARKETS IN EQUITIES

In the primary market, a company seeking official listing of its shares on the stock exchange must meet the AASE's official listing requirements. Australia has national listing. The securities of all listed companies are quoted on all six exchanges, and they are subject to common official listing requirements. The business rules of all exchanges are essentially identical.

Although the underwriting of new issues is handled by both stockbrokerage firms and merchant banks, each new listing must be sponsored by an AASE member. An industrial company seeking an official listing must have a minimum of A\$ 300,000 of shareholders' equity and 300 shareholders. A company won't be admitted to the official list unless it has established firm proposals for the investment and/or expenditure of at least 50 percent of the funds raised by a prospectus. The underwriting fee is generally 5 percent. The State Companies Act governs the constitution and administration of companies; their provisions must be met before an official listing will be approved.

New issues can be distributed as new floats, preemptive entitlements, and private placements to institutions. These are methods of raising capital where existing shareholders may buy new shares in the company, usually below the current market price. Shares to existing shareholders can be distributed at a predetermined ratio through a rights issue, an entitlement issue, or a bonus issue.

In the secondary market, shares may be traded both on and off the exchange floor through personal contact or by telephone between members. All off-the-floor transactions are made at prices based on prices recorded on the floor; they must be reported immediately to the exchange. All securities can be dealt off the exchange floor.

THE PRIMARY AND SECONDARY MARKETS IN DEBT SECURITIES

In the primary market, most Australian corporate bonds are issued through public offerings underwritten by stockbrokerage firms. Commonwealth government bonds are tendered by federal and state governments and their agencies. They are regulated by the Australian Loan Council. Interest payments are made semiannually. There are a few offerings of unlisted corporate bonds.

In the secondary market, listed government and corporate debt securities are traded on the exchanges through members acting as agents or principals. In addition, and in contrast to the secondary equity market, commercial banks and investment banking institutions operate an unofficial secondary market in government debt securities outside the exchanges. Short-term marketable debt securities are traded by commercial banks and investment banking firms on the unofficial secondary market.

THE AUSTRALIAN OPTIONS MARKET

The Australian Options Market was founded in 1976 as a division of the Sydney Stock Exchange. The options market is administered by the Options Clearing House Pty., Ltd. (OCH). The OCH is a wholly owned subsidiary of the Sydney Stock Exchange that registers all domestically traded option contracts on the options market. The OCH is a clearinghouse for all options transactions except options traded on the International Options Market (IOM).

The underlying securities on which options are traded are selected by the exchange. Currently, put and call options are listed on 11 Australian companies that comprise some of the largest and most actively traded securities on the exchange. They include: Australia and New Zealand Banking Group, Broken Hill Proprietary Company, Bougainville Copper, CRA, CSR, Energy Resources of Australia, Elders IXL, MIM Holdings, Santos, Westpac Banking Corporation, Western Mining Corporation Holdings, and Woodside Petroleum. An option contract represents 1,000 shares of the underlying security.

In 1985, the Australian Options Market became international when it entered the IOM and formed trading and clearing linkages with the European Options Exchange in Amsterdam, and the Montreal and Vancouver Stock Exchanges in Canada. Initially, trading has been limited to gold, silver, and selected foreign currencies, but it may expand to include other instruments. With the international linkage, it will be possible for investors to continually trade options on selected instruments because the exchanges' electronic linkage spans a 24-hour time zone. When trading ceases on one exchange, the "order book" is transmitted to the next exchange's opening and so on throughout the world. All internationally traded options are administered through the International Options Clearing Corporation (IOCC). Refer to Chapter 16 for more information on these options markets.

Unlike trading in securities, options are traded by competitive market makers called registered traders who act as principals or agents for clients. A registered trader is required by the exchange to provide a continuous and orderly market in option trading and is obligated to make a market in at least one contract when called upon. Registered traders must also maintain appropriate price relationships among the option series for each stock they deal in.

FIGURE 15.2   All Shares Ordinary Index

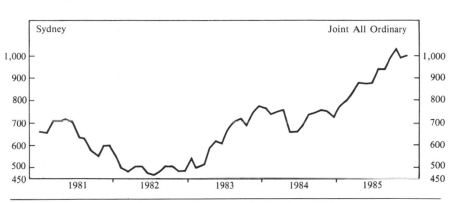

SOURCE: *Euromoney Yearbook*, Euromoney Publications, 1986.

TAXATION

There is a 15 percent withholding tax on cash dividends. Stock dividends in the form of bonus shares are tax-free if they are paid solely out of a company's annual surplus. A 10 percent withholding tax is levied on interest payments. Capital gains aren't subject to withholding taxes if the securities are held longer than 12 months; otherwise, they are taxed as short-term profits.

STOCK MARKET INDEX

The ASE All Ordinaries Share Price Index is the most quoted index. It is a sample of 260 companies covering nearly 90 percent of Australian market capitalization. The base value is 500 as of January 1, 1980. See Figure 15.2. Table 15.1 lists 10 of the largest capitalized companies in Australia. They are included in the ASE All Ordinaries Index.

THE SYDNEY STOCK EXCHANGE

Although its origins date to 1871, the present Sydney Stock Exchange was incorporated in 1964 as a public company. The need for a stock exchange grew out of Sydney's rapid development as a financial and commercial center during the second half of the 19th

TABLE 15.1 Selected Information on the 10 Largest Companies by Market Capitalization as of April 25, 1986

Company	Business	U.S.$ Million	Percent Total
Broken Hill Prop.	Energy sources	6,835	9.5
CRA	Nonferrous metals	2,368	3.3
Westpac	Banking	2,319	3.2
Coles Myer	Merchandizing	1,966	2.7
ANZ Group Holdings	Banking	1,838	2.6
News Corp	Publishing	1,714	2.4
Nat'l. Aust. Bank	Banking	1,649	2.3
Boral	Building materials	1,363	1.9
CSR	Multi-industry	1,264	1.8
Pacific Dunlop	Multi-industry	2,430	1.5
Totals		U.S.$ 22,383	31.2%

Total stock market capitalization U.S.$ 72 billion

SOURCE: Morgan Stanley Capital International Perspective, Geneva, Switzerland.

century. Members of the stock exchange own and administer it; however, they must meet stringent financial and certification qualifications. The exchange seeks to break even or operate at a small surplus. Each year, the membership elects a committee of 10 including a chairman, vice chairman, and treasurer who administer the exchange.

In 1984, the exchange had listed 1,457 equity securities and 2,390 debt securities. The official list was comprised of 633 industrial companies, 327 mining and Oil companies, and 40 public utilities.

The exchange plans to install an automated trading system (ATS) for automatic execution of orders in selected stocks up to a predetermined volume. The automated market system (AMT) will provide electronic maintenance and execution of odd-lot orders, small parcels, and fixed-interest and unlisted debt securities.

Types of Securities Traded

Securities traded on the exchange include: ordinary and preference shares, rights, warrants, convertible bonds, debentures, corporate bonds, government bonds, and semigovernment bonds.

Trading Hours

The exchange is open Monday through Friday. Official hours for trading on the floor are from 10 A.M. to 12:15 P.M. and from 2 P.M. to 3:15 P.M.

Commissions

Commissions are fully negotiable between buyers and sellers.

Clearance and Settlements

A centralized clearinghouse system is being developed to clear and settle transactions from broker to broker. Cash transactions must be settled within 10 business days. A system of forward dealing allows clients to buy securities on margin and settle the transaction within six weeks. Australian brokers can't accept a client's order to sell short, and an Australian broker can't sell short to a client.

THE SYDNEY FUTURES EXCHANGE

The Sydney Futures Exchange (SFE) is a separate organization from the Sydney Stock Exchange and the AASE. The SFE was founded in 1960 as a central market to trade wool futures. During its early years, it was known as the Sydney Greasy Wool Futures Exchange, but it changed its name in 1972 to the Sydney Futures Exchange.

Over the years, the SFE has evolved into a financial futures exchange that lists a variety of futures and futures option contracts on commodities, precious metals, stock indexes, and Australian Treasury securities. Trading practices, margining procedures, clearing, and settlement are similar to U.S. exchanges, except that both long and short positions in options on futures are marginable. In the United States, options on futures are only marginable on the short positions; long (purchased) options must be paid for in cash. Cash settlement is permitted by the SFE on certain contracts instead of physical delivery of the underlying asset.

In 1985, the SFE established trading and settlement linkages with the Commodity Exchange of New York (COMEX) to trade dually listed and fungible futures and options contracts. These trading and settlement linkages set the stage for 24-hour trading of gold futures and options contracts.

The SFE's membership includes individuals, partnerships, brokerage firms, and banks. Exchange membership is divided into three categories: floor members, local members, and full associate members. Floor members may deal on the exchange floor for themselves or for their clients. Local members may deal on the exchange floor only for their own account. Full associates may deal off the exchange floor for clients or for their own accounts. All contracts must be traded on the exchange floor and be registered and cleared through the International Commodity Clearing House (ICCH). Since May 1985, the SFE has been phasing in options on bank-accepted bills, U.S. dollars, and the ASA Ordinary Share Index.

TABLE 15.2   Contract Specifications for Selected Contracts

Futures Contracts	Contract Size
All Ordinaries Share Price Index	100 × ASE Index
90-day bank-accepted bills	A$ 500,000
U.S. dollars	U.S.$ 100,000
Two-year Commonwealth Treasury bonds	A$ 200,000
10-year Commonwealth Treasury bonds	A$ 100,000
Gold	50 troy ounces
Silver	1,000 troy ounces

Options are available on the: 90-day bank-accepted bills, All Ordinaries Share Price Index, and U.S. dollars futures contracts. If these contracts are successful, more options contracts will be listed for trading.

TABLE 15.3   Futures Contracts for the All Ordinaries Share Price Index, 90-Day Bank-Accepted Bills, and U.S. Dollars

All Ordinaries Share Price Index
Contract Unit:
A sum of money equal to 100 times the Australian Stock Exchanges All Ordinaries Share Price Index expressed as dollars.
Cash Settlement Price:
The closing quotation for the Australian Stock Exchanges All Ordinaries Share Price Index on the business day prior to the last day of trading; it's calculated to one decimal place.
Mandatory Cash Settlement:
All brought and sold contracts at the close of trading in the contract month are settled by the clearinghouse at the index value for cash settlement.
Quotations:
Prices are quoted in the same form as the ASE All Ordinaries Share Price Index expressed to one decimal place, with a minimum fluctuation of 0.1 index point (equal to $10 per contract).
Contract Months:
March, June, September, and December up to 18 months ahead.
Termination of Trading:
The second to last business day of the contract month. Trading ceases at noon.

90-Day Bank-Accepted Bills
Contract Unit:
$A 500,000 face value of 90-day bank-accepted bills of exchange.
Standard Delivery:
Five 90-day bank-accepted bills each with a face value of $100,000, or one 90-day bank-accepted bill with a face value of $500,000, maturing 85–95 days from settlement day.
Quotations:
100 minus the annual percentage yield to the second decimal place. (The minimum fluctuation of 0.01 percent equals approximately $11 per contract varying with interest rates.)
Delivery Months:
Spot month plus the next six consecutive calendar months, then March, June, September, and December up to two years ahead.
Termination of Trading:
The Wednesday prior to the second Friday of the delivery month. Trading on this day ceases at noon.
Settlement Day:
The second Friday of the delivery month.

TABLE 15.3 *(concluded)*

U.S. Dollars
Contract Unit:
$U.S. 100,000.
Cash Settlement Rate:
The U.S. dollar hedge settlement rate of exchange (converted to Australian dollars per one U.S. dollar and calculated to the nearest 0.0001 Australian dollar per U.S. dollar) displayed by Australian Associated Press-Reuters Economic Services on its monitor on the morning of that day. If no such rate is calculated and disseminated by AAP-Reuters, the settlement rate is the rate provided that morning to the Australian Bankers Association by the chairman bank of the Australian Bankers Association.
Mandatory Cash Settlement:
All bought and sold contracts at the close of trading are settled by the clearinghouse at the cash settlement rate of exchange.
Quotations:
Prices are quoted in Australian dollars per U.S. dollar in multiples of 0.0001 Australian dollar (equal to $10 per contract).
Contract Months:
Each successive calendar month up to 12 months ahead.
Termination of Trading:
The third Wednesday of the contract month. Trading ceases at noon.

SOURCE: Sydney Futures Exchange.

TABLE 15.4   Two-Year and 10-Year Commonwealth Treasury Bond Futures Contracts

Two-Year Commonwealth Treasury Bonds
Contract Unit:
Commonwealth government Treasury bonds with a face value of $200,000, a nominal coupon rate of 10 percent per annum and a term to maturity of two years, no tax rebate allowed.
Cash Settlement Price:
The arithmetic mean on the last day of trading of yields to two decimal places provided by 12 dealers, brokers, and banks, at which they would buy and sell Treasury bonds as described in the contract specifications, excluding the two highest buying and the two lowest selling quotations.
Mandatory Cash Settlement:
All bought and sold contracts in existence at the close of trading in the contract month are settled by the clearinghouse at the cash settlement price.
Quotations:
Prices are quoted in yield per annum per 100 dollars face value in multiples of 0.01 percent. For quotation purposes, the yield is deducted from 100. (The minimum fluctuation of 0.01 percent equals approximately $34 per contract, varying with interest rates.)
Contract Months:
March, June, September, and December up to 24 months ahead.
Termination of Trading:
The fifteenth day of the cash settlement month or the next succeeding business day where the fifteenth day is not a business day. Trading ceases at noon.

10-Year Commonwealth Treasury Bonds
Contract Unit:
Commonwealth government Treasury bonds with a face value of $100,000, a nominal coupon rate of 12 percent per annum and a term to maturity of 10 years, no tax rebate allowed.
Cash Settlement Price:
The arithmetic mean on the last day of trading of yields to two decimal places provided by 12 dealers, brokers, and banks, at which they would buy and sell Treasury bonds as described in the contract specifications, excluding the two highest buying and the two lowest selling quotations.
Mandatory Cash Settlement:
All bought and sold contracts in existence at the close of trading in the contract month are settled by the clearinghouse at the cash settlement price.
Quotations:
Prices are quoted in yield per annum per 100 dollars face value in multiples of 0.01 percent. For quotation purposes, the yield is deducted from 100. (The minimum fluctuation of 0.01 percent equals approximately $60 per contract, varying with interest rates.)
Contract Months:
March, June, September, and December up to 12 months ahead.
Termination of Trading:
The fifteenth day of the cash settlement month or the next succeeding business day where the fifteenth day is not a business day. Trading ceases at noon.

SOURCE: Sydney Futures Exchange.

TABLE 15.5 Silver and Gold Futures Contracts

Silver

Contract Unit:

One thousand fine troy ounces of silver.

Standard Delivery:

The equivalent of one thousand troy ounces (50 ounces more or less) assaying not less than 999 parts per thousand fine silver, cast in not more than two bars by an approved refiner.

Quotations:

In multiples of one cent per troy ounce (equal to $10 per contract).

Delivery Months:

March, June, September, and December up to 24 months ahead.

Termination of Trading:

The twenty-first day of the delivery month, or if this is not a business day, the business day prior. On this day, spot month prices may not exceed a price five percent above the previous trading day's Comex spot settlement price converted at the reigning currency hedge market settlement price for U.S. dollars. Trading ceases at noon.

Gold

Contract Unit:

Fifty fine troy ounces.

Standard Delivery:

The equivalent of 50 troy ounces (five percent more or less) assaying not less than 995 parts per thousand fine gold, cast in bars by an approved refiner.

Quotations:

In Australian dollars in multiples of 10 cents per troy ounce (equal to $5 per contract).

Delivery Months:

March, June, September, and December up to 24 months ahead.

Termination of Trading:

The twenty-second day of the delivery month or, if this is not a business day, the business day prior. Trading ceases at noon.

SOURCE: Sydney Futures Exchange.

CHAPTER SIXTEEN

The Kingdom of the Netherlands

The Kingdom of the Netherlands comprises the Netherlands and the Netherlands Antilles (also called the Dutch West Indies), islands located in the Caribbean. The Netherlands is a small but densely populated country in Northern Europe situated on the North Sea. West Germany borders the Netherlands on the east, and Belgium is the southern neighbor. More than half the country lies below sea level, and it requires the maintenance of an extensive system of dams, dikes, and pumping installations to keep the land dry. Nearly 60 percent of the population lives in low-lying areas of the country. The Netherlands covers an area of 16,185 square miles. In 1985, the population was 14.5 million. Amsterdam is the capital and financial center of the country.

Dutch is the official language of the Netherlands, but English and German are widely understood. Even though the guilder (G) is the official currency, the Dutch florin (DFl.) is also used in commercial transactions. One Dutch florin equals one guilder. The terms are interchangable. See Figure 16.1.

GOVERNMENT

The Netherlands is a constitutional monarchy with a parliamentary system. The central power is vested in the Crown (the monarch and the government) and the States General. The States General (Parliament) is comprised of two chambers. The Upper Chamber has 75 members who are elected by the provincial councils. The

---

FIGURE 16.1   Exchange Rate for Dutch Guilders

SOURCE: The Federal Reserve Bank of St. Louis.

Lower Chamber has 150 members who are elected directly by the Dutch people. The Upper Chamber has the legislative power to approve or reject bills, but it can't initiate them or amend them. The Lower Chamber has the right to amend bills and the right to propose legislation.

Together with the sovereign and the ministers, Parliament forms the legislature. Executive power rests with the sovereign and the ministers. The monarch has only nominal powers, although he or she has a role in times of government crisis. The seat of government is in The Hague.

The sovereign appoints the ministers on recommendation of the *formateur*, usually the person who will become the prime minister. The parties forming the government divide the total number of ministerial posts in proportion to the number of seats they occupy in the States General. Ministers form the Council of Ministers to coordinate government policy.

The country has three principal parties; the Christian Democrat Appeal (CDA) is the leading party. The Labour Party (PvdA) and the People's Party for Freedom and Democracy (VVD) are the other major parties.

The Council of State is the highest advisory body; its views on every bill must be heard. The sovereign, as head of state, is the president. The council, consisting of 28 members, advises the monarch, gives an opinion on draft bills, and has jurisdiction over disputes between state agencies.

The Netherlands is a member of the European Community (EC) and Benelux. Belgium, Luxembourg, and the Netherlands form the a queen's commissioner. The members of the provincial councils elect members of the Upper Chamber of the States General.

INTERNATIONAL RELATIONS

The Netherlands is a member of the European Community (EC) and Benelux. Belgium, Luxembourg, and the Netherlands form the economic union of Benelux, which was formed for total economic integration among the three countries. The Treaty of Benelux Economic Union became effective in 1960, and it is a model for the European Community's goal of creating genuine internal markets for the exchange of goods and services.

THE ECONOMY

The Netherlands is one of the richest nations in the world with a per capita income of $8,500. The basis for prosperity is industry, which developed rapidly in the postwar period. Shipping and foreign trade are important components of the economy. Over 70 percent of all exports are industrial products shipped to Western Europe. Rotterdam is one of the busiest ports in the world. Even though the Netherlands lacks many natural resources, it has abundant supplies of natural gas and fossil fuels.

Through an ambitious land reclamation program that began in the 13th century, the country has expanded its area of inhabitable lands by 20 percent by damming and pumping ocean water from land below sea level. These reclaimed areas of sea, known as *polders,* are used for intensive farming and construction of new communities. Because over 50 percent of the Netherlands is below sea level, water and flood control management are essential priorities for the Dutch government.

The Delta and Zuyderzee projects are modern engineering feats of water control and land reclamation. Reclamation of fertile land from the sea has helped the Netherlands become self-sufficient in producing food. Fishing is still an important part of the economy.

Apart from the energy sector, mining is confined to quarrying and extracting salt in the eastern and northern districts of the country.

Energy is a major sector of the economy, and it is based on the production of crude oil and natural and liquified gases. Royal Dutch Petroleum is the second largest oil company in the world. It makes a significant contribution to the country's export earnings.

The Netherlands is self-sufficient in meeting energy needs. The government is active in implementing energy policy in the Netherlands. As half-owner of Gasunie, it controls the supply of natural gas to domestic and export markets. Gasunie was formed in 1963 after the discovery of the huge gas fields at Schlochtern in the northern part of the country.

In 1985, energy supplies were as follows: natural gas, 48 percent; oil, 38 percent; coal, 9 percent; and nuclear energy, 1.8 percent. Energy-related products accounted for 22 percent of all exports. Petroleum-based products such as base chemicals, paints, and plastics accounted for 18 percent of all exports.

The Dutch economy has benefited greatly from the establishment of the European Economic Community (EEC), which allowed for easy export of agricultural and industrial products to member countries. Recently, the Netherlands has become a net exporter to the EEC. The removal of trade barriers within the EEC and consequent competition has stimulated Dutch industry and promoted industrial expansion. In 1985, Dutch exports of food, beverage, and tobacco products accounted for 22 percent of total exports.

The service sector, private and public, accounts for over 58 percent of total gross domestic product (GDP). As the economy has become increasingly developed, the service sector provides more jobs. The service sector employs 60 percent of the labor force; the industrial sector employs 31 percent, and the agriculture sector employs 6 percent.

The Netherlands exports over 72 percent of its goods and services to the European Community (EC), and it imports 56 percent of its goods from the EC. West Germany, Belgium, Luxembourg, France, the United Kingdom, and the United States are important trading partners.

In the postwar period, the Dutch government encouraged joint cooperation of industry and multinational firms to rebuild the economy and reduce unemployment. Consequently, large international firms have their headquarters and manufacturing plants in the Netherlands.

In 1982, the Dutch government created the MIP Equity Fund to attract high-tech industries to the Netherlands. It is the world's largest venture capital fund. The state owns 57 percent of the fund; the remaining 43 percent is held by private financial institutions. The MIP fund seeks electrical engineering, semiconductor, and computer companies that will establish companies in the Netherlands.

MONEY AND BANKING

De Nederlandsche Bank, founded in 1814, is the central bank and issuer of banknotes for the Netherlands. The bank was nationalized in 1948. The central bank acts as the state's bank, banker's bank, and lender of last resort. Its monetary policy instruments include the bank rate, an open-market policy, intervention in the foreign exchange market, fixing reserve requirements, and monitoring the credit conditions of financial institutions. Since 1982, the central bank has continued a system of credit monitoring with state and private banks. Nonresidents have free access to the country's capital markets.

The banking system is comprised of commercial banks, cooperative banks, savings banks, mortgage banks, and two government-owned PTT institutions—the Postal Cheque and Giro Service, and the State Postal Savings Bank. Dutch banks are permitted to be members of the Amsterdam Stock Exchange and to underwrite securities. Two large commercial banks, AMRO and ABN, underwrite most new issues.

THE AMSTERDAM STOCK EXCHANGE (ASE)

The Amsterdam Stock Exchange (ASE) is one of the oldest exchanges in the world. During the unparalleled expansion in commerce, shipping, and trade that occurred in the late 16th century and the early 17th century, funds flowed to Amsterdam's financial markets. This period saw the development of merchant banking, which financed shipping and trade between nations and their colonies.

Against this background of developing money and capital markets, the stock exchange played a modest role. Only when the United East India Company and the Dutch West India Company, were established in the early 1600s did the structure and role of the modern stock exchange take its present form. Shares in these companies were issued to investors and traded at an exchange. The companies held physical certificates for shareholders. They were transferable between buyers and sellers at the exchange.

The Amsterdam Stock Exchange, founded in 1876 as a private association, is the sole stock exchange in the Netherlands. The Stock Exchange handles all trading of Dutch securities, and it is administered by the Vereniging voor de Effectenhandel (VVDE). The VVDE has a guarantee fund and several committees that regulate the conduct of members.

The ASE has an international orientation because there are more foreign than domestic shares traded on the exchange; many are U.S. company shares. The ASE has a reputation of innovation that includes:

1. Starting a program known as the Amsterdam Security Account System (ASAS) for trading the original shares (not depository receipts) of foreign companies in their respective currencies. No physical handling of certificates is required. All settlements and transfers are done by book entry. Transactions involving selected American, British, and Japanese securities can be settled through ASAS.
2. Creating a parallel market, which offers small and medium-sized companies easier access to capital markets.
3. Developing a market for trading odd-lot Eurobonds. These transactions use less than U.S.$ 100,000 cleared through the ASAS.
4. Initiating and creating a communications system, known as the Interbourse Data Information System, in which European bourses can electronically exchange trading data.
5. Creation of a new trading system known as the Amsterdam Interprofessional Market System (AIM). Banks and brokers

are allowed to negotiate with clients on a net basis (without charging a commission). The transactions must relate to shares or bonds quoted on the official market and have a value of at least Dfl. 1 million for shares and Dfl. 2.5 million for bonds. Transactions between banks and brokers must be channeled through the *hoekman* on the central market; it links AIM and the existing market. The *hoekman* is a member of the stock exchange who acts as an intermediary between banks and stockbrokers. He can act both as agent and as a dealer for his own account but can not deal with public investors.

In 1978, the first European Options Exchange (EOE) was created to trade American-style put and call options on Dutch shares, precious metals, currencies, and Dutch government bonds. The EOE has clearing linkages with the Montreal Stock Exchange, the Vancouver Stock Exchange, and the Sydney Stock Exchange for trading and settling fungible options. No financial futures market exists in the Netherlands.

Bond and equity trading occurs on one of three markets in the Netherlands:

1. The official market, which lists over 2,000 companies.
2. The parallel market, started in 1982, where approximately 50 companies are listed.
3. The unofficial market, which is relatively inactive.

PRIMARY MARKETS

Banks underwrite and manage equity and bond issues. A bank can take over or guarantee an entire issue. Alternatively, a bank can act as a selling agent and leave the underwriting risk to the company. The offering price is negotiated between the lead underwriter and the issuer.

All proposed bond issues, except for convertible bonds, must be registered with De Nederlandisha Bank. The central bank maintains a calendar of issues and determines the ones to be issued; the central bank also approves the issuance of shares. Applications for admission to official listing must be made by a member of the stock exchange. Formal ministerial approval is required for listing shares on the official and parallel markets.

SECONDARY MARKET

All firms trading in securities listed on the official and parallel markets must be ASE members, and if they aren't VVDE members, they must be licensed under the Securities Trades Act.

Banks and brokers are obliged to place all orders through *hoekmannen,* who function as competing market makers in certain securities. *Hoekmannen* can trade for their own accounts, but they can't deal with the public. They are not obligated to trade under all market conditions as a specialist would be.

TAXATION

A 25 percent withholding tax is applicable to cash dividends paid to nonresidents and residents. Capital gains on equities and debt securities aren't subject to a withholding tax. There is no withholding tax on interest paid on bonds and interest-bearing accounts. The Netherlands has double taxation treaties with many countries.

TABLE 16.1 Selected Information on the 10 Largest Companies by Market Capitalization on the Amsterdam Stock Exchange as of April 25, 1986.

Company	Business	U.S.$ Million	Percent Total
Royal Dutch Pet.	Petroleum	20,966	34.4
Philips	Electrical	5,604	9.2
Unilever	Food processing	5,588	9.2
Nationale-Nederland	Banking	3,523	5.8
AKZO	Banking	2,709	4.4
ABN Bank	Banking	1,975	3.2
AMRO Bank	Banking	1,934	3.2
AMEV	Banking	1,800	3.0
Heineken	Beverages	1,713	2.8
AEGON	Insurance	1,484	2.4
Totals		U.S.$ 47,296	77.6%

Total stock market capitalization U.S.$ 61 billion

SOURCE: Morgan Stanley Capital International Perspective, Geneva, Switzerland.

FIGURE 16.2   ANP/CBS General Index

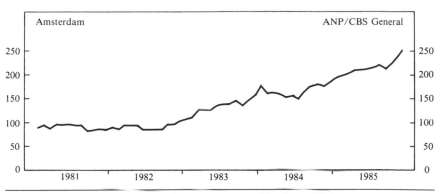

SOURCE: Euromoney Yearbook, Euromoney Publications, 1986.

STOCK EXCHANGE INDEX

The ANP/CBS General Index is the primary stock exchange index most frequently quoted. Large international corporations comprise nearly 50 percent of the index's weighting. Table 16.1 lists the 10 largest companies in the Netherlands that are included in the ANP/CBS General Index. See Figure 16.2.

GENERAL INFORMATION ON THE AMSTERDAM STOCK EXCHANGE

Stock Exchange Authorities

The Stock Exchange Association is governed by a council of 17 members. Five council members are independent nonmembers of the exchange; the remaining 12 represent member firms. There are 147 member firms representing banks, brokers, and *hoekmannen* firms. The main Dutch banks are exchange members. There are two categories of members: (1) banks and brokers and (2) *hoekmannen*. *Hoekmannen* are competing market makers who don't deal with the public. They act as intermediaries between banks and brokers. *Hoekmannen* trade all securities in both official and parallel markets.

Trading Hours

The exchange is open Monday through Friday. Official trading occurs in two sessions: The first session lasts from 10 A.M to 4:30 P.M. During the first session, securities will be quoted and traded continuously. The second session lasts from 4:30 P.M. to 10 P.M. From 4:30 P.M. until the closing of the New York Stock Exchange, transactions can be made in the following international securities: AKZO, KLM, Philips, Royal Dutch Pet, and Unilever.

Types of Securities

Types of Securities	Official Market	Parallel Market
Dutch bonds	1,296	2
Foreign bonds	155	1
Dutch shares	214	32
Dutch shares in investment companies	45	10
Foreign shares in investment companies	25	1

Types of Orders

The following orders are acceptable on the exchange with respect to price and time:

Order at Best Price.   If executed, the customer receives the full execution at the next price quoted after receipt of the order.
Limited order.   No purchase can be made above a specified price. No sale can be made below a specified price.
Sans Forcer Order.   The broker or bank has the right to determine the method of execution in installments and completion time.
Stop-Loss Order.   A stop-loss order is executed at any price as soon as the price limit is reached.
Yield Order.   Yield orders are executed at a price where a given, prearranged yield is obtained.
Day Order.   A day order is valid for the day only.
Standing Order.   A standing order is valid until a specified cancellation time, which is usually until the end of the next month.

Clearing and Settlement

Settlement of bond and equity transactions requires delivery within 10 days of the commitment. Margin trading isn't permitted, but customers can make loans from financial institutions using securities as collateral.

Transaction Costs

Commission charges range from 0.36 percent to 1.5 percent of the market value for bonds. Commissions for shares can range from 0.7 to 1.5 percent of the market value. For transactions in shares exceeding Dfl. 1 million, commissions are negotiable. For transactions in bonds exceeding Dfl. 2.5 million, commissions are negotiable.

Stamp Duty

Stamp duty is levied on purchases and sales of securities at a rate of 0.12 percent. The maximum is limited to Dfl. 1,200 per transaction.

THE EUROPEAN OPTIONS EXCHANGE (EOE) (EUROPESE OPTIEBEURS)

The European Options Exchange (EOE) was founded in 1978, and it is the world's fifth largest options exchange. The Amsterdam Stock Exchange (ASE) provided a large part of the initial capital to create the EOE, although the EOE is independent of the ASE. The EOE was modeled after the Chicago Board Options Exchange (CBOE) in that American-style put and call options are traded and standardized according to size, strike prices, and expiration dates. The expiration months run in three-, six-, and nine-month cycles. The maximum life of any option is nine months. Equity options cover 100 shares of the underlying stock and they are priced in Dutch guilders. The exception is Petrofina, which covers 10 shares and is priced in Belgian francs. The options can be traded and exercised at any time.

The EOE lists 32 classes of options on selected Dutch shares, foreign shares, Dutch government bonds, foreign currencies, and gold and silver options. Options trading on 16 listed stocks accounted for 80 percent of the total turnover. The EOE has its own stock index, which is based on 15 underlying Dutch stocks listed on the EOE.

Trading is conducted Monday through Friday from 8 A.M. to 2:30 P.M. Each option class has a pit with two video terminals; one displays calls and the other displays puts. Information is displayed on current options being traded, the previous close, and information about the underlying instrument. Options expire on the third Friday of the expiration month.

The EOE uses the market-maker system for executing orders. Orders are filled by open outcry on the trading floor by competing market makers. Market makers can trade for customer accounts and their own accounts. Limit orders are handled by the EOE, and order-book officials execute trades when the market matches the limit price.

The EOE was the first exchange to establish an electronic linkage with the Montreal Stock Exchange, the Vancouver Stock Exchange, and the Sydney Stock Exchange for trading, clearing, and settling trades in gold, silver, and currency options. Investors can trade the same contract on all four exchanges 20 hours a day; they can open a position in one market and close it in another market. A limit order can be carried forward through time zones until it is filled. The International Options Clearing Corporation (IOCC) clears trades on the four exchanges. See Figure 16.3.

The EOE intends to expand the number of listed options and clearing linkages with other option exchanges. For example, a linkage between the American Stock Exchange (AMEX) and the EOE may be established to trade options on the Major Market Index (MMI) that are currently listed on the AMEX. The details of this relationship are unclear.

FIGURE 16.3   Clearing Linkages between the Option Exchanges

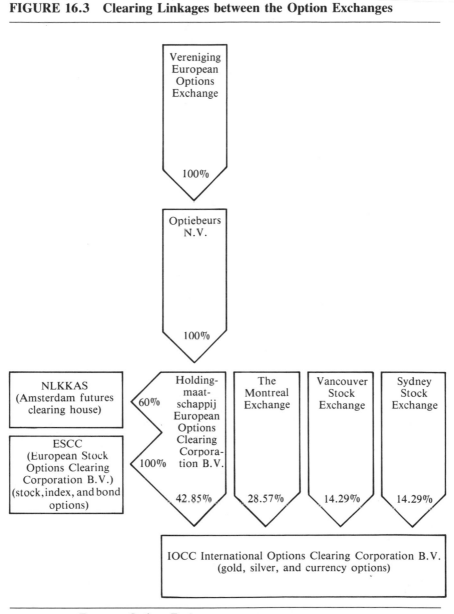

SOURCE: European Options Exchange.

TABLE 16.2   Contract Specifications

Equities	*Unit of Trading*
Algemene Bank Nederland	100 shares per option unless otherwise
Aegon	specified
Ahold	
Akzo	
Amsterdam-Rotterdam Bank	
Gist-Brocades	
Heineken	
Hoogoves	
KLM	
Nationale Nederlanden	
Philips	
Royal Dutch/Shell	
Robeco	
Unilever	
Petrofina	10 shares
Elsevier	
Amev	
Nedloyd	

Precious Metals	*Unit of Trading*
Gold	10 troy ounces in dollars
Silver	250 troy ounces in dollars

Currencies	*Unit of Trading*	
Dollar/Guilder	$	10,000 in guilders
Dollar/deutsche mark	$	10,000 in marks
Pound/dollar	£	12,500 in dollars
Pound/dollar	£	100,000 in dollars
Pound/guilder	£	10,000 in guilders
ECU/dollar	ECU	10,000 in dollars

Dutch Government Bonds	*Unit of Trading*
12 ¾ % State Loan 1981	Fl 10,000 nominal value;
11 ¼ % State Loan 1982	10 bonds of Fl 1,000
9 ½ % State Loan 1983	
8 ½ % State Loan 1984-I	
8 ½ % State Loan 1984-II	
7 ½ % State Loan 1983-I	

SOURCE: European Options Exchange.

The Scandinavian Countries

Scandinavia is comprised of five countries: Sweden, Norway, Finland, Denmark, and Iceland. Although there are five Scandinavian countries, only four have an economic base covered in this book. Sweden, Norway, Finland, and Denmark all have their own stock exchanges. All four countries have strong political and economic ties to each other. Norway and Finland were once part of Sweden. The most dominant country in the Scandinavian group is Sweden, which will be our primary focus. We will also compare the economies, political systems, and financial markets of Norway, Finland, and Denmark. The official currencies of Scandinavia are: the Swedish krona (SEK), Danish krone (DKK), Norwegian krone (NOK), and Finnish markka (FIM). See Figure 17.1.

THE KINGDOM OF SWEDEN

The Kingdom of Sweden is the fourth largest country in Europe covering an area of 173,800 square miles. The population is approximately 8.3 million. Over 30 percent of the population is concentrated in the cities of Stockholm, Göteborg, and Malmö. Stockholm is the capital and financial center. The Swedish people enjoy one of the highest standards of living in the world. Sweden occupies the eastern part of the Scandinavian peninsula; it shares a boundary with Norway on the west and Finland on the east.

Sweden is a mountainous land covered with dense forests. Timber is an important export commodity. Only 8 percent of the

FIGURE 17.1   Exchange Rate for the Swedish Krona

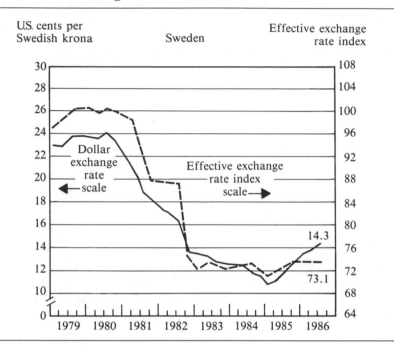

SOURCE: Federal Reserve Bank of St. Louis.

land is used for farming The country is agriculturally self-sufficient. Sweden lacks fossil fuel resources, but it has abundant supplies of iron ore, uranium, and minerals. Sweden's electrical energy is supplied by hydroelectric plants.

GOVERNMENT

Sweden is a constitutional monarchy. The country is ruled by a parliamentary form of government. Under the Constitution of 1975, the *Riksdag* is the sole governing body. The prime minister presides over the *Riksdag* and its 349 members, who are elected for three-year terms. Sweden's major political parties are the Social Democrats, the Conservative Party, the Center Party, the Liberal Party, and the Communist Party.

Sweden's government fosters an extensive welfare system supported by high taxes levied on individuals and business. The central and local governments employ 33 percent of the workforce in administering government and social welfare programs; this is a severe financial drain on the economy.

INTERNATIONAL RELATIONS

Sweden is a member of numerous international organizations that promote economic cooperation. It is a member of the European Economic Community (EEC), the European Free Trade Association (EFTA), the Organization for Economic Cooperation and Development (OECD), the United Nations, the International Monetary Fund (IMF), the General Agreement on Tariffs and Trade (GATT), and the North Atlantic Treaty Organization (NATO).

THE ECONOMY

Historically, Sweden's economy has been severely affected by crude oil prices. Low oil prices are a boon to the Swedish economy. The country must import all oil and most of its coal. The only natural energy supply is hydroelectric power, which is insufficient to meet the burgeoning demands of a highly technological society.

Sweden's economy depends heavily on foreign trade, especially the exports of motor vehicles, machinery, electrical products, wood products, and pulp and paper goods. Imports and exports account for 30 percent of the gross domestic product (GDP). Sweden exports 47 percent of all its goods to the European Community (EC) and imports 54 percent of its goods from the EC. The European Free Trade Association (EFTA), West Germany, the United Kingdom, the United States, and other Scandinavian countries are important trading partners.

In recent years, a dramatic shift has occurred in industrial production away from traditional industries such as pulp production and shipbuilding to more technological industries such as chemicals, pharmaceuticals, and engineering. The engineering industry exports more than 50 percent of its production. The electrical products group, which includes telecommunications, household appliances, and electrical generators and engines, accounts for nearly 10 percent of value added by all manufacturing.

The chemical and plastics industries account for 9 percent of total value added by all manufacturing. Growth has been strong in pharmaceuticals, organic chemicals, and plastics. Sweden is a net importer of chemicals and plastics. Sweden manufactures explosives, bleaches for cellulose, fertilizers, paints, and bulk chemicals.

Although Sweden is a free-trade state, there is significant government involvement in certain private-sector enterprises. Swedish shipbuilding was nationalized in the 1970s. The shipbuilding industry has suffered from a worldwide glut and demand for more specialized ships. In 1977, the Sweden steel works were consolidated into one company (Svenskt Stal AB); the government owns 75 percent of its shares. The Swedish government also controls the transportation and communications industries.

Statsforetag AB (Swedish State Company, Ltd.) is a primary industry umbrella used by the Swedish government. It encompasses shipbuilding, engineering, construction, and other important industries. The government has a majority interest in approximately 110 companies; the largest interests are in the mining, forestry, steel, and paper industries.

SWEDEN'S SOCIAL WELFARE SYSTEM

Sweden has a comprehensive system of social services including public health, child allowances, housing subsidies, and social security insurance. The responsibility for social services is shared between the central government and local authorities. The main sources of revenue for the public sector include central government and local income taxes, social security contributions, and value-added tax (VAT). Taxes are also levied on wealth, inheritances, and gifts. The highest individual tax rate is 80 percent. Social services accounted for 75 percent of total income transfers to households.

Sweden's social welfare system hurts capital formation. The high tax rates imposed on businesses and individuals discourage savings and investment for private enterprise. A conservative government that lowered individual and corporate tax rates, dismantled social welfare programs, and provided incentives for capital investment would improve the Swedish economy and its capital markets.

MONETARY AND BANKING SYSTEMS

The Swedish banking system is composed of 15 commercial banks, 12 regional cooperative banks, and 150 savings banks. The three largest banks are Skandinaviska Enskilda Banken, Post-och Kretit-banken, and Svenska Handelsbanken. As of 1985, these banks had nearly 79 percent of all commercial deposits in Sweden. Commercial banks can be Stockholm Stock Exchange members.

Sveriges Riksbank, an agency of the *Riksdag,* is Sweden's Central Bank. Its responsibilities include:

1. Issuing bank notes.
2. Functioning as a central depository for Sweden.
3. Developing and maintaining monetary and foreign exchange policies by fixing the discount rate, engaging in open market operations, and regulating banking and credit sectors of the economy.

Monetary policy is determined primarily by additional liquidity created by large central government budget deficits and deficits for current accounts. With government consent, the Sveriges Riksbank can:

1. Impose cash and liquidity reserve requirements.
2. Impose investment ratios for insurance companies and banks.
3. Impose credit ceilings for banks.
4. Impose maximum interest rates on loans and deposits.
5. Control bond issues.

The Sveriges Riksbank has relied on open-market operations to control interest rates and cash and liquidity reserve requirements. There are no restrictions on discount borrowing, but banks are penalized through an increase in interest rates proportional to a bank's increase in borrowing.

FOREIGN EXCHANGE POLICY

Sveriges Riksbank issues the foreign exchange rate policy in accordance with the Exchange Control Act and the Exchange Control Ordinance. Payments are made through authorized banks. To be authorized, a bank must have a permit from the *Riksbank.* Permits are granted for direct investments, loans from abroad, and sales of listed shares. In this manner, the *Riksbank* monitors and controls the flow of capital and Swedish krona in and out of the country.

THE SECURITIES MARKETS

The Stockholm Stock Exchange (SSE) is Sweden's only stock exchange, and it is the largest exchange in Scandinavia with a total market capitalization of U.S.$ 43 billion. SSE operations are governed by the Law on the Stockholm Stock Exchange of 1979. The Bank Inspection Board, an agency of the Swedish government, supervises SSE operations.

The Swedish Companies Act of 1975 requires that each company listed on the SSE must publish annual and interim reports to shareholders. The SSE also requires that a listed company promptly disclose to the public and the SSE certain events affecting the company. The 1985 Securities Market Law implemented insider trading rules that prohibit company management, officers, and directors from trading securities based on unpublished information.

There are three official lists at the stock exchange:

1. List A—contains shares A:I and A:II, which differ in minimum share capital, equity, and number of shares issued daily.
2. List O:I—contains government bonds, mortgage bank bonds, and premium bonds issued daily.
3. List O:II/III—contains other listed bonds issued weekly.

List A includes two types of securities traded on the SSE. The first, A-I securities, must have share capital of at least SEK 10 million and a minimum of 1,000 shareholders. The second, A-II, must have at least SEK 2 million in share capital, SEK 4 million in total equity, and at least 400 shareholders. In 1986, of the 171 companies listed on the SSE, 125 companies were classified as A-I and 46 companies were classified as A-II.

Non-nationals aren't allowed to own either domestic debt securities or the common shares of banks, finance companies, and brokerage firms. Listed shares are divided into free and restricted shares. Restricted shares represent a majority of the voting and economic interests in a company. Because this book's purpose is foreign investment, we will focus on free shares.

Free shares can be purchased by non-nationals. Free shares represent a minority of the company's voting and economic interests. The major drawback to trading free shares is that the market for them is illiquid and volatile. Of the 171 companies listed on the SSE, only 30 percent give quotations on free shares. The Sveriges Riksbank determines companies that can sell free shares through licensing agreements. The license specifies the limitations for selling free shares.

Sweden has an active over-the-counter (OTC) market that has experienced solid growth in recent years. The OTC market is the seat of bond trading, foreign securities, and semiofficial OTC trading by banks and brokers acting as market makers. Since 1982, many companies prefer to have their shares traded on the OTC market. In 1984, there were approximately 70 OTC-traded companies with an aggregate market capitalization of SEK 6 billion, which represented 14 percent of the total market capitalization.

The Swedish market is dominated by institutional investors such as insurance companies, pension plans, and charitable foundations. Individuals invest in the market through unit investment trusts (mutual funds). In recent years, foreign investment has been increasingly important.

THE EQUITY MARKET

In the primary market, new equity offerings are usually distributed by commercial banks and brokers. The new securities of listed companies are offered on a subscription basis to existing shareholders or primarily distributed on a best-efforts basis. Since 1979, this requirement has been relaxed, and Swedish companies can offer equity securities that don't grant preemptive rights to existing shareholders.

In the secondary market, securities are traded on the SSE by automated auction market and by after-auction market trading. During the market auction or "call over" of the list of traded securities, orders to buy and sell at the same price are matched by computer. The shares are called in a predetermined order in six alphabetical groups. After the auction market is closed, SSE members deal among themselves to fill unmatched orders. Dealings may continue after official SSE hours.

All brokers can trade off the exchange, but they must report all transactions to the SSE before the following day's auction market. Prices of shares purchased and sold after completion of the auction market or outside the SSE may be determined without reference to prices determined by the auction market.

Prior to July 1984, brokerage commissions were fixed by the Bank Inspection Board. Since then, commissions have been negotiable.

THE DEBT MARKET

Non-nationals aren't permitted to purchase domestic debt securities in Sweden. The government of Sweden is the primary issuer of debt obligations. In 1985, SEK 68 million of primary debt offerings were issued with an annual turnover of SEK 14.5 million. Until 1985, the dominant portion of bond trading occurred off the exchange. After January 1986, all bond trading had to be reported to the SSE.

TAXATION

Under Swedish law, payments of dividends to nonresidents are subject to Swedish withholding taxes. The applicable withholding rate is 15 percent on dividends paid by Swedish issuers. Capital gains on shares are fully taxed as income if they are held for less than two years. If they are held for more than two years, 40 percent of the gain is taxed as income.

For Swedish government bonds, capital gains are fully taxed as income if they are held for less than two years. If they are held for two to three years, 75 percent of the gain is taxed; if they are held for three to four years, 50 percent of the gain is taxed; and if they are held for four to five years, 25 percent of the gain is taxed as income. Gains on bonds held for more than five years are free of capital gains.

Capital losses may be offset only against capital gains with the same reduced rates as the gains, depending on the holding period. Capital losses can be carried forward for six years.

STOCK EXCHANGE INDEX

The Affarsvarlden Index is the primary SSE index. The index is heavily weighted with securities representing the engineering sectors, such as chemicals, pharmaceuticals, plastics, electrical products, automobiles, shipbuilding, and machinery.

GENERAL INFORMATION ON THE STOCKHOLM STOCK EXCHANGE

Stock Exchange Authorities

The board of governors has 11 members; six are appointed by the government, one is appointed by the *Riksbank,* two are appointed by the SSE, and two are appointed by trade and industry associations. Brokerage of securities may be carried by members licensed as authorized stock brokers. There are 26 members of the SSE, including commercial banks, savings banks, and private firms.

Trading Hours

The SSE is open Monday through Friday. Official trading occurs from 9:30 A.M. to 2:30 P.M.

Number of Listings

The SSE lists common shares, preferred shares, and mutual fund shares for 170 companies. In addition, the exchange lists convertible and government bonds.

Types of Orders

The following orders are permitted on the exchange:

1. Market order.
2. Limit order.
3. Good for the day.
4. Good-until-cancelled—Unlike U.S. exchanges, all orders entered on the SSE are assumed to be good-until-cancelled unless they are specified as only good for the day.

TABLE 17.1   Selected Information on the 10 Largest Companies by
Market Capitalization on the Stockholm Stock Exchange
as of April 25, 1986

Company	Business	U.S.$ Million	Percent Total
Volvo	Automobiles	3,239	7.5
Electrolux	Electrical	2,257	5.2
ASEA AB	Electrical	2,208	5.1
Saab-Scania	Automobiles	2,171	5.0
Skandinav Enskilda Bank	Banking	1,768	4.1
SCA	Insurance	1,590	3.7
Ericsson	Office equipment	1,537	3.6
Skanska	Construction	1,368	3.2
SKF	Banking	1,315	3.2
Astra	Health care	1,300	3.0
Totals		U.S.$ 18,753	43.5%

Total stock market capitalization U.S.$ 43 billion

SOURCE: Morgan Stanley Capital International Perspective, Geneva, Switzerland.

Transactions and Settlement

Transactions must be for cash and settled within five business days
unless a special one-month delayed delivery rule is invoked. The
one-month delayed delivery rule applies to selling abroad. The
majority of foreign sales come from securities held in Sweden.

Transaction Costs

A-I Type of securities:
   0.45 percent on the first SEK 500,000.
   0.30 percent on the remainder of the purchase or sale.
A-II Type of securities:
   0.65 percent on the value of the purchase and sale.
Table 17.1 shows the 10 largest companies listed on the Stockholm
Stock Exchange, ranked according to market capitalization.

The remainder of the chapter briefly describes the economies
of Denmark, Norway, and Finland. The capital markets of these
countries are small and illiquid. No options or financial futures
markets exist. Investors aren't encouraged to make direct investments in these countries unless a special situation exists and one is

TABLE 17.2 A Comparison of Selected Market Statistics for Equity Securities

Country	Market Capitalization	Number of Listed Companies	Average Daily Turnover
Sweden	$43.0 billion	171	$86.4 million
Denmark	16.2	252	8.9
Norway	9.6	164	17.7
Finland	7.1	51	4.8

SOURCE: Scandinavia Fund.

aware of all the risks. The Scandinavia Fund, listed on the American Stock Exchange, offers a means of investing in these countries. Refer to Chapter 2 for more information.

Table 17.2 provides a view of Scandinavian equity markets in comparing market capitalization, number of listed companies, and average daily turnover.

THE KINGDOM OF DENMARK

The Kingdom of Denmark is a constitutional monarchy with a parliamentary system of government. Denmark is the southernmost of the Scandinavian countries bounded by the North Sea, the Baltic Sea, and the Federal Republic of Germany. Denmark is a peninsula with several islands covering an area of 16,631 square miles. The population is 5.1 million. The Danish people, with a per capita income of $12,950, enjoy one of the highest standards of living in the world. Copenhagen is the capital and financial center. The Danish krone (DKK) is the official currency.

THE ECONOMY

In 1985, Denmark's gross domestic product (GDP) was DKK 605 billion. The services sector (trade, transportation, and finance) accounted for 66 percent of the GDP; the industrial sector (manufacturing, construction, and utilities) accounted for 28 percent of the GDP; and fishing and agricultural accounted for only 6 percent of the GDP. Foreign trade accounted for 38 percent of all exports and 37 percent of all imports in the 1985 GDP. The European Community (EC) accounted for 43 percent of all exports and 48 percent of all imports. The Federal Republic of Germany, the United Kingdom, and Sweden are Denmark's main trading partners.

Business services constitute 40 percent of the total gross domestic product (GDP). Mining and manufacturing comprise 21 percent of the total GDP. Denmark's main exports are food, machinery, electrical products, and chemicals.

Oil is key to the Danish economy because Denmark is dependent on foreign oil. Although Denmark has North Sea continental shelf rights, treaties with Norway and the United Kingdom preclude Denmark from oil exploration. In 1985, fuel imports were 5.3 percent of the total GDP.

Denmark has had balance of payment deficits since 1981. The government borrows heavily to finance social programs. In 1984, the central government's budget deficit became a staggering DKK 28 billion.

The Denmarks Nationalbank is the central bank of Denmark. The central bank administers foreign exchange control. Nearly all transactions are free of restrictions. For nonresidents, Danish kroner are fully convertible into any other currency.

THE COPENHAGEN STOCK EXCHANGE

The Copenhagen Stock Exchange (CSE) is Denmark's only stock exchange. It has a market capitalization of $16.2 billion with 252 companies listed. Table 17.3 lists the most actively traded securities on the CSE.

THE KINGDOM OF NORWAY

With an area of 125,056 square miles, exclusive of overseas territories, and a population of 4.2 million people, Norway is the northernmost of the Scandinavian countries. It is bordered on the west by the Atlantic and Arctic Oceans, on the south by the North Sea, and on the east by Sweden. It is a mountainous country with only three percent of the land cultivated for farming. Norway is a constitutional monarchy with a parliamentary form of government. The official currency is the Norwegian krone (NOK).

TABLE 17.3   The 10 Most Actively Traded Companies on the
Copenhagen Stock Exchange as of April 25, 1986

Company	Market Value DKK in Millions
Superfos A/S	1,368
Novo Industri A/S	5,770
A/S Kobenhavns Handelsbank	5,034
Den Danske Bank A/S	5,660
A/S Det Oestasiatiske Kompagni	1,997
De Danske Sukkerfabrikker	2,990
Privatbanken A/S	3,558
Dampshipseelkapet of 1912	7,139
Sophus Berendsen A/S	2,041
Jyske Bank A/S	2,337

Total stock market capitalization U.S.$ 16.2 billion.

SOURCE: Annual Report of the Copenhagen Stock Exchange.

THE ECONOMY

Norway's economy is heavily dependent on foreign trade. Its principal exports are oil, gas, and petroleum products. Norway exports 67 percent of its products to the European Community (EC) and imports 48 percent from the EC. The United Kingdom, West Germany, Sweden, and the United States are Norway's main trading partners.

Unlike other Scandinavian countries, Norway has an abundant supply of oil and gas from the North Sea. The discovery of petroleum in the Norwegian sector of the North Sea has bolstered the Norwegian economy. In contrast to Denmark and Sweden, Norway benefits from high oil prices. Low oil and gas prices are detrimental to the Norwegian economy. Oil and gas production accounted for 17 percent of the gross domestic product (GDP) and 52 percent of total exports. Norway also benefits from abundant hydroelectric power, which provides almost all of its electricity.

Norges Bank is the central bank of Norway. All transfers of capital to and from Norway, except current transactions, certain trade credits, and portfolio transactions in listed shares are subject to prior government approval. Norges Bank is responsible for approvals except the issuance of debt securities and borrowings abroad regarding the importing of ships.

THE OSLO STOCK EXCHANGE

The Oslo Stock Exchange (OSE) is Norway's stock exchange. The OSE lists equity and debt securities. The stock exchange lists 164 companies with a market capitalization of U.S.$ 9.6 billion. The OSE is regulated by the Law Relating to Bourses, which was adopted in 1931, and it operates with supervision from the Norwegian Ministry of Commerce. The Security Trading Act, adopted in 1985 to prevent insider trading, requires listed companies to disclose material information and sales of their shares by management.

There are two official equity lists on the OSE. The listing requirements for admission to Bourse 1 are more stringent than for admission to Bourse 2. Bourse 1 admits companies with at least NOK 10 million in share capital and 500 shareholders. Bourse 2 was established in 1984 for companies with at least NOK 2 million in share capital and more than 200 shareholders. New equity issues are distributed by brokers and banks.

Non-nationals aren't permitted to purchase debt securities. The dominant issuer of Norwegian debt is the government of Norway. Table 17.4 lists the most actively traded securities on the OSE.

THE REPUBLIC OF FINLAND

The Republic of Finland is the only Scandinavian country that isn't a constitutional monarchy. It is a parliamentary democracy. Finland covers 130,119 square miles and has a population of 4.9 million. Finland is bordered by Sweden on the west, the Soviet Union on the east, and Norway on the north. Like Norway and Sweden, Finland is a mountainous country 70-percent covered by forests. Less than nine percent of the land is cultivated. Helsinki is the capital and financial center. Finland's per capita income is $9,720. The population is 93 percent Finnish and 6 percent Swedish. The Finnish markka is the official currency (FIM).

TABLE 17.4 The 10 Most Actively Traded Companies on the Oslo Stock Exchange as of December 1986

Company	Market Value NOK in Millions
Norsk Hydro A.S.	12,623
Elkem A/S	1,315
A/S Kosmos	1,780
Dyno Industrier A.S.	1,375
Orkla Industrier A.S.	1,252
Hafslund	2,529
Borregaard A.S.	1,527
A/S Storebrand Norden	1,686
Actinor A.S.	1,735
Kvaerner Industrier A/S	1,858

Total stock market capitalization: U.S.$ 9.6 billion

SOURCE: Oslo Stock Exchange.

THE ECONOMY

The gross domestic product (GDP) for 1985 was estimated at FIM 337.6 billion, which represented an annual growth of three percent since 1982. The export of goods and services represented 31 percent of the gross domestic product (GDP). Finland's leading exports are forestry and paper products, machinery, transport equipment, and base metals. The European Community (EC), EFTA, Comecon, and the Soviet Union are major export and import partners for Finland. Unlike other Scandinavian countries, the Soviet Union is an important trading partner; it accounts for 21 percent of total exports and imports.

Leading imports include mineral fuels and lubricants, machinery, and chemicals. Services account for 58 percent of the total GDP. Manufacturing, mining, and quarrying represent 26 percent of the gross domestic product (GDP). Agriculture (excluding forestry) represents 4.5 percent of the GDP. About 10 percent of all land is devoted to farming.

The Bank of Finland is the central bank. It regulates foreign exchange in Finland. Most current transactions are unrestricted, and the related payments are handled by commercial banks. Most capital transactions require prior central bank approval.

TABLE 17.5   The 10 Most-Actively Traded Companies on the Helsinki
Stock Exchange as of December 1986

Company	Market Value FIM in Millions
OY Nokia AB	2,325
Pojhola	1,745
Suomen Sokeri OY	1,478
Farmos-Yhtyma OY	512
Union Bank of Finland	3,418
OY Wartsila AB	1,283
Kymi-Stromberg OY	1,100
Kesko OY	820
Amer-Yhtyma	792
Rauma-Repola OY	1,215
Total stock market capitalization U.S.$ 7.1 billion	

SOURCE: Market News, Unitas, Ltd.

THE HELSINKI STOCK EXCHANGE

The Helsinki Stock Exchange (HSE) is Finland's sole stock exchange. It's the smallest capital market in Scandinavia with a market capitalization of $7.1 billion. Only 51 companies are listed on the HSE. HSE activities, the banks, and brokers are supervised by the HSE Committee of Ethics. There are no laws governing the HSE activities or trading.

Admission of equity securities for HSE listing is authorized by the HSE board of directors. To qualify for listing, a company must have fully paid capital of at least FIM five million and total equity of FIM 10 million. Each issue registered on the HSE must have at least 700 shareholders. Companies with securities listed on the HSE are required by the Finnish Companies Act to make annual reports available to shareholders.

Nonnationals aren't permitted to purchase debt securities. Bonds issued by Finland's government and by mortgage credit institutions dominate the fixed-interest market.

Table 17.5 lists the most actively traded equity securities on the HSE.

CHAPTER EIGHTEEN

Hong Kong

Hong Kong is a British colony located along the coast of Southern China. It covers approximately 408 square miles. Hong Kong consists of a mainland and a group of islands; it has the largest deep-water port on the southern China sea coast. In 1985, the population was 5.4 million people; 98 percent are Chinese. Hong Kong has one of the highest population densities in the world. Victoria is the capital of Hong Kong. Chinese (cantonese dialect) and English are the official languages. English is widely spoken in government, commerce, and industry. The Hong Kong dollar (HK$) is the official currency. One HK$ equals 100 cents. See Figure 18.1.

The Chinese imperial government gave Hong Kong Island to Great Britain in 1841. The Kowloon Peninsula was acquired by Britain in 1860. The mainland area of the New Territories and outlying areas were leased for 99 years in 1898. The lease won't be renewed in 1997 as stated by the Sino-British Joint Declaration.

GOVERNMENT

Hong Kong is administered by the Hong Kong government as a British-ruled overseas territory. The head of state is the queen. The governor, who is appointed by the queen, is responsible for all aspects of the territory as the commander-in-chief. The two constitutional bodies are the Executive Council, which advises the governor on important policy matters, and the Legislative Council.

FIGURE 18.1 Exchange Rate for the Hong Kong Dollar
(quarterly averages)

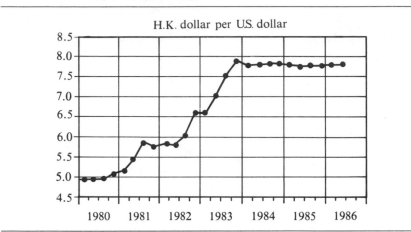

H.K. dollar per U.S. dollar

SOURCE: The Federal Reserve Bank of St. Louis.

Through the United Kingdom, Hong Kong is represented in several international organizations including the International Monetary Fund and the United Nations. In its own right, Hong Kong is a member of the General Agreement on Tariffs and Trade (GATT) and the Asian Development Bank.

Although the population is concentrated on Hong Kong Island and the Kowloon Peninsula, the entire territory of Hong Kong will revert to China in 1997. The future of Hong Kong is stated in the Sino-British Joint Declaration signed in December 1984. The declaration and its annexes state that Hong Kong will be a Special Administrative Region (SAR) of China commencing July 1, 1997. The SAR will retain its own government and legislature and a high degree of autonomy, and existing legal and economic systems will be unchanged for 50 years after establishing the new Hong Kong SAR. A basic law for the SAR is being drafted by a joint drafting committee representing interests in Hong Kong and China.

THE ECONOMY

Hong Kong has a private-enterprise economy with well-developed industrial, financial, and service sectors. Hong Kong has limited natural resources and depends on imports of food and raw materials for most of its basic requirements. In 1985, the GDP was HK$ 181.3 billion. The total value of trade in 1985 was HK$ 466.5 billion, which represents 257 percent of the GDP. Hong Kong has active trading arrangements with the United States, China, Japan, the United Kingdom, West Germany, Taiwan, and Singapore.

Hong Kong exports over 44 percent of its goods and services to the United States, but it imports only 9.5 percent of its requirements from the United States. China and Japan are the main origin of imports; they account for a combined total of 48 percent. Clothing, textiles, and fabrics are the primary exports; they account for 22 percent of the total.

Re-export businesses constitute a major sector of the economy; they account for 44 percent of all exports. Hong Kong industries import semimanufactured goods to re-export as finished products in the form of clothing, toys, watches, clocks, radios, and electronic components and parts. Re-export trade is important to the United States because labor costs can be reduced significantly by employing skilled Hong Kong workers to assemble and finish products shipped from the United States. Hong Kong is the world's largest exporter of textile goods.

The main GDP contributions come from the services sector, which includes real estate, insurance, financial services, and tourist-related businesses. This sector represents 62 percent of the GDP. The manufacturing sector represents 25 percent of the GDP.

HONG KONG AND THE PEOPLES REPUBLIC OF CHINA

With the opening of trade between Western nations and the Peoples Republic of China (PRC), Hong Kong is an entrepôt where nations can gain access to the huge Chinese consumer markets. The PRC has made definite moves to develop a more market-oriented economy in which private enterprises will exist. As an example, in September 1986, the PRC, under Deng Xiaoping's regime, reopened the Shanghai Stock Exchange after it was closed in 1950 during the Maoist revolution. The Shanghai Stock Exchange, run by the Shanghai Investment & Trust Company, lists only a small number of issues for trading, but this is the first step in developing an efficient economy responsive to competitive production and pricing by encouraging capital formation through private ownership of businesses.

The political and business leaders of Hong Kong will play a vital role in modernizing the industrial, financial, and service sectors of China. This will be done by introducing efficient and competitive forms of business and management organization. In future years, the economies of Hong Kong and China will blend the pragmatic and endurable characteristics of western capitalism and Maoist communism.

MONEY AND BANKING

Hong Kong has no central bank. Most of the usual functions of a central bank, such as supervision of financial institutions, management of foreign exchange reserves, and supervision of currency are carried out by select government agencies. The Hong Kong & Shanghai Banking Corporation and Standard Chartered Bank are authorized to issue bank notes. The Hong Kong Association of Banks sets the maximum rates of interest payable on deposits with licensed banks, and it has a statutory obligation to consult the government on interest rates.

The financial sector has increased in importance over the past decade. Hong Kong is a major regional financial center for international banks, insurance companies, and realty and brokerage firms.

There are no foreign exchange restrictions in Hong Kong. Between 1972 and 1983, the H.K. dollar was allowed to float freely. In October 1983, the H.K. dollar was pegged to the U.S. dollar at an exchange rate of U.S.$ 1 = H.K.$ 7.80. To issue Hong Kong dollar bank notes, a deposit must be made in U.S. dollars at the fixed rate with the Hong Kong Government Exchange Fund. Certificates of indebtedness are issued to the banks against these deposits, and they may be redeemed by the fund at any time.

THE SECURITIES MARKETS

The Hong Kong Stock Exchange began trading in 1891. Trading expanded to the Far East Stock Exchange in 1969, the Kam Ngan Exchange in 1971, and the Kowloon Stock Exchange in 1972. The Stock Exchange of Hong Kong Limited (SEHK) was formed in 1986 when the four exchanges (Far East, Kam Ngan, Hong Kong, and Kowloon) were unified in one modern, automated exchange. In 1986, there were 678 members of SEHK, and 224 companies were listed on the SEHK. The Hong Kong Exchange is twelfth largest in the world with $41 billion in total market capitalization. Unlike other capital markets, there is no substantial over-the-counter (OTC) market in Hong Kong equities.

The SEHK operates within the framework of the securities ordinance, which requires registration of dealers, dealing partnerships, and investment advisers. The protection of the investors ordinance prohibits fraudulent means of inducing investors to buy or sell securities. While rules and legislation against insider trading exist, there are no penalties for violating these rules.

Membership on the stock exchange is restricted to stockbrokers and stockbrokerage companies. Members must be registered with the commissioner for securities' office. They are allowed to trade as principals for their own account and as broker orders for customers.

Banks can't become members of the exchange. Securities are usually deposited and administered by brokers and commercial banks that serve as custodians for securities. A few commercial banks have adequate computerized accounting facilities to do collective deposits of securities. The purchase and sale of securities aren't subject to any restrictions, but all transactions must be supported by relative contract notes and *ad valorem* duty must be paid. Transactions are usually settled on the same day or within one business day.

Equity Market

Listed companies may issue new shares as rights issues, public offerings, placement, gratis issue, or any other method recognized by the listing committee of SEHK. To become listed on the stock exchange, a company must have a minimum of HK$ 20 million paid in capital, and a public offering must have at least HK$ 5 million. A listed firm must submit the company's annual report and an unaudited interim financial statement to the SEHK.

Fixed-Interest Market

Markets for fixed-interest securities are inactive. In 1986, there were only eight debt securities quoted on the stock exchange. There is only one Hong Kong government bond listed; it is closely held and rarely traded.

TABLE 18.1   Selected Information on the 10 Largest Companies by
Market Capitalization as of April 25, 1986

Company	Business	U.S.$ Million	Percent Total
Hongkong Shanghai	Banking	3,547	8.7
Hongkong Telephone	Communications	2,264	5.5
Swire Pacific	Multi-industry	2,221	5.4
Hutchinson Whampoa	Multi-industry	2,130	5.2
China Light & Power	Utility	2,113	5.2
Hang Seng Bank	Banking	1,818	4.5
Hongkong Land	Real estate	1,752	4.3
Hongkong Electric	Utility	1,593	3.9
Hongkong Kowloon	Trading company	1,423	3.5
Cheung Kong	Real estate	1,081	2.6
Totals		U.S.$ 19,942	48.8%

Total stock market capitalization: U.S.$ 41 billion

SOURCE: Morgan Stanley Capital International Perspective, Geneva, Switzerland.

Stock Exchange Index

The Hang Seng Index is the primary index used to monitor the SEHK. It has 33 major companies weighted by market capitalization. Although fairly narrow, the Hang Seng Index represents 70 percent of total market capitalization. Table 18.1 lists the 10 largest capitalized companies in Hong Kong. They are included in the composition of the Hang Seng Index. The base rate on July 31, 1964 was 100. See Figure 18.2.

Taxation

There are no taxes on capital gains and dividends. There is a 15 percent withholding tax on interest payments.

FINANCIAL FUTURES MARKETS

The Hong Kong Futures Market (HKFE) was established in 1976 as a marketplace for agricultural and metal futures. In 1985, a stock index futures contract on the Hang Seng Index began trading. The I.C.C.H. Ltd. registers and clears all futures contracts traded on the HKFE, and it acts as manager of the Hong Kong Commodities

FIGURE 18.2 Hang Seng Index

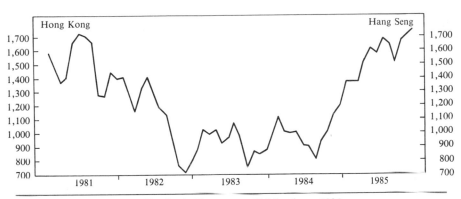

SOURCE: *Euromoney Yearbook*, Euromoney Publications, 1986.

Guarantee Corporation Ltd. (HKCG). The HKCG is responsible for ensuring fulfilled futures contracts. In addition to the rules and regulations of the HKFE, I.C.C.H., and the HKCG, these organizations operate within a framework of the Commodities Trading Ordinance under the supervision of the commodity trading commission.

The Hang Seng Stock Index futures contract is valued at HK$ 50 times the index price. For example, if the Hang Seng Index is quoted at 1,720, the value of the index contract is: HK$ 50 × 1,720 = HK$ 86,000, or approximately U.S.$ 11,025, at an exchange rate of 1 U.S.$ = HK$ 7.80. A buyer or seller of an index futures contract is required to deposit with a broker initial margin funds that represent a percentage of the contract value and to meet all variation margin calls while holding the contract.

GENERAL INFORMATION ON THE HONG KONG EXCHANGE

Stock Exchange Authorities

Stock exchange officials, the general assembly, and members are all authorities at the exchange. Members make up the general assembly, which elects a chairman, vice chairmen, a council, and committee members. The general assembly is the supreme administrative body of the exchange.

Stock Market Hours

The exchange is open Monday through Friday. The morning session is from 10:30 A.M. to 12:30 P.M., and the afternoon session is from 2:30 P.M. to 3:30 P.M.

Types of Securities

Equities. The equities available on the Hong Kong exchange include:

1. Common shares.
2. Preferred shares.
3. Cumulative preferred shares.
4. Warrants.

Loan Stock (Debt Securities). The debt securities available on the Hong Kong exchange include:

1. Convertible loan stock.
2. Warrant issues.
3. Convertibles.
4. Corporate straight debt securities (very limited trading).
5. Government bond (only one issue that is not traded).

Only registered shares are permitted in Hong Kong. Shares are registered on the books of an issuing company in an owner's name.

Transaction Charges

Commissions are negotiable between buyers and sellers. The minimum commission is HK$ 25. Sellers must pay a stamp tax of HK$ 5.

Settlement

All transactions are settled in cash either on the same day or within one business day of the commitment. Neither margins nor forward transactions are permitted.

CHAPTER NINETEEN

The Republic of Singapore

The Republic of Singapore consists of 50 islands covering approximately 238 square miles. Singapore is situated at the foot of the Malay Peninsula. A causeway across the Straits of Johore joins the main island, Singapore, to the Malaysian mainland. The city of Singapore is the capital and financial center of the republic. The population of Singapore in 1985 was 2.6 million; over 53 percent of whom live in the city. Approximately 76 percent of Singapore's citizens are Chinese, 15 percent are Malaysian, and 6 percent are Indian or Sri Lankan. The official languages are Malay, Mandarin Chinese, Tamil, and English. English is widely used for business and administration. The Singapore dollar (S$) is the official currency; S$ 1 = 100 cents. See Figure 19.1.

Singapore began as a settlement founded by Sir Thomas Stamford Raffles in 1819. During World War II, the country was occupied by the Japanese, but it was returned to British sovereignty after the war. Singapore gained independence from Britain in 1963 when it became a state in the federation of Malaysia. In 1965, Singapore left the federation and became an independent and sovereign republic.

GOVERNMENT

The Constitution of Singapore provides for a parliamentary system of government based on universal adult suffrage. The life of Parliament is five years unless it is dissolved earlier. The head of state is

**FIGURE 19.1 Exchange Rate for the Singapore Dollar
(quarterly averages)**

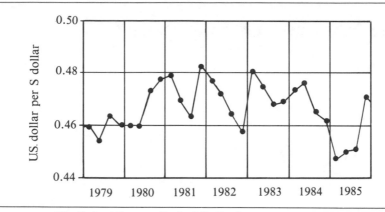

SOURCE: The Federal Reserve Bank of St. Louis.

the President, who serves a term of four years. The President appoints the prime minister. On the advice of the prime minister, the President appoints other ministers from Parliament to form a cabinet. The laws of the country are based on the British system. Legislation becomes law after passage by Parliament and approval by the President.

INTERNATIONAL RELATIONS

Singapore follows a policy of nonalignment and free trade. It is a member of ASEAN, the Asian Development Bank, the International Monetary Fund, and the United Nations.

THE ECONOMY

Singapore is heavily dependent on exports, which were equivalent to 300 percent of the GDP in 1985. The economy is based on trade, financial and business services, transportation, communication, manufacturing, and construction. Re-export businesses account for sizable percentages of trade activity with the United States. Re-export industries involve taking semi-manufactured goods and turning out finished products for sale.

Singapore exports over 21 percent of its goods and services to the United States, and it imports about 15 percent of its requirements. Japan, Malaysia, Hong Kong, China, and Middle Eastern countries are also active trading partners with Singapore.

During the 1970s, Singapore experienced real growth in the GDP of 8 percent per annum. In 1985, the real GDP dropped sharply (-1.8 percent versus $+8.2$ in 1984) due to the decline in Singapore's key industries, particularly petroleum and mineral-fuels industries. Increased labor costs and reduced domestic demand also contributed. Singapore has no natural energy resources.

Singapore has to import most of its food since production from agriculture and fishing is insufficient to feed the population.

MONEY AND BANKING

The regulation of all financial institutions is the responsibility of the Monetary Authority of Singapore (MAS), which acts as the central bank in regulating the money supply and credit. Unlike central banks in other countries, the MAS doesn't have currency-issuing ability. The Singapore board of commissioners of the currency issues bank notes and coinage. The board is under statutory obligation to maintain 100 percent backing for currency in external assets. In 1985, there were 130 commercial banks, 55 merchant banks, 34 finance companies, and 8 money brokers.

There have been no foreign exchange controls in Singapore since 1978. The Singapore dollar isn't fixed to any currency; it floats freely against other currencies. The value of the Singapore dollar is determined based on its relationship with trading partners.

THE SECURITIES MARKET

There is a close connection between the Singapore Stock Exchange and the Malaysian Stock Exchange in Kuala Lumpur; many issues are traded on both exchanges. The Singapore and Malaysian securities markets have developed side-by-side, and for many years they shared a single market for shares. In 1973, the Malaysian government terminated the convertibility of Malaysian and Singapore currencies. This action ended the official link between Malaysian and Singapore markets. Two separate markets were then established:

1. The Stock Exchange of Singapore Ltd. (SES).
2. The Kuala Lumpur Stock Exchange of Malaysia.

The Singapore market is the 15th largest in the world with total market capitalization of U.S.$ 23 billion. In 1985, there were 25 member firms trading 316 stocks, 122 stocks were incorporated in Singapore, 183 stocks were incorporated in Malaysia, and 11 stocks were incorporated overseas.

Securities markets are governed by regulations and laws including the Securities Industry Act of 1986, the Securities Industry Regulations of 1986, the Companies Act, and the Singapore Code on Takeovers and Mergers. Under these laws, the Security Industry Council acts as an adviser in matters relating to the securities industry.

Investor protection is given by the stock exchange's corporate disclosure policy, which covers immediate disclosure of material information, insider trading, and confirmation of rumors or reports. In addition, listed companies are required to furnish prompt and adequate information on matters affecting the value of their securities. The Fidelity Guarantee Fund and the imposition of personal liability on the principals in stock exchange firms safeguard the investing public if a member firm fails to meet its commitments.

Stock exchange membership is restricted to stockbrokerage firms holding a license under the Securities Industry Act. There is no limit to the number of members. There are three types of stock exchange dealers:

1. Stockbroker–A principal of a member firm who can trade for his or her own account and is personally liable for his or her activities.
2. Dealer–A paid brokerage firm employee who represents a member on behalf of the firm.
3. Remisier–A commission agent, usually not an employee of a member firm, who transacts business for a member firm.

The completion of a share transaction involves two steps: (*a*) delivery of the share scrip to the seller, and (*b*) buyer payment in settling the first business day following delivery. Delivery requires physical transfer of certificates between member firms. There are three types of delivery and settlement of transactions permitted by the exchange:

1. Immediate trades–transactions are settled the next business day.
2. Ready trades–all shares traded from Monday–Friday have to be delivered on any business day but no later than Tuesday of the following week.
3. Transactions with delayed delivery–transactions are settled on a basis not to exceed one month.

EQUITY MARKET

Initial offerings of equity securities can be made by public issues or private placement. In the secondary market, equities are traded on the SES through securities companies that act as brokers. A round-lot transaction for shares is 1,000. Odd-lot orders are allowed but can't be executed as quickly as round-lot transactions. There is no significant over-the-counter (OTC) market.

Listed companies are assigned in two sections: the first section and the second section. Securities that qualify for first-section trading must meet the following criteria:

1. Minimum paid capital of S$ 5 million.
2. Minimum number of shareholders is 500.
3. Total turnover of company shares is at least 5 percent of the paid capital or 250,000 shares per annum—whichever is lower.
4. Payment of an annual dividend of at least 5 percent.

Other listed companies that can't meet criteria for the first section are classified under the second trading section unless the stock exchange committee decides otherwise.

FIXED-INTEREST MARKET

Trading in debentures, loan stocks, and bonds in Singapore is minimal. They account for less than 2 percent of the total value of the Singapore Stock Market. A minimum order is S$ 100.

FIGURE 19.2   Straits Times Index

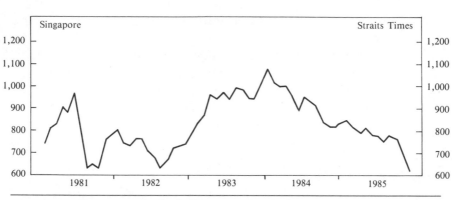

SOURCE: *Euromoney Yearbook*, Euromoney Publications, 1986.

TAXATION

Under current laws, there is no tax on capital gains. Dividend and interest income is subject to a 40 percent withholding tax. There is no double taxation treaty between the United States and Singapore that allows U.S. residents to utilize this tax as a credit against U.S. tax obligations.

STOCK EXCHANGE INDEX

The Stock Exchange of Singapore Index (SES) is a capitalization-weighted index of 32 stocks. Base: December 31, 1973 = 100. See Figure 19.2. Table 19.1 lists the 10 largest capitalized companies in Singapore which are included in the SES Index.

GENERAL INFORMATION ON THE SINGAPORE STOCK EXCHANGE

Stock Exchange Authorities

The general meeting of the stock exchange elects a committee of five members. This committee appoints a general manager who handles administration for the Committee.

TABLE 19.1 Selected Information on the 10 Largest Companies by Market Capitalization as of April 25, 1986

Company	Business	U.S.$ Million	Percent Total
Singapore Airlines	Airlines	1,781	7.9
OCBC Oversea Chinese	Banking	1,353	6.0
Singapore Press Hld.	Publishing	638	2.8
Development Bank	Banking	620	2.7
United Overseas Bank	Banking	527	2.3
Sime Darby	Multi-industry	482	2.1
Malayan Bank	Banking	434	1.9
Harrison's M. Plant.	Rubber	409	1.8
Genting	Plantation	355	1.6
Consolidated Plant.	Rubber	343	1.5
Totals		U.S.$ 6,942	30.6%

Total stock market capitalization. U.S.$ 23 billion

SOURCE: Morgan Stanley Capital International Perspective, Geneva, Switzerland.

Stock Market Hours

The stock exchange is open Monday through Friday for two trading sessions a day. The first session lasts from 10 A.M. to 12:30 P.M. The second session lasts from 2:30 P.M. to 4 P.M.

Floor Trading Practices

Dealings occur in the exchange trading hall where quoted securities are assigned to particular score boards (post system) according to their division in first and second trading sections and subdivision in categories of securities and groups.

Determination of Prices

Trading is a continuous auction process where bids and offers are both communicated verbally and by hand signals. A trading slip records the agreed price of a transaction between buyer and seller.

Types of Orders

The stock exchange permits market orders and price-limit orders valid either for the day or good-until-cancelled.

Types of Listings

Listings on the Singapore Stock Exchange include equity and fixed-interest securities.

Equity. Equity issues include:
Ordinary shares.
Preference shares.
Warrant.

Fixed Interest. Fixed-interest issues include:
Straight bonds.
Convertible bonds.
Warrant issues.
Floating-rate notes.

THE SINGAPORE INTERNATIONAL MONETARY EXCHANGE (SIMEX)

The Singapore International Monetary Exchange (SIMEX), formed in 1983, has the most advanced clearing system for linking two financial futures markets in the world. SIMEX was the first international financial futures exchange in Asia to establish a clearing linkage between Singapore and Chicago. In 1984, SIMEX started to trade financial futures contracts in 100 troy-ounce gold, foreign currencies, Eurodollars, and U.S. Treasury bond contracts. In September 1986, the Nikkei stock average futures contract began trading. The Nikkei Stock Average Index is comprised of 225 stocks of Japanese companies listed on the first section of the Tokyo Stock Exchange.

In partnership with the Chicago Mercantile Exchange (CME), SIMEX introduced a mutual offset system of trading financial futures contracts that are transferred back to or liquidated on the CME. The closing prices of all open positions are market-to-market each day to reflect profits and losses in customer accounts. Contracts traded on the SIMEX are fungible with contracts traded on the CME. They are subject to the same initial and variation margin requirements and delivery specifications. The rules and regulations of SIMEX are similar to the CME. SIMEX is a nonprofit organization, and it has no affiliation with the Singapore Stock Exchange (SES).

MUTUAL OFFSET

Because of the time difference between Singapore and Chicago, the mutual offset system represents a major step toward 24-hour trading in financial futures. The mutual offset system allows customers to manage overnight price movement risk and to offset in a liquid market. The expanded trading hours allow access to two exchanges open at different hours. Transaction costs and margin requirements are reduced since positions are maintained with one clearinghouse designated by the customer.

CLASSES OF MEMBERS

There are three classes of members on SIMEX:

1. Clearing members.   This class is authorized to clear trades and accept customer business. Minimum capital required is S$ 2 million.
2. Corporate nonclearing members.   This class is authorized to accept customer business; all trades must be qualified by and cleared through a clearing member. Minimum capital is S$ 1 million.
3. Individual nonclearing members.   This class trades for their own accounts but may fill orders for other members; all trades must be qualified by and cleared through a clearing member.

MARKET SUPERVISION AND REGULATION

Futures trading in Singapore is controlled by the Futures Trading Act. The Futures Trading Act confers upon the Monetary Authority of Singapore (MAS) the responsibility of monitoring and regulating futures markets. SIMEX has adopted the rules and regulations, compliance, audit, and surveillance procedures of the Chicago Mercantile Exchange. As further safeguards for customer accounts, SIMEX has established:

a. A common bond system that protects the financial integrity of the clearinghouse in case of default by member firms.
b. Segregation of customer accounts from the firm account.
c. A gross margining system requiring the deposit of full margins for both long and short positions with the clearinghouse.

FINANCIAL FUTURES CONTRACTS TRADED

There are seven contracts traded. However, the number of new listings will probably expand since the SIMEX is a new exchange. More detailed contract specifications are presented in Tables 19.2 and 19.3.

Contract Name	Contract Size	Trading Hours Singapore Time
Gold	100 fine troy oz.	9:30 A.M.–5:15 P.M.
Eurodollar	US$ 1,000,000	9:35 A.M.–5:20 P.M.
Treasury Bond	US$ 100,000	8:00 A.M.–5:00 P.M.
Japanese Yen	Yen 12,500,000	9:00 A.M.–5:05 P.M.
Deutsche Mark	DM 125,000	9:25 A.M.–5:10 P.M.
British Pound	BP 25,000	9:30 A.M.–5:15 P.M.
Nikkei 225	Y 500 × index value of Nikkei Stock Index	8:00 A.M.–2:15 P.M.

THE NIKKEI STOCK AVERAGE FUTURES CONTRACT

The Nikkei Stock Average futures contract is based on the Nikkei Stock Index, which is composed of 225 companies representing 34 industry groups in Japan's economy. The index is computed at one-minute intervals by the Quotation Information Center K.K. (QUICK), a subsidiary of Nihon Keisai Shimbun (NKS). The Nikkei 225 Index can be used as a proxy on the Tokyo stock market because it tracks the Tokyo Stock Exchange Index (TSE) very closely. The index futures contract is settled for cash upon expiration; physical securities are never delivered between buyers and sellers.

TABLE 19.2

British Pound

Contract size: £25,000 per contract
Ticker symbol: £
Contract months: March, June, September, December, and the spot month.
Trading hours: Singapore Time 9:30 A.M.–5:15 P.M.
London time: 1:30 A.M.–9:15 A.M.
Chicago time: 7:30 P.M.–3:15 A.M.
Minimum price fluctuation: US $0.005 per £ Value of 1 tick = U.S. $12.50
Daily price limit: None
Last trading day: Second business day immediately preceding the delivery day of the
  contract month.
Delivery date: Third Wednesday of the contract month. If the day is not a business day
  (in the country of delivery) delivery will be made on the next business day.

Eurodollar

Contract size: U.S. $1,000,000
Ticker symbol: ED
Contract months: March, June, September, December, and the spot month.
Trading hours: Singapore Time 9:35 A.M.–5:20 P.M.
London time: 1:35 A.M.–9:20 A.M.
Chicago time: 7:35 P.M.–3:20 A.M.
Minimum price fluctuation: 0.01% of 1 percentage point Value of 1 tick = U.S. $25
Daily price limit: None
Last trading day: Second business day (immediately preceding the delivery day of the
  contract month.
Delivery date: Last day of trading.

Deutsche Mark

Contract size: 125,000 DM per contract
Ticker symbol: DM
Contract months: March, June, September, December, and the spot month.
Trading hours: Singapore Time 9:25 A.M.–5:10 P.M.
London time: 1:25 A.M.–9:10 A.M.
Chicago time: 7:25 P.M.–3:10 A.M.
Minimum price fluctuation: US $0.0001 per DM Value of 1 tick = U.S. $12.50
Daily price limit: None
Last trading day: Second business day immediately preceding the delivery day of the
  contract month.
Delivery date: Third Wednesday of the contract month. If the day is not a business day
  (in the country of delivery) delivery will be made on the next business day.

Japanese Yen

Contract size: 12,500,000 ¥ per contract
Ticker symbol: JY
Contract months: March, June, September, December, and the spot month.
Trading hours: Singapore Time 9:00 A.M.–5:05 P.M.
London time: 1:20 A.M.–9:05 A.M.
Chicago time: 7:20 P.M.–3:05 P.M.
Minimum price fluctuation: US $0.000001 per ¥ Value of 1 tick = U.S. $12.50
Daily price limit: None
Last trading day: Second business day immediately preceding the delivery day of the
  contract month.
Delivery date: Third Wednesday of the contract month. If the day is not a business day
  (in the country of delivery) delivery will be made on the next business day.

SOURCE: Singapore International Monetary Exchange.

TABLE 19.3

Gold

Contract size: 100 troy ounces
Ticker symbol: GD
Contract months: February, March, April, June, August, September, October, and December.
Trading hours: Singapore time 9:30 A.M.–5:15 P.M.
London time: 1:30 A.M.–9:15 A.M.
Chicago time: 7:30 P.M.–3:15 A.M.
Minimum price fluctuation: US $0.10 Value of 1 tick = U.S. $10
Daily price limit: 250 ticks
Last trading day: Trading terminates on the business day preceding the fifth last business day of the delivery month.
Delivery date: The first to the last business day of the delivery month.

Nikkei Stock Average

Contract size: ¥500 times Nikkei Stock Average futures price
Ticker symbol: NK
Contract months: March, June, September, December
Trading hours: Singapore time 8 A.M.–2:15 P.M.
London times: 12 A.M.–6:15 A.M.
Chicago time: 6 P.M.–12:15 A.M.
(Monday to Friday except Singapore holidays)
Minimum price fluctuation: 5.0 points Value of 1 tick = ¥2,500 (about US $16)
Daily price limit: None
Last trading day: Third Wednesday of the contract month.
Delivery date: Last day of trading

U.S. Treasury Bond

Contract size: U.S. $ 100,000 face value Treasury Bonds
Ticker symbol: U.S.
Contract months: March, June, September, December.
Trading hours: Singapore time 8 A.M.–5 P.M.
London time: 12 A.M.–9 A.M.
Chicago time: 6 P.M.–3 A.M.
Minimum price fluctuation: 1 thirty-second (1/32) point per 100 points Value of 1 tick = U.S. $31.25
Daily price limit: 96 thirty-seconds (96/32) or 3 percentage points
Last trading day: Seven business days prior to last business day of the month.
Last delivery day: Last business day of the month.
Deliverable grade: U.S. Treasury bonds with a nominal 8 percent coupon that is callable are not callable for at least 15 years, or is not callable, had a maturity of at least 15 years from delivery date.
Delivery system: Federal Reserve book entry, wire transfer system.

SOURCE: Singapore International Monetary Exchange.

The Nikkei Stock Average futures contract benefits for investors are:

1. A short futures contract can be used as portfolio insurance for investors with diversified holdings of Japanese equities. A short position in the Nikkei futures can hedge the systematic risks of the market for investors who hold a portfolio of equities without having to liquidate any securities from the portfolio.

2. An investor can make a proxy commitment to buying a broad base of Japanese equities by buying an index futures contract. For example, an investor holding cash may want to own a broad base of Japanese securities that represent the market without making individual stock selection.

3. An investor can position spread transactions between the stock markets of the United States and Japan by spreading the S&P 500 Index (traded on the CME) against the Nikkei Stock Average to profit from differences in value between the two markets. An investor may believe that the S&P 500 Index is overvalued compared to the Nikkei stock index. The investor could sell S&P 500 Index futures on the CME and buy Nikkei Stock Average futures on the SIMEX to profit.

The main disadvantage of the Nikkei Stock Average futures contract is the difficulty in doing index arbitrage or program trading. Program trading involves buying a group of stocks on the Tokyo Stock Exchange and selling index futures contracts on the SIMEX to lock in a yield spread. Eventually this problem may be overcome by linkages in both trading and clearing between the Tokyo Stock Exchange and SIMEX.

The chapter concludes with several examples of how investment managers can utilize the Nikkei Stock Average futures contract to gain market participation and to hedge portfolio risks in the Japanese securities market. Refer to Chapter 8 for more information on Japanese economy and markets. For clarity, exchange rates are kept constant and transaction costs are omitted.

EXAMPLE 19.1

Scenario: An investment manager owns $500,000 worth of Japanese securities in a portfolio. At an exchange rate Yen/U.S.$ = 220, he owns ¥ 110 million worth of Japanese securities. He believes that the Japanese stock market will decline by 7 percent over the next four months, but he doesn't want to sell securities. He adopts the following strategy to obtain portfolio insurance against a declining market:

Market data:	Yen Value	U.S. Dollar Value
Nikkei-225 Index	19,000	
Index value	¥ 9.5 mln	$ 43,181
Yen/U.S.$	¥ 220	$ 0.004545
Market value	¥ 110.0 mln	$ 500,000
Margin per contract	¥ 500,000	$ 2,273

He sells 11 Nikkei Stock Average index futures contracts on the SIMEX when the index is at 19,000. This is equivalent to ¥ 104.5 million, or $475,000 worth of Japanese securities. He deposits $25,003 with a broker. Four months later he buys back the 11 contracts when the index is at 17,500 for a gain of 1,500 points on the index.

Buy/Sell	Index	Factor	Total Value	Yen/U.S.$	U.S.$ Value
Sell	19,000	500	¥ 9.50 mln	220	$43,181
Buy	17,500	500	¥ 8.75 mln	220	$39,773

$$\text{Profit per contract} = \$ \ 3,408.00$$
$$\text{Profit for 11 contracts} = \$37,488.00$$

$$\text{Return on margin} = \frac{\$37,488}{\$25,003} \times 100 = 150 \ \%$$

EXAMPLE 19.2

Scenario: An investment manager wants to hold approximately $300,000 worth of Japanese securities in her portfolio. At an exchange rate Yen/U.S.$ = 220, she wants to buy ¥ 66 million worth of Japanese securities. She believes that the Japanese stock market will appreciate five percent over the next three months. She adopts the following strategy:

Market Data:

Nikkei-225 Index	18,000	
Index value	¥ 9.0 mln	$ 40,909
Yen/U.S.$	¥ 220	$ 0.004545
Market value	¥ 66.0 mln	$ 300,000
Margin per contract	¥ 500,000	$ 2,273

She buys seven Nikkei Stock Average index futures contracts on the SIMEX when the index is at 18,000. This is equivalent to ¥ 63 million, or $286,363 worth of Japanese securities. She deposits $15,911 with a broker. Three months later, she sells the seven contracts when the index is at 18,800 for a gain of 800 points on the index.

Buy/Sell	Index	Factor	Total Value	Yen/U.S.$	U.S.$ Value
Buy	18,000	500	¥ 9.0 mln	220	$40,909
Sell	18,800	500	¥ 9.4 mln	220	$42,727

$$\text{Profit per contract} = \$ \ 1,818.72$$
$$\text{Profit for 7 contracts} = \$12,727.90$$

$$\text{Return on margin} = \frac{\$12,727.90}{\$15,911.00} \times 100 = 80\ \%$$

CHAPTER TWENTY

Sources of Information and Computer Databases

There are numerous sources of written literature, charting services, investment advisory services, and computer databases available to meet the tailored information needs of individual, corporate, and institutional investors. Information can be classified into the following areas:

1. Financial information on specific companies such as balance sheets, income statements, and earnings forecasts.
2. Analysis of macroeconomic and political events such as political parties, monetary data, balance of trade figures, leading economic indicators, and central bank policies and activities.
3. Credit risk analysis of countries and their governments.
4. Statistical data for technical analysis such as stock prices, foreign currency prices, and volume data.
5. Forecasts on the direction of stock index prices, interest rates, bond yields, and foreign exchange rates.

We have selected a sample of representative sources to highlight the speciality services provided. Some of the publications are printed only in a foreign language.

Specific information on the stock, options, and futures exchanges can be obtained by contacting the public relations departments of each exchange. Most exchanges provide general information, annual statistical summaries, and annual reports about their operations that may be useful. Brokerage firms furnish clients with research reports on foreign companies. However, most of the reports are limited to actively traded Canadian companies and companies traded as ADRs. The central bank and leading commercial banks of each country publish voluminous statistical data and economic research material that is useful for analyzing historic and present trends in macroeconomic variables and foreign currencies.

Financial information on a specific company can be obtained by writing a company's director of investor relations. Most exchanges require that listed companies file annual reports with appropriate regulatory authorities. Large U.S. accounting firms such as Coopers & Lybrand, Price Waterhouse, and Touche Ross provide their clients with excellent booklets on the financial accounting practices of companies by country.

GLOBAL FINANCIAL INFORMATION SERVICES

The following publications are printed daily or weekly. They provide current financial news, feature articles, foreign currency quotations, interest rates, money and banking statistics, and selected price data on foreign securities:

> *New York Times,* 229 West 43rd St., New York, NY 10036.
> *The Wall Street Journal,* 200 Burnett Rd., Chicopee, MA 01021.
> *Asian Wall Street Journal,* 200 Burnett Rd., Chicopee, MA 01021.
> *Financial Times,* 75 Rockefeller Plaza, New York, NY 10019.
> *Investors Daily,* PO Box 24933, Los Angeles, CA 90024.
> *Barron's,* 200 Burnett Rd., Chicopee, MA 01021.
> *The Economist,* 10 Rockefeller Plaza, New York, NY 10020.

The following periodicals provide feature articles, interviews, and commentaries on the global financial markets:

> *Bank Credit Analyst,* 3463 Peel Street, Montreal, Canada, H3A 1W7.
> *The Economist Intelligence Unit,* 10 Rockefeller Plaza, New York, NY 10020.

Euromoney, Nestor House, Playhouse Yard, London, U.K. EC4V 5EX. This is a monthly publication that provides well-written feature articles on foreign companies and financial markets. Supplements to *Euromoney* are devoted to more in-depth material. The publisher also has *Euromoney Online* for accessing information via computer terminals.

Morgan Stanley Capital International Perspective, 1633 Broadway, New York, NY 10019. This is a monthly publication printed in English, French, and German. It provides well-organized data in the form of charts and valuation ratios.

Intermarket Magazine, 401 South LaSalle, Chicago, IL 60605.

Futures Magazine, 219 Parkade, Cedar Falls, IA 50613.

Business Environment Risk Information, 1355 Redondo Avenue, Long Beach, CA 90804.

Institutional Investor, 488 Madison Avenue, New York, NY 10022.

Money Market Services, 490 El Camino Real, Belmont, CA 94002.

International Economic Conditions, Federal Reserve Bank of St. Louis, St. Louis, MO.

Standard & Poor's Corporation, 25 Broadway, New York, NY 10004.

Value Line Investment Survey, 711 Third Avenue, New York, NY 10017.

COMPUTER DATA BASES

Dow Jones News/Retrieval, P.O. Box 300, Princeton, NJ 08540.

Reuters News Service, 445 South Figueroa, Los Angeles, CA 90017.

Telerate, One World Trade Center, New York, NY 10048. This is an extensive data base of information on foreign securities, interest rates, and foreign currencies.

Euromoney Online, Nestor House, Playhouse Yard, London EC4V 5EX.

Compuserve Information Service, 5000 Arlington Centre Blvd., Columbus, OH 43220.

CHARTING SERVICES

The following services provide charts of selected foreign stock market indexes, companies, foreign currencies, and interest rates.

Commodity Perspective, 327 LaSalle St., Chicago, IL 60604.

Commodity Chart Service, 75 Montgomery St., Jersey City, NJ 07302.

Financial Futures Charting Service, Data Lab Corporation, 200 West Monroe, Chicago, IL 60606.

Morgan Stanley Capital International Perspective, 1633 Broadway, New York, NY 10019.

Daily Graphs, P.O. Box 24933, Los Angeles, CA 90024.

PUBLICATIONS ON SPECIFIC COUNTRIES AND THEIR MARKETS

Japan
The Japan Stock Journal
The Japan Company Handbook
Kyodo News Service

United Kingdom
The Financial Times
The London Times
Extel Service
Bondholder's Register

West Germany
Amtliches Kursblatt Der Frankfurter Wertpapierbörse. This is a daily publication in German that lists statistical data of securities by industry group traded on the Frankfurt Stock Exchange. No articles or news items are included.

Canada
Daily Record, Toronto Stock Exchange.
Bulletin, Toronto Stock Exchange.

Switzerland
Titlebulletin, Telekurs, AG.
Kursblatt Der Zurcher Effektenbörse. A daily publication in German with market data on the Zurich exchange.

France

Le Monde. Leading French daily newspaper with a business section covering world and national business news; it contains market data on listed securities of the Paris Bourse.
Cote Officielle
Informations Sur Operations Titres

Italy

La Repubblica. This is the leading Italian daily newspaper with a business section covering the Milan Stock Exchange.
Listino Ufficiale Della Borsa Valori
Gazzetta Ufficiale

Australia

Australian Financial Review
National Times

Netherlands

Official Pricelist, Amsterdam Stock Exchange.

Sweden

Offciell Kurslista, Stockholm Stock Exchange.

Hong Kong

Price List
Weekly Report

Singapore

Business Times
Financial News
Companies Handbook
Singapore Stock Exchange Journal

BIBLIOGRAPHY

Books

Appel, Gerald, and W. Frederick Hitschler. *Stock Market Trading Systems*. Homewood, Ill.: Dow Jones-Irwin, 1980.

Baughn, William H., and Donald R. Mandick. *The International Banking Handbook*. Homewood, Ill.: Dow Jones-Irwin, 1983.

Beidleman, Carl R. *Financial Swaps*. Homewood, Ill.: Dow Jones-Irwin, 1985.

Bernstein, Leopold A. *Analysis of Financial Statements*. Homewood, Ill.: Dow Jones-Irwin, 1985.

Bookstaber, Richard M., and Roger G. Clark. *Option Strategies for Institutional Investment Management*. Reading, Mass.: Addison-Wesley 1983.

Casey, Douglas. *Strategic Investing*. New York: Simon & Schuster, 1982.

Cetron, Marvin. *The Future of American Business—The U.S. in World Competition*. New York: McGraw-Hill, 1985.

Chandler, Lester V. *The Economics of Money and Banking*. New York: Harper & Row, 1964.

Coninx, Raymond G. F. *Foreign Exchange Dealer's Handbook*. Homewood, Ill.: Dow Jones-Irwin, 1986.

Coopers & Lybrand. *International Financial Reporting and Auditing*, 1984.

Day, Adrian. *International Investment Opportunities: How and Where to Invest Overseas Successfully*. New York: William Morrow, 1983.

————. *Investing without Borders*. Alexandria, Va.: Alexandria House Books, 1982.

Duchek, Charles, and Carol Harding. *Trading in Foreign Currencies*. Chicago: American TransEuro Corp., 1978.

Edwards, Robert D., and John Magee. *Technical Analysis of Stock Trends*. Springfield, Mass.: John Magee, 1957.

Erdman, Paul. *Paul Erdman's Money Book*. New York: Random House, 1984.

Fabozzi, Frank J., and Harry I. Greenfield, eds. *The Handbook of Economic and Financial Measures*. Homewood, Ill.: Dow Jones-Irwin, 1984.

Fabozzi, Frank J., and Irving J. Pollack, eds. *The Handbook of Fixed Income Securities*. Homewood, Ill.: Dow Jones-Irwin, 1983.

Fong, H. Gifford, and Frank J. Fabozzi. *Fixed Income Portfolio Management*. Homewood, Ill.: Dow Jones-Irwin, 1985.

George, A. M., and I. H. Giddy. *International Finance Handbooks,* Vol. I and II. New York: John Wiley & Sons, 1983.

Goldenberg, Susan. *Trading*. New York: Harcourt Brace Jovanovich, 1986.

Hollender, Keith. *Scripophily*. New York: Facts on File, 1982.

Kaufman, Henry. *Interest Rates, The Markets, and the New Financial World*. New York: Times Books, 1986.

Keys, L. J. *A Guide to World Money and Capital Markets*. London: McGraw-Hill, 1981.

Krefetz, Gerald. *How to Read and Profit from Financial News*. New York: Ticknor & Fields, 1984.

Levine, Sumner N., ed. *Investment Manager's Handbook*. Homewood, Ill.: Dow Jones-Irwin, 1980.

Lurie, Adolph. *How to Read Annual Reports*. Englewood Cliffs, N.J.: Prentice-Hall, 1984.

McMillan, Lawrence G. *Options as a Strategic Investment*. New York: Institute of Finance, 1980.

Melton, William C. *Inside the Fed*. Homewood, Ill.: Dow Jones-Irwin, 1985.

Nix, William E., and Susan W. Nix. *The Dow Jones-Irwin Guide to Stock Index Futures and Options Markets*. Homewood, Ill.: Dow Jones-Irwin, 1984.

Nix, William E., and Kermit Zieg. *The Commodity Options Markets*. Homewood, Ill.: Dow Jones-Irwin, 1978.

Pring, Martin J. *How to Forecast Interest Rates*. New York: McGraw-Hill, 1981.

————. *International Investing Made Easy*. New York: McGraw-Hill, 1981.

————. *Technical Analysis Explained*. New York: McGraw-Hill, 1980.

Rebell, Arthur L., and Gail Gordon. *Financial Futures and Investment Strategy*. Homewood, Ill.: Dow Jones-Irwin, 1984.

Rudd, Andrew, and Henry K. Clasing, Jr. *Modern Portfolio Theory*. Homewood, Ill.: Dow Jones-Irwin, 1982.

Shearlock, Peter, and Andrew Hutchinson, eds. *Finance Director International 1986,* U.K. Edition. London: Sterling Publishing Group PLC, 1986.

Stigum, Marcia. *Money Market Calculations: Yields, Breakevens, and Arbitrage.* Homewood, Ill.: Dow Jones-Irwin, 1981.

————. *The Money Market.* Homewood, Ill.: Dow Jones-Irwin, 1983.

Stobaugh, Robert, and Daniel Yerkin, eds. *Energy Future—Report of the Energy Project at the Harvard Business School.* New York: Random House, 1979.

Vertin, James R., ed. *International Equity Investing.* Homewood, Ill.: Dow Jones-Irwin, 1984.

Warfield, Gerald. *How to Buy Foreign Stocks and Bonds.* New York: Harper & Row, 1985.

Williams, Arthur III. *Managing Your Investment Manager.* Homewood, Ill.: Dow Jones-Irwin, 1986.

Winston, Patrick H., and Karen A. Prendergast, eds. *The AI Business.* Cambridge, Mass.: MIT Press, 1984.

Wolverton, Van. *VisiCalc—Worksheets for Business.* San Jose, Calif.: VisiPress, 1983.

Woodwell, Donald R. *Automating Your Financial Portfolio.* Homewood, Ill.: Dow Jones-Irwin, 1983.

Articles and Reports

Adam, Nigel, and Norman Peagram. Amsterdam Stock Exchange. Supplement to *Euromoney*, May 1985.

Lim, Peck Quek, and John Carson Parker. "The Rise of the Singapore Stock Market." Supplement to *Euromoney*, December 1984.

Spehar, George. Focus: Index Arbitrage, Vol. 1, Issue 1, Stock Index Futures and Options. Bear, Stearns & Co., September 9, 1985.

Spehar, George. Focus: Hedging with Stock Index Futures, Vol. 1, Issue 2, Stock Index Futures and Options. Bear, Stearns, & Co., October 31, 1985.

Madura, Jeff, and Wallace Reiff. "A Hedge Strategy for International Portfolios," *Journal of Portfolio Management,* Fall 1985, pp. 70–74.

Ibbotson, Roger C., Lawrence B. Siegel, and Kathryn S. Love. "World Wealth: Market Values and Returns," *Journal of Portfolio Management*, Fall 1985, pp. 4–23.

Selected articles from 1984 to 1986: Foreign Economic Trends and Their Implications for the United States. Washington, D.C.: U.S. Department of Commerce.

Selected articles from 1982 to 1986: *Euromoney*.

Selected articles from 1984 to 1986. The Economist Intelligence Unit. London: Economist Publications Ltd.

Ostrander, Judy T., ed. Investment Information Sources. Los Angeles Public Library; Business and Economics Department, October, 1980.

The Federal Reserve Bank. Annual Reports. Washington, D.C.

De Nederlandsche Bank n.v. Annual Reports. Amsterdam, The Netherlands.

The Bundesbank. Annual Reports. Frankfurt, Federal Republic of Germany.

INDEX